T0207358

Lecture Notes in Computer Science

Lecture Notes in Artificial Intelligence   **14644**
Founding Editor

Jörg Siekmann

Series Editors

Randy Goebel, *University of Alberta, Edmonton, Canada*
Wolfgang Wahlster, *DFKI, Berlin, Germany*
Zhi-Hua Zhou, *Nanjing University, Nanjing, China*

The series Lecture Notes in Artificial Intelligence (LNAI) was established in 1988 as a topical subseries of LNCS devoted to artificial intelligence.

The series publishes state-of-the-art research results at a high level. As with the LNCS mother series, the mission of the series is to serve the international R & D community by providing an invaluable service, mainly focused on the publication of conference and workshop proceedings and postproceedings.

Mayumi Bono · Yasufumi Takama · Ken Satoh ·
Le-Minh Nguyen · Setsuya Kurahashi
Editors

New Frontiers in Artificial Intelligence

JSAI-isAI 2023 International Workshops
JURISIN, SCIDOCA, EmSemi and AI-Biz
Kumamoto, Japan, June 4–6, 2023
Revised Selected Papers

Springer

Editors
Mayumi Bono
National Institute of Informatics
Tokyo, Japan

Yasufumi Takama ⓘ
Tokyo Metropolitan University
Tokyo, Japan

Ken Satoh ⓘ
National Institute of Informatics
Tokyo, Japan

Le-Minh Nguyen ⓘ
Japan Advanced Institute of Science
and Technology
Nomi, Ishikawa, Japan

Setsuya Kurahashi ⓘ
University of Tsukuba
Tokyo, Japan

ISSN 0302-9743   ISSN 1611-3349 (electronic)
Lecture Notes in Artificial Intelligence
ISBN 978-3-031-60510-9   ISBN 978-3-031-60511-6 (eBook)
https://doi.org/10.1007/978-3-031-60511-6

LNCS Sublibrary: SL7 – Artificial Intelligence

Preface

The fifteenth JSAI International Symposium on Artificial Intelligence (JSAI-isAI) was held on June 4–6, 2023, at Kumamoto-Jo Hall, Kumamoto, Japan. JSAI-isAI has hosted several international workshops every year since 2009, and they are supported by JSAI. It has provided a unique and intimate forum where AI researchers gather and share their knowledge in a focused discipline. Since 2022, JSAI-isAI has been held with the JSAI Annual Conference (JSAI Annual Conference) to achieve synergies between the two events. Although JSAI is a Japanese society and is mainly run in Japanese, the JSAI Annual Conference has an international session, providing a forum for presentations and exchanging opinions in English. For the first time in 2023, The JSAI Annual Conference participants could participate and present their papers at JSAI-isAI free of charge, and more participants than ever before were seen taking part in JSAI-isAI and engaging in active discussions, and presenters at JSAI-isAI had the same framework for submission recommendations to New Generation Computing (published by Springer), the international journal of JSAI, as presenters at the JSAI Annual Conference. JSAI-isAI 2023 hosted four workshops (JURISIN 2023, SCIDOCA 2023, EmSemi 2023, and AI-Biz 2023) and had 6 invited talks, 1 special panel session, and 46 oral presentations for 94 participants from 21 countries.

The seventeenth International Workshop on Juris-informatics (JURISIN 2023) detailed legal issues from the perspective of information science. It covered various topics, including models of legal reasoning, argumentation agents, legal ontologies, legal knowledge bases, computerized legal education, AI legal problems, legal document analysis, and natural language processing for law. The seventh International Workshop on Scientific Document Analysis (SCIDOCA 2023) was an annual international workshop focusing on various aspects and perspectives of scientific document analysis for their efficient use and exploration. The first International Workshop on Embodied Semiotics (EmSemi 2023) focused on developing a "multimodal semiotic" approach to the existing semiotics discussed in the fields of linguistics and philosophy of language, focusing on phenomena such as gestures and signs in language interactions which have not yet been clearly characterized as symbols. The International Workshop on Artificial Intelligence of and for Business (AI-Biz 2023) focused on the vast business and AI technology fields. It covered various topics, including investment strategy, stock market, mergers and acquisitions, online advertisement, knowledge extraction, power market, collaborative multi-agent, visualization, COVID-19 infections, classification, fake news, and wide and deep learning.

This volume is the post-proceedings of JSAI-isAI 2023. From the 23 papers submitted to JURISIN 2023, the 8 papers submitted to SCIDOCA 2023, the 11 papers submitted to EmSemi 2023, and the 10 papers submitted to AI-Biz 2023, 15 papers were selected based on a single-blind review by at least two reviewers and the quality of the extended versions of the papers was carefully checked by the program committee members. The acceptance rate was about 28%, ensuring the quality of the post-proceedings. JSAI-isAI

2023 was held in a hybrid format and was the first event after the removal of entry restrictions due to the impact of COVID-19, and it also saw participants from abroad. We hope this book will introduce readers to the state-of-the-art research outcomes of JSAI-isAI 2023 and motivate them to organize and participate in JSAI events in the future.

March 2024

Mayumi Bono
Yasufumi Takama
Ken Satoh
Katsumi Nitta
Le-Minh Nguyen
Setsuya Kurahashi

Organization

Program Committee Chairs

Mayumi Bono	National Institute of Informatics, Japan
Yasufumi Takama	Tokyo Metropolitan University, Japan
Ken Satoh	National Institute of Informatics, Japan
Le-Minh Nguyen	Japan Advanced Institute of Science and Technology, Japan
Setsuya Kurahashi	University of Tsukuba, Japan

JURISIN 2023

Workshop Chairs

Ken Satoh	National Institute of Informatics, Japan
Katsumi Nitta	National Institute of Informatics, Japan

Steering Committee

Yoshinobu Kano	Shizuoka University, Japan
Takehiko Kasahara	Toin University of Yokohama, Japan
Le-Minh Nguyen	Japan Advanced Institute of Science and Technology, Japan
Makoto Nakamura	Niigata Institute of Technology, Japan
Yoshiaki Nishigai	Chiba University, Japan
Katsumi Nitta	National Institute of Informatics, Japan
Yasuhiro Ogawa	Nagoya City University, Japan
Seiichiro Sakurai	Meiji Gakuin University, Japan
Ken Satoh	National Institute of Informatics, Japan
Satoshi Tojo	Asia University, Japan
Katsuhiko Toyama	Nagoya University, Japan
Masaharu Yoshioka	Hokkaido University, Japan

Advisory Committee

Trevor Bench-Capon	University of Liverpool, UK
Henry Prakken	University of Utrecht & University of Groningen, The Netherlands
John Zeleznikow	Victoria University, Australia
Katsumi Nitta	National Institute of Informatics, Japan
Robert Kowalski	Imperial College London, UK
Kevin Ashley	University of Pittsburgh, USA

Program Committee

Michał, Araszkiewicz	Jagiellonian University, Poland
Ryuta Arisaka	Kyoto University, Japan
Marina De Vos	University of Bath, UK
Kripabandhu Ghosh	Indian Institute of Science Education and Research Kolkata, India
Saptarshi Ghosh	Indian Institute of Technology Kharagpur, India
Randy Goebel	University of Alberta, Canada
Guido Governatori	Independent Researcher, Australia
Tokuyasu Kakuta	Chuo University, Japan
Yoshinobu Kano	Shizuoka University, Japan
Mi-Young Kim	University of Alberta, Canada
Le-Minh Nguyen	Japan Advanced Institute of Science and Technology, Japan
Makoto Nakamura	Niigata Institute of Technology, Japan
Katsumi Nitta	National Institute of Informatics, Japan
Yasuhiro Ogawa	Nagoya City University, Japan
Juliano Rabelo	University of Alberta, Canada
Seiichiro Sakurai	Meiji Gakuin University, Japan
Ken Satoh	National Institute of Informatics, Japan
Akira Shimazu	Japan Advanced Institute of Science and Technology, Japan
Satoshi Tojo	Asia University, Japan
Katsuhiko Toyama	Nagoya University, Japan
Bart Verheij	University of Groningen, The Netherlands
Yueh-Hsuan Weng	Tohoku University, Japan
Masaharu Yoshioka	Hokkaido University, Japan
Thomas Ågotnes	University of Bergen, Norway

SCIDOCA 2023

Workshop Chairs

Le-Minh Nguyen	Japan Advanced Institute of Science and Technology, Japan
Yuji Matsumoto	RIKEN Center for Advanced Intelligence Project, Japan

Program Committee

Le-Minh Nguyen	Japan Advanced Institute of Science and Technology, Japan
Noriki Nishida	RIKEN Center for Advanced Intelligence Project, Japan
Vu Tran	Institute of Statistical Mathematics, Japan
Yusuke Miyao	University of Tokyo, Japan
Yuji Matsumoto	RIKEN Center for Advanced Intelligence Project, Japan
Yoshinobu Kano	Shizuoka University, Japan
Akiko Aizawa	National Institute of Informatics, Japan
Ken Satoh	National Institute of Informatics, Japan
Junichiro Mori	University of Tokyo, Japan
Kentaro Inui	Tohoku University, Japan
Nguyen Ha Thanh	National Institute of Informatics, Japan
Nguyen Minh Phuong	Japan Advanced Institute of Science and Technology, Japan

AI-Biz 2023

Workshop Leader

Takao Terano	Chiba University, Japan

Workshop Co-leaders

Setsuya Kurahashi	University of Tsukuba, Japan
Hiroshi Takahashi	Keio University, Japan

Steering Committee

Chang-Won Ahn	Vaiv Company Inc., South Korea
Ernesto Carella	University of Oxford, UK
Reiko Hishiyama	Waseda University, Japan
Manabu Ichikawa	Shibaura Institute of Technology, Japan
Yoko Ishino	Yamaguchi University, Japan
Hajime Kita	Kyoto University, Japan
Hajime Mizuyama	Aoyama Gakuin University
Chathura Rajapaksha	University of Kelaniya, Sri Lanka
Masakazu Takahashi	Yamaguchi University, Japan
Alfred Taudes	Vienna University, Austria
Shingo Takahashi	Waseda University, Japan
Takashi Yamada	Yamaguchi University, Japan
Matthias Raddant	Kiel University, Germany
Chao Yang	Hunan University, China

Sponsored by

The Japanese Society for Artificial Intelligence (JSAI)

Contents

SCIDOCA 2023

AI-Biz 2023

JURISIN 2023

Seventeenth International Workshop on Juris-informatics (JURISIN 2023)

Legal informatics is the study of legal issues from an informatics point of view. JURISIN is an international workshop on legal informatics and has been held annually in Japan JURISIN is an international workshop on legal informatics and has been held annually in Japan since 2007. Relevant topics range from models of legal reasoning, argumentation agents, legal ontologies, legal knowledge bases, computerized legal education, AI legal problems, legal document analysis, natural language processing for law, etc. The traditional field of "artificial intelligence and law" is also included in JURISIN's relevant topics.

JURISIN 2023 was held on June 6 and 7, 2023 as part of the International Workshop Series (is-AI) organized by the Japanese Society for Artificial Intelligence. Each paper submitted to the workshop was reviewed by three program committee members, and as a result, 21 papers were accepted. The accepted papers covered a wide variety of topics, including legal decision making, ontology of legal knowledge, privacy protection, and applications of language models. In addition to these 21 oral presentations, there were two invited talks, "Awareness and Reliability in Legal Reasoning – from the viewpoint of modal logic –" by Satoshi Tojo of Asia University and "Rules, Computation and Reasoning" by Denis Merigoux of Inria, France.

After the conclusion of JURISIN 2023, the authors of the papers revised their papers and resubmitted them for post-proceedings based on the reviewers' comments and discussions at the workshop. Each of these resubmitted papers was reviewed again by three reviewers, and nine papers were accepted. The nine papers are included in this LNAI.

We would like to thank the JURISIN 2023 steering committee, the program committee, all those who submitted papers, and the organizing committee of is-AI for the publication of the JURISIN 2023 post-proceedings.

March 2024

Ken Satoh
Katsumi Nitta

Compliance Checking in the Energy Domain via W3C Standards

Joseph K. Anim$^{(\boxtimes)}$, Livio Robaldo, and Adam Wyner

Swansea University, Swansea, UK
{joseph.anim,livio.robaldo,a.z.wyner}@swansea.ac.uk

Abstract. This paper investigates the use of W3C standards, specifically RDF, OWL, SPARQL, and SHACL, to automate legal compliance checking. We consider in particular in-force regulations for extracting oil and gas in Ghana to exemplify our proposed model. This paper models some selected norms from these regulations into a sample RDF ontology along with inference rules to check their compliance with respect to a given state of affairs. The paper's main finding is that inferences enabled by OWL and SHACL shapes are not expressive enough to represent some existing legal requirements, specifically those imposing constraints on metadata about RDF individuals. To achieve the required expressivity, it is proposed that SHACL-SPARQL rules should be instead used.

Keywords: Compliance checking · W3C standards · symbolic AI

1 Introduction

Due to the ever-growing regulations upon which compliance procedures are conducted, the quantum of documents that companies must submit to prove their compliance with the regulations governing their activities has increased and is increasing in volume[1]. In addition, lawyers mostly check compliance and prepare due diligence documents manually. However, this has several disadvantages: it is highly time-consuming, it is error-prone, and it creates an avenue for corruption as it makes it difficult to understand when errors were either caused by unintentional oversights or they were done on purpose.

LegalTech technologies aim at mitigating these problems [4]. Automatizing repetitive operations allows one to save time, enhances accuracy, and makes the whole process easily accountable, which in turn makes corruption less feasible.

Currently, most approaches to LegalTech are based on Machine Learning (ML), see, e.g., [5,14,15,17,31]. However, ML makes it difficult to handle *specific and exact* values, as it is often required when checking compliance of due diligence documents as well as drawing inferences from the values. The accuracy of ML

---

[1] https://www.thomsonreuters.com/en-us/posts/investigation-fraud-and-risk/cost-of-compliance-2021.

Joseph K. Anim has been supported by the Ghana Scholarship Secretariat (see https://www.scholarshipgh.com).

M. Bono et al. (Eds.): JSAI-isAI 2023 Workshops, LNAI 14644, pp. 3–18, 2024.
https://doi.org/10.1007/978-3-031-60511-6_1

is intrinsically limited by the Pareto principle, a.k.a., the 80/20 rule; thus it provides results that are correct in *most* cases but not *all* [23].

Furthermore, ML tends to behave like a "black box" unable to explain its decisions; as a consequence, often it is even impossible to explain the difference between the $\sim$80% of correct results from the $\sim$20% of incorrect ones.

To address these limitations, symbolic representations and rules have been proposed and used even though they require more manual efforts. Symbols correspond to human-understandable concepts and rules represent how we reason with the symbols, thus the chain of logical derivations on symbols could provide intelligible explanations of AI decision-making. To mitigate the fact that symbolic representations and rules require more manual efforts, *standardized formats should be used*, thus allowing the funnelling of efforts from more people, which in turn facilitates reusability and sharing of resources.

This paper presents a methodology for compliance checking based on main W3C standards for the Semantic Web. The methodology is exemplified on Ghanaian regulations for extraction of oil and gas, which we will use as case study.

We believe that it is crucial to research and implement symbolic compliance checkers that are compatible with the mentioned W3C standards because more and more (big) data is becoming available in RDF format. Matching and annotating big data with legislative information will produce even more and richer big data. Thus, the importance of using the same standardized formats, namely the W3C standards, to achieve interoperability.

In addition, legal ontologies encoded in RDF/OWL have been increasingly proposed and used within existing LegalTech applications [16,18,26,28]. Legal ontologies specify relevant legal concepts, individuals, constraints, etc. such as duties and rights from legislation, as well as their relationship with the concepts of the domain to which the norms apply, e.g., finance, health, or the energy domain.

By using legal ontologies, states of affairs need to be checked against the constrains of the ontology in order to check for compliance. The present paper proposes a novel approach to compliance checking using SHACL-SPARQL rules, discussed below. In contrast to prior work, e.g., [10] and [27], which respectively use OWL restrictions and SHACL shapes together with SHACL Triple rules, the current work uses SHACL-SPARQL rules which are able to extract metadata, aggregate it, then perform some process on the aggregated information. This is not feasible via OWL restrictions, SHACL shapes, or SHACL Triple rules. The framework is exercised with respect to an ontology representing regulations in the oil and gas domain.

2   Background - W3C Standards for the Semantic Web

As mentioned earlier, the objective of this paper and of our research as a whole is to devise computational methods for compliance checking fully compatible with main W3C standards, in order to foster interoperability with available big data.

W3C has already defined several formats to empower the Semantic Web[2]. This paper will use RDF and OWL to encode the ontology, both the TBox (terminological box), which represents the domain knowledge, and the ABox (assertive box), which represents the states of affairs.

Then, we will use SPARQL and SHACL to compute and query new knowledge from the explicitly asserted RDF triples. Specifically, we will model norms as SHACL-SPARQL rules; these rules will then be executed on the states of affairs encoded in RDF to infer which individuals comply with the norms rather than violating them.

2.1   RDF and OWL

RDF (Resource Description Framework) is a language which represents information about resources on the World Wide Web. RDF represents metadata about web resources, such as the title, author, and modification date of a web page, etc. However, RDF has evolved such that it can be used to represent any general information about identifiable things on the web. The intent behind RDF was to allow applications to process and exchange information without this information losing its intended meaning. This will ensure that information can be exchanged even between applications that were not developed to use or work with the original information.

RDF is therefore used for creating ontologies, i.e., application-neutral networks of concepts, which are called "RDF resources" (classes, individuals, and properties). RDF includes basic constructs to declare them as well as to relate them to one another.

RDF has been mainly designed to *describe* knowledge. Thus, it has very limited reasoning capabilities. In RDF, it is only possible to infer whether certain RDF resources belong to certain classes via the constructs `rdfs:subClassOf`, `rdfs:domain`, and `rdfs:range`.

OWL (Ontology Web Language) augments RDF by adding more reasoning capabilities. OWL allows specification of many more constraints than RDF, which in turn enable more inferences about the RDF resources. In particular, OWL introduces constructs that allow to infer when certain RDF resources do *not* belong to certain classes, e.g., the construct `owl:disjointWith`. These constructs in particular amplify the reasoning capabilities of the language, which in turn has led to investigations about the trade-off between expressivity and computational complexity of the inferences.

These investigations have identified three main sub-languages of OWL: OWL full, OWL DL, and OWL lite. OWL full and OWL lite feature, respectively, full and very reduced expressivity but, consequently, also full and very reduced computational complexity. OWL DL has intermediate expressivity and complexity between OWL full and OWL lite; DL stands for "Description Logic", the logic

---

[2] See the list at https://www.w3.org/2001/sw/wiki/Main_Page.

that OWL DL refers to[3]. Thus, for applications in which the computational time is relevant, it is advisable to use OWL DL or OWL lite in place of OWL full.

Several OWL reasoners have been already proposed in the literature to compute inferred ontologies from the explicitly asserted one, e.g., HermiT[4]. [9] presents a comparison among some of these OWL reasoners. [9] highlights that the reasoners vary significantly with regard to the relevant aims and characteristics, so that each specific case study, especially if in an industrial context, deserves a careful and critical choice of the reasoner to be employed.

2.2   SPARQL and SHACL

As part of the Semantic Web activity, the RDF Data Access Working Group released in 2004 the first public working draft of an RDF querying language which was known as SPARQL. Since then, further operators to add, delete, and update the triples in the ontology as well as to deduce new information from them has been added to SPARQL. Nowadays SPARQL is a rich language for both querying and manipulating RDF datasets [21].

SPARQL query are generally embedded and executed within other software or programming languages; examples are the SPARQL plug-in for the Protégé editor and the Jena libraries for Java. Therefore, the order in which SPARQL queries are executed is decided by the user or programmatically in the logic of the software: SPARQL does not provide constructs to relate the queries of one to another, for instance, to establish some execution order on them.

On the other hand, SHACL is a W3C recommendation more recent than SPARQL: it was originally proposed in 2017 for the purpose of validating RDF datasets. SHACL allows to specify special constraints, called "SHACL shapes" on RDF resources. External validators allow to check whether an RDF dataset is valid or not with respect to a set of SHACL shapes. SHACL is more expressive than OWL, and it may be therefore used to augment the inferential capacities. In particular, SHACL includes non-monotonic operators such as negation-as-failure. These are not allowed in OWL, which is a monotone language.

Furthermore, SHACL constraints are more flexible and easier to edit than OWL ones because, while the latter are all executed *at once*, in SHACL we may *decouple* complex validation tasks into (simpler) sequential modules. This is possible thanks to the introduction of SHACL rules[5] that enable non-ontological types of operations such as collecting data from RDF resources located in "distant" parts of the ontology or computing partial results needed for the validation [20]. SHACL allows in particular to specify *priorities* on the rules, and so to define sequences or even flow charts of rules, in a rather controlled fashion.

There are two kinds of SHACL rules: SHACL Triple rules, which can add a *single* RDF triple to the inferred ontology, and SHACL-SPARQL rules, which

---

[3] Description Logic refers to a *family* of logics that are less expressive than First-order Logic; OWL DL more specifically refers to the description logic **SHOIN-D** [13].

[4] http://www.hermit-reasoner.com.

[5] https://www.w3.org/TR/shacl-af.

embed SPARQL queries in the form CONSTRUCT-WHERE. In SHACL-SPARQL rules, for each subgraph that satisfies the WHERE clause, the subgraph in the corresponding CONSTRUCT clause is added to the inferred ontology. Therefore, contrary to SHACL Triple rules, SHACL-SPARQL rules may add more than one RDF triple to the inferred ontology. Moreover, the expressivity of SHACL-SPARQL rules add to the richness of SPARQL the possibility of establishing *orders* between SPARQL inferences, thus creating the controlled sequences or flow charts of such inferences.

3 Related Works

As explained in the Introduction, approaches in LegalTech (indeed, in AI in general) may be classified in two main categories: approaches based on statistical reasoning, i.e., Machine Learning (ML), and approaches base on logical reasoning, such as the one proposed in this paper.

ML approaches are predominant, also for compliance checking; examples are [31] and [15]. In these approaches, ML is used to detect anomalies, i.e., behaviours or outcomes that diverge from the general trend identified statistically.

For instance, [15] observed that, in current real-world Enterprise Resource Planning (ERP) systems, the rules for VAT compliance are mostly maintained manually by ERP VAT experts, due to the large amount of variables involved, which are in turn subject to changes in regulations, laws, tax rates, or internal business strategies and preference criteria of the different industries and companies. Therefore, it is rather easy for the ERP VAT experts to make mistakes (see [15]). In light of this, [15] developed a supervised learning classifier for the VAT tax code determination process able to identify and notify anomalies in the results of the calculations.

The objective of our approach differs substantially from the one of [15] or similar anomaly detection ML-based solutions. Our research aims at defining a standardized methodology for encoding the if-then rules coming from the in-force regulations or the companies' internal business strategies. In addition, we envision a future in which the if-then rules coming from the in-force regulations are directly provided by the appointed public authorities, rather than being (re)encoded by each company, each in the specific format of the ERP system used. Consequently, each company will only have to encode the if-then rules related to the company's internal business strategies and preference criteria. In this scenario, ML-based algorithms such as [15]'s can be still used to detect anomalies: the two solutions are fully orthogonal.

In our view, the standardized methodology that we advocate should be defined in terms of the W3C standards RDF and SHACL, both because they provide the required expressivity, as this paper will show, and because they are at the basis of the World Wide Web, i.e., they are widely used worldwide and they enable interoperability with external available knowledge bases, which could lead to higher coverage and accuracy of the applications.

However, the present paper is not the first attempt to check compliance on RDF data. Some of the first approaches are [7,8,12,19]. These approaches use

RDF/OWL to model the TBox while the states of affairs and separate knowledge bases of rules are encoded in special *separated* XML formats such as SWRL [12], LKIF-rules [7], RuleML [8] and LegalRuleML [19].

More recently, but in the same vein, [11] made a preliminary proposal to extend the LegalRuleML meta model [3] and to represent normative rules via SPARQL queries. [11] is, to our knowledge, the first proposal that models normative reasoning by employing W3C standards only. The solution presented in this paper is therefore rather close to [11]'s; however, while [11] only uses SPARQL, our formalization will use SHACL in conjunction with SPARQL.

Another relevant approach is [6], which encodes legal rules within OWL2 decidable profiles in order to keep computational complexity under control. In [6], norms are represented as property restrictions that refer to the subsets of individuals that comply with the norms. Compliance checking is then enforced via OWL2 subsumption. However, the authors themselves acknowledge (see [6], §3.3) that their approach does not really involve legal reasoning, which is defeasible in nature, and it is only limited to GDPR policy validation.

Similarly to [6,10] and [27] distinguish compliant and non-compliant individuals by introducing, respectively, special OWL subclasses and special SHACL shapes. Contrary to [6], however, [10] and [27] can model defeasible inferences.

For instance, the OWL ontology in [10] include two classes `Supplier` and `Vehicle`. The individuals in `Supplier` are obliged to communicate their contractual conditions to their consumers (R1), while vehicles cannot drive over 90 km/h (R2). To implement R1 and R2, `Supplier` and `Vehicle` respectively include a boolean datatype property `hasCommunicatedConditions` and a float datatype property `hasDrivingSpeed`. Then, two subclasses `SupplierR1compliant` and `VehicleR2compliant` are defined, the former including individuals in `Supplier` for which `hasCommunicatedConditions` is true, the latter including individuals in `Vehicle` for which `hasDrivingSpeed` is lower than 90. Compliance checking is then enforced by simply applying OWL2 subsumption. In other words, OWL "is-a" inferences will populate `SupplierR1compliant` and `VehicleR2compliant` with only the individuals that comply with the two norms.

In this setting, exceptions may be added by defining complement subclasses via the OWL2 tags at disposal, e.g., `owl:disjointWith`. These subclasses will define the subsets of individuals that *violate* the norms; thus, by imposing the set the individuals that comply with a norm as `owl:disjointWith` the one that violate it, the correct inferences are achieved.

The solution in [27] is very close to the one of [10], the crucial difference being that [27] uses SHACL shapes in place of OWL2 subclasses/restrictions to validate the values of the relevant attributes, e.g., `hasCommunicatedConditions` and `hasDrivingSpeed`, in the example above. In [27], SHACL Triple rules are used to compute the values of these attributes. These rules collect partial data from the RDF triples, and so they facilitate the representation of the norms by decoupling it in multiple sequential steps. Once the SHACL Triple rules have computed the values of the attributes, the SHACL shapes are executed in order to validate these values. Individuals with invalid attribute values are labelled as non-compliant. Finally, defeasibility is modeled via negation-as-failure: whenever exceptions hold, corresponding SHACL Triple rules defeat other ones, so that the inferences associated with the latter are blocked.

Finally, very recently [26] propose to efficiently check compliance of RDF data via the DLV2 reasoner [2], which allows for the embedding of SPARQL queries within Answer Set Programming (ASP) clauses. The results in [26] shows that DLV2 can process data much faster than available libraries for SHACL.

The next sections will highlight that the approaches in [10,11,27], and [26] are all inadequate, as the expressivity of the underlying formats does not suffice to represent certain kinds of norm that we may find in existing legislation.

Specifically, [10] and [27] are unable to handle compliance on *aggregate data* from the ontology, which are indeed *metadata* about the individuals in the ABox. For example, as described below, we would like to extract metadata (i.e., not specified per se by the ontology) such as the number of Ghanaian technical core employees at a company and the number of all technical core employees at that company, bring them together (aggregate), then use them to *calculate* whether the former is at least 20% of the latter, as required by the regulation.

Aggregate data cannot be computed via OWL "is-a" inferences or via SHACL shapes and Triple rules. On the other hand, to compute aggregate data we need the expressivity offered by SPARQL.

After aggregate data are calculated, we need to compute proportions among them, e.g., 20%, and make mathematical comparisons. In order to execute these computations in the right order (first the aggregate data, then the proportions, and then the mathematical comparisons), we will use the *priority operator* provided by SHACL. No equivalent priority operators are provided in SPARQL or ASP, that is why the frameworks in [11] and [26] are also inadequate.

In light of this, this paper will propose a novel revision of the framework in [27] in which SHACL shapes and Triple rules are replaced by SHACL-SPARQL rules in order to extract metadata, aggregate it, then perform some process on the aggregated information. The ontology and SHACL-SPARQL rules are used in a compliance checking framework depicted in Fig. 1.

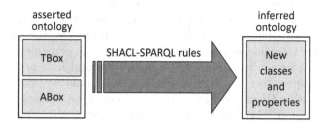

Fig. 1. The compliance checking framework

4   Case Study: Extracting Oil and Gas in Ghana

In Ghana, the oil and gas upstream industry has recently seen a lot of foreign investments from international corporations. It is expected these investments will further grow in the near future, due to the conflict in Ukraine and the consequent need for new alternative sources of oil and gas. The explorations have led to several oil and gas discoveries[6], among which it is worth mentioning the Offshore Cape Three Points (OCTP), which is estimated to hold about 41 billion cubic meters of non-associated gas and 500 million barrels of oil.

These discoveries are in turn expected to greatly contribute to the Ghanaian gross domestic product. It has been estimated that the oil and gas industry will contribute approximately 15.94 billion GHS (around 2.76 billion U.S. dollars) to Ghana's gross domestic product in 2024 [29].

As a result, the upstream oil and gas industry has become one of a heavily regulated sector in Ghana. Companies operating in this domain are required to submit several due diligence documents to auditing agencies such as the Ghana Petroleum Commission in order to check for regulatory compliance with respect to the in-force regulations[7]. In this work, we focus on the Local Content and Local Participation Regulations L.I 2204, henceforth named as "L.I 2204" only.

The L.I 2204 aims at ensuring the participation of Ghanaians and the use of indigenous materials in the upstream oil and gas industry. Simply put, the L.I 2204 is intended to prevent foreign companies from bringing their own employees and materials from abroad. Rather, they are allowed to extract the country's oil and gas only on condition they create employment and other economical benefits for the local population.

In particular, the regulation 7(2)(B) of the L.I 2204 requires companies in the upstream oil and gas industry to provide annually a "Local Content Plan", which includes several sub-plans (Employment Plan, Training plan, Insurance services plan, etc.), wherein the company specifies information about the impact of the company's business in the Ghanaian local economy.

The overall aim of our work is to design and implement a LegalTech application to assist the compilation and the assessment of the Local Content Plan. The present paper represents the first step of this research journey: it aims to present a first prototype of an ontology that can be used to collect and store data about companies in the upstream oil and gas industry, then used to automatically check their compliance with the L.I 2204. That is, companies are expected to use a Web interface to the Local Content Plan and determine their obligations with respect to the L.I 2204. Further data could be integrated in the ontology from other Ghanaian institutions and sources, e.g., the environmental protection agency (EPA), and double-checked against the information entered by the company. These double-checks, not implemented in our current work, are of course intended to detect (possibly unintentional) oversights and errors as well as to speed up and assist the compilation of the Local Content Plan by

---

[6] See https://www.gnpcghana.com/operations.html.

[7] Listed at https://www.petrocom.gov.gh/laws-regulations.

self-inserting the data already known. In our prototype, companies are expected to enter data about the bank supporting their financial operations, the law firm that is assisting their business, and their employees.

Some of the legal requirements that the Local Content Plan is intended to assess are the following:

(1) a. Is the E&P company banking with a Ghanaian bank?
     b. Is the E&P company hiring the legal services of a Ghanaian law firm?
     c. Is the E&P company employing at least 30% of Ghanaian management staff?
     d. Is the E&P company employing at least 20% of Ghanaian technical core staff?
     e. Etc.

We created a small ontology including some of the relevant classes and properties (TBox) from our domain. We populated the ontology with some sample individuals and relations between them (ABox). Then, we modeled some sample legal requirements, among which those in (1a–e), as SHACL-SPARQL rules.

These rules create additional classes and properties to distinguish compliant and non-compliant individuals, and populate the classes with these individuals. By executing the rules on the (asserted) ontology, a new (inferred) ontology is obtained. The latter will therefore represent which companies comply or not with the modeled legal requirements as well as the *explanations* why they do or do not comply with these requirements.

The hypothetical LegalTech application for the Local Content Plan will query the inferred ontology via simple SPARQL queries, in order to generate a report of the compliance assessment. Note that the inferred triples are not saved and stored together with the original asserted ontology. The additional classes and properties have the sole purpose of classifying the companies as compliant or non-compliant. Once these have been identified and communicated to the LegalTech application, the inferred ontology is simply discharged.

The next two subsections illustrate part of the asserted ontology and some SHACL-SPARQL queries[8].

4.1   The (Asserted) Ontology

We modeled the domain of the Local Content Plan as an ontology in OWL. The ontology includes classes referring to the sets of relevant entities. Some of these classes are shown in Fig. 2.

Figure 2 shows the classes of legal entities, activities, areas, and structures involved in the modeled legal requirements as well. For example, `SectorCompany` denotes the set of all companies in the upstream oil and gas industry operating in Ghana. Individuals from one class can be related to individuals from another

---

[8] The full ontology and list of queries is available on https://github.com/liviorobaldo/jurisin2023ca, together with Java software to execute the latter on the former thus obtaining the inferred ontology.

12   J. K. Anim et al.

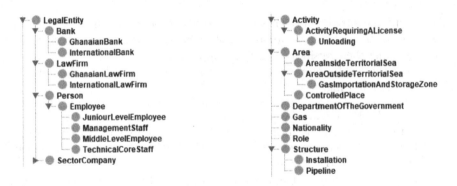

Fig. 2. Some of the classes in the ontology for the Local Content Plan

class by object properties. For instance, each individual in `Employee` is related with an individual in `Nationality` via an object property "`is`"; `Nationality` is a value partition including the individuals `ghanaian`, `italian`, `american`, etc.

On the other hand, individuals in `SectorCompany` are associated with information specifying the areas they operate, the activities they carry out in these areas, the structures used within these activities, the type of gas (`methane`, `propane`, `butane`, etc.) they work with, etc.

The ontology has been then populated with sample individuals in order to test the SHACL-SPARQL rules. Figure 3 shows some of these individuals and object properties (e.g., `employs`, `is`, `bank-with`). Two sample companies are considered: `companyc` and `companye`. The former banks with a Ghanaian bank while the latter banks with an international bank. Furthermore, `companyc` employs four technical core employees, having all Ghanaian nationality, while `companye` employs two technical core employees, having respectively Italian and American nationality.

It is then evident that `companyc` complies with legal requirements (1a) and (1d) while `companye` violates both of them. The SHACL-SPARQL rules described in the next section allows to infer these compliance checking results.

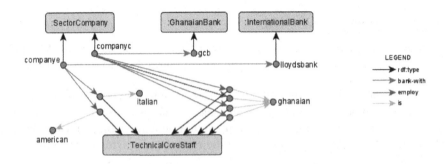

Fig. 3. Sample individuals for the case study

4.2   The SHACL/SPARQL Rules

The previously referenced computational artefact includes around twenty-nine SHACL-SPARQL queries to implement some selected legal requirements from the L.I 2204. While these are all downloadable from the GitHub repository, space constraints limit showing and describing all of them in detail; we will focus only on the ones that implement (1a) and (1d).

The two SHACL-SPARQL rules that implement (1a) are shown together in (2). The rules embed a SPARQL query in the form `CONSTRUCT-WHERE` within the SHACL property `sh:construct`. As specified in the `WHERE` clause, the first rule collects all companies that bank with a Ghanaian bank (`?x :bank-with ?y. ?y rdf:type :GhanaianBank.`). The `CONSTRUCT` clause:

- creates a *new* class `BLCCompliantSectorCompany` in the inferred ontology (`:BLCCompliantSectorCompany rdf:type rdfs:Class.`)
- asserts `BLCCompliantSectorCompany` as subclass of the class `SectorCompany` (`:BLCCompliantSectorCompany rdfs:subClassOf :SectorCompany.`)
- asserts the individuals `?x` that satisfy the `WHERE` clause as instances of this new class (`?x rdf:type :BLCCompliantSectorCompany.`)

The second rule in (2) is very similar to the first one. The rule collects all individuals that bank with an international bank and asserts them as instances of a newly created class `BLCNonCompliantSectorCompany`.

Thus, the two rules together distinguish individuals that comply with (1a) from those that do not: the LegalTech application will query the inferred ontology by listing all individuals belonging to either `BLCCompliantSectorCompany` or `BLCNonCompliantSectorCompany` via simple SPARQL queries.

```
(2) sh:rule [rdf:type sh:SPARQLRule;
        sh:prefixes[sh:declare [sh:prefix"rdf";sh:namespace"..."], ... ];
        sh:construct """
          CONSTRUCT{ :BLCCompliantSectorCompany rdf:type rdfs:Class.
                 :BLCCompliantSectorCompany rdfs:subClassOf :SectorCompany.
                 ?x rdf:type :BLCCompliantSectorCompany. }
          WHERE{ ?x :bank-with ?y. ?y rdf:type :GhanaianBank. }""";];

    sh:rule [rdf:type sh:SPARQLRule;
        sh:prefixes[sh:declare [sh:prefix"rdf";sh:namespace"..."], ... ];
        sh:construct """
          CONSTRUCT{ :BLCNonCompliantSectorCompany rdf:type rdfs:Class.
                 :BLCNonCompliantSectorCompany rdfs:subClassOf :SectorCompany.
                 ?x rdf:type :BLCNonCompliantSectorCompany. }
          WHERE{ ?x :bank-with ?y. ?y rdf:type :InternationalBank. }""";]
```

Although the rules in (2) employ a different technology than [10]'s and [27]'s, the expressivity and the "modus operandi" of the three approaches is exactly the same. In other words, [10] and [27] are also designed to populate two classes such as `BLCCompliantSectorCompany` and `BLCNonCompliantSectorCompany` with all individuals that respectively comply with or not with (1a).

By contrast, it is not possible to implement the legal requirement (1d) via OWL classes/restrictions, as in [10], or via SHACL shapes, as in [27]. (1d) requires to *count* both the number of Ghanaian technical core employees and the number of all technical core employees, and then to *calculate* whether the former is at least 20% of the latter. OWL "is-a" inferences and SHACL shapes are not expressive enough to query *metadata* of RDF individuals. On the contrary, SPARQL offers the desired expressivity thanks to its *aggregate functions*[9] and its *arithmetic functions*[10].

However, SPARQL alone is not enough to implement (1d) because the two operations of counting the sets of technical core employees and calculating the proportion among these sets cannot be done via a single rule. SHACL provides the missing ingredient by allowing to *decouple* the implementation of the legal requirement into two *sequential* rules. By using SHACL-SPARQL rules as proposed here, the problem can be addressed.

The two SHACL-SPARQL rules that count the number of Ghanaian technical core employees and the total number of such employees are shown in (3).

```
(3) sh:rule [rdf:type sh:SPARQLRule; sh:order 0;
      sh:prefixes[sh:declare [sh:prefix"rdf";sh:namespace"..."], ... ];
      sh:construct """
      CONSTRUCT {?x :gh_tec_emp ?gh_tec_emp.}
      WHERE{ SELECT ?x (count(?y) as ?gh_tec_emp)
            WHERE{ ?x rdf:type :SectorCompany.
                   ?x :employ ?y.
                   ?y rdf:type :TechnicalCoreStaff.
                   ?y :is :ghanaian.} GROUP BY ?x}"""]

    sh:rule [rdf:type sh:SPARQLRule; sh:order 0;
      sh:prefixes[sh:declare [sh:prefix"rdf";sh:namespace"..."], ... ];
      sh:construct """
      CONSTRUCT {?x :tec_emp ?tec_emp.}
      WHERE{ SELECT ?x (count(?y) as ?tec_emp)
            WHERE{ ?x rdf:type :SectorCompany.
                   ?x :employ ?y.
                   ?y rdf:type :TechnicalCoreStaff.} GROUP BY ?x}"""]
```

In (3), sh:order is the SHACL operator to order the rules. These are executed from the lowest value of sh:order to the highest one. The two rules associate every sector company ?x with, respectively, their numbers of Ghanaians technical core employees and their number of overall technical core employees via two newly created datatype properties gh_tec_emp and tec_emp.

A separate rule, shown in (4) and executed *after* the ones in (3), because its sh:order is equal to 1, calculates the proportion between the values of the datatype properties gh_tec_emp and tec_emp, asserted via the previous rules.

---

[9] https://en.wikibooks.org/wiki/SPARQL/Aggregate_functions.
[10] https://en.wikibooks.org/wiki/SPARQL/Expressions_and_Functions.

(4) asserts all individuals for which the proportion is lower than 20% as instances of a newly created class `Nc_Gh_Tec_Emp`.

```
(4)    sh:rule [rdf:type sh:SPARQLRule; sh:order 1;
          sh:prefixes[sh:declare [sh:prefix"rdf";sh:namespace"..."], ... ];
          sh:construct """
            CONSTRUCT{ :Nc_Gh_Tec_Emp rdf:type rdfs:Class.
                       ?x rdf:type :Nc_Gh_Tec_Emp. }
            WHERE{ ?x rdf:type :SectorCompany.
                   ?x :gh_tec_emp ?gh_tec_emp.
                   ?x :tec_emp ?tec_emp.
                   FILTER(?gh_tec_emp<(?tec_emp*0.2)). }"""]
```

Finally, the LegalTech application can again retrieve the list of individuals belonging to the class `Nc_Gh_Tec_Emp`, i.e., the list of sector companies that do not comply with (1d), via a simple SPARQL query.

5   Conclusions and Future Works

This paper contributes the means to automatise compliance checking with Semantic Web technologies. The main motivation behind researching solutions grounded on W3C standards is the hypothesis that, in the future, these standards will likely serve as the basis of symbolic explainable Artificial Intelligence, particularly for LegalTech applications.

Some recent approaches along these lines, e.g., [6] and [10], propose solutions for compliance checking based on OWL2 inferences; the main motivation behind this technological choice is to keep the framework *decidable*.

Although controlling computational complexity is of course crucial, it should be privileged over the expressivity of the inferences only when there is really no other way to make the application working in reasonable time.

This paper provided evidence that OWL2 inferences are not enough expressive for representing several compliance checks required by existing regulations, specifically those checking and aggregating *metadata* of RDF individuals.

Subsection 4.2 above exemplified this kind of checks out of a real-world legal requirement that we found in the Local Content and Local Participation Regulations for extracting oil and gas in Ghana. Companies in the oil and gas upstream industry are required to employ at least 20% of Ghanaian technical core staff. In order to represent this requirement, we had to use SHACL-SPARQL rules: SPARQL provides aggregate and arithmetic operators, while SHACL allows to build sequences or flow charts of operations by specifying priorities on the rules.

Although we have not conducted (yet) any empirical investigation about the frequency of this kind of norms in existing regulations, we believe they are rather frequent. Regulations often impose legal constraints on, for instance, *sums* of money or *minimum/maximal* numerical values, or they require to *count* number of days/requests/attempts/etc., etc. All these constraints require to process metadata about RDF individuals. Therefore, their implementation requires the same expressivity offered by SHACL-SPARQL rules but not by OWL or SHACL shapes and Triple rules.

On the other hand, the computational complexity of SPARQL and SHACL does not seem to be significantly problematic (cf. [1,21]), nor, more generally, the one of compliance checkers based on sets of explicit if-then rules (cf. [30]). In fact, SHACL-SPARQL rules may be easily converted into other rule-based logical languages such as Answer Set Programming [24], for which automated reasoners with very good computational performance are available.

In future work, we will further enrich the ontology and evaluate it. Furthermore, an important direction of research is to incorporate time management in the ontology (cf. [25]), for which we plan to import existing ontologies such as OWL-Time[11] and the Time-indexed Value in Context ontology [22]. In this regard, we also intend to use a combination of SHACL and SPARQL since SPARQL vocabulary includes operators to compare dates.

On the contrary, OWL vocabulary does not include operators for comparing dates thus the formalization of time management in OWL seems to be harder, if not impossible. Therefore, we believe that our future works will further prove the main conclusion of this paper, i.e., that OWL is not expressive enough to check compliance with existing norms, many of which require to satisfy temporal deadlines or fix the maximal duration of certain permitted actions.

Indeed, the need to incorporate time management in our formalization stems from a lacuna that we found in the LI 2204: even if it is mandatory for contractors, subcontractors, licensees, and allied entities to employ a percentage of Ghanaians at certain levels of employment (management staff, technical core staff, etc.), yet a provision has not been made to define *the point in time* in which these Ghanaian employees must be employed in relation to the submission of the annual local content plan. In other words, a contractor, subcontractor, licensee, or allied entity can merely meet the LI 2204's legal requirements by employing the required percentage of Ghanaians *one day before* submitting the local content plan and by dismissing them *one day after* the submission. By playing this "trick", the legal requirement would be formally complied with, but the purposes for which LI 2204 was enacted would be obviously nullified.

The identified gap in LI 2204 could be simply solved by establishing a temporal threshold, i.e., a borderline date before which all Ghanaian employees must be employed in relation to the submission of annual local content plan. For instance, the legislation could specify that only employees hired *at least six months* prior the submission date of the local content plan can be considered.

Once the threshold has been fixed, compliance can be checked via SHACL rules that employ the SPARQL operators for comparing dates. Only if the comparison shows that a Ghanaian employee was employed before the threshold date, then the employee can count towards the required percentage.

Time management will allow us to model several further legal requirements arising from both legislation and contractual clauses. For instance, our ontology could be extended in order to associate each employee with the minimal period

---

[11] https://www.w3.org/TR/owl-time.

(e.g., number of years) in which, by contract, s/he must be employed before s/he can be dismissed. SHACL rules will calculate the period of employment from the start and end date of the employment and compare it with the stipulated minimal employment period to check compliance with the contractual requirement.

References

1. Ahmetaj, S., David, R., Ortiz, M., Polleres, A., Shehu, B., Šimkus, M.: Reasoning about explanations for non-validation in SHACL. In: Proceedings of 18th International Conference on Principles of Knowledge Representation and Reasoning (2021)
2. Alviano, M., et al.: The ASP system DLV2. In: Balduccini, M., Janhunen, T. (eds.) LPNMR 2017. LNCS (LNAI), vol. 10377, pp. 215–221. Springer, Cham (2017). https://doi.org/10.1007/978-3-319-61660-5_19
3. Athan, T., Boley, H., Governatori, G., Palmirani, M., Paschke, A., Wyner, A.: LegalRuleML: from metamodel to use cases. In: Morgenstern, L., Stefaneas, P., Lévy, F., Wyner, A., Paschke, A. (eds.) RuleML 2013. LNCS, vol. 8035, pp. 13–18. Springer, Heidelberg (2013). https://doi.org/10.1007/978-3-642-39617-5_4
4. Boella, G., Caro, L.D., Humphreys, L., Robaldo, L., Rossi, P., van der Torre, L.: Eunomos, a legal document and knowledge management system for the web to provide relevant, reliable and up-to-date information on the law. Artif. Intell. Law **24**(3), 245–283 (2016)
5. Boella, G., Caro, L.D., Rispoli, D., Robaldo, L.: A system for classifying multi-label text into EuroVoc. In: Proceedings of the International Conference on Artificial Intelligence and Law (ICAIL). ACM (2013)
6. Bonatti, P.A., Ioffredo, L., Petrova, I.M., Sauro, L., Siahaan, I.S.R.: Real-time reasoning in OWL2 for GDPR compliance. Artif. Intell. **289**, 103389 (2020)
7. Ceci, M.: Representing judicial argumentation in the semantic web. In: Casanovas, P., Pagallo, U., Palmirani, M., Sartor, G. (eds.) AICOL -2013. LNCS (LNAI), vol. 8929, pp. 172–187. Springer, Heidelberg (2014). https://doi.org/10.1007/978-3-662-45960-7_13
8. De Vos, M., Kirrane, S., Padget, J., Satoh, K.: ODRL policy modelling and compliance checking. In: Fodor, P., Montali, M., Calvanese, D., Roman, D. (eds.) RuleML+RR 2019. LNCS, vol. 11784, pp. 36–51. Springer, Cham (2019). https://doi.org/10.1007/978-3-030-31095-0_3
9. Dentler, K., Cornet, R., ten Teije, A., de Keizer, N.: Comparison of reasoners for large ontologies in the OWL 2 EL profile. Semant. Web **2**(2), 71–87 (2011)
10. Francesconi, E., Governatori, G.: Patterns for legal compliance checking in a decidable framework of linked open data. Artif. Intell. Law **31**(3), 445–464 (2022)
11. Gandon, F., Governatori, G., Villata, S.: Normative requirements as linked data. In: Wyner, A.Z., Casini, G. (eds.) Legal Knowledge and Information Systems, vol. 302. IOS Press (2017)
12. Gordon, T.F.: Constructing legal arguments with rules in the legal knowledge interchange format (LKIF). In: Casanovas, P., Sartor, G., Casellas, N., Rubino, R. (eds.) Computable Models of the Law. LNCS (LNAI), vol. 4884, pp. 162–184. Springer, Heidelberg (2008). https://doi.org/10.1007/978-3-540-85569-9_11
13. Horrocks, I.: OWL: a description logic based ontology language. In: van Beek, P. (ed.) CP 2005. LNCS, vol. 3709, pp. 5–8. Springer, Heidelberg (2005). https://doi.org/10.1007/11564751_2

14. Humphreys, L., et al.: Populating legal ontologies using semantic role labeling. Artif. Intell. Law **29**(2), 171–211 (2021)
15. Lahann, J., Scheid, M., Fettke, P.: Utilizing machine learning techniques to reveal VAT compliance violations in accounting data. In: IEEE 21st Conference on Business Informatics (CBI), vol. 1. IEEE (2019)
16. Leone, V., Caro, L.D., Villata, S.: Taking stock of legal ontologies: a feature-based comparative analysis. Artif. Intell. Law **28**(2), 207–235 (2020)
17. Nanda, R., et al.: A unifying similarity measure for automated identification of national implementations of European union directives. In: Proceedings of the International Conference on Artificial Intelligence and Law (ICAIL). ACM (2017)
18. Palmirani, M., Martoni, M., Rossi, A., Bartolini, C., Robaldo, L.: PrOnto: privacy ontology for legal compliance. In: 18th EU Conference on Digital Government (2018)
19. Palmirani, M., Governatori, G.: Modelling legal knowledge for GDPR compliance checking. In: 31st Conference on Legal Knowledge and Information Systems (2018)
20. Pareti, P., Konstantinidis, G., Norman, T.J., Şensoy, M.: SHACL constraints with inference rules. In: Ghidini, C., et al. (eds.) ISWC 2019. LNCS, vol. 11778, pp. 539–557. Springer, Cham (2019). https://doi.org/10.1007/978-3-030-30793-6_31
21. Pérez, J., Arenas, M., Gutierrez, C.: Semantics and complexity of SPARQL. ACM Trans. Database Syst. **34**(3), 1–45 (2009)
22. Peroni, S.: The semantic publishing and referencing ontologies. In: Peroni, S. (ed.) Semantic Web Technologies and Legal Scholarly Publishing. LGTS, vol. 15, pp. 121–193. Springer, Cham (2014). https://doi.org/10.1007/978-3-319-04777-5_5
23. Reed, W.J.: The Pareto, Zipf and other power laws. Econ. Lett. **74**(1), 15–19 (2001)
24. Robaldo, L., et al.: Compliance checking on first-order knowledge with conflicting and compensatory norms - a comparison among currently available technologies. Artif. Intell. Law (2023). https://doi.org/10.1007/s10506-023-09360-z
25. Robaldo, L., Caselli, T., Russo, I., Grella, M.: From Italian text to TimeML document via dependency parsing. In: Gelbukh, A. (ed.) CICLing 2011. LNCS, vol. 6609, pp. 177–187. Springer, Heidelberg (2011). https://doi.org/10.1007/978-3-642-19437-5_14
26. Robaldo, L., Pacenza, F., Zangari, J., Calegari, R., Calimeri, F., Siragusa, G.: Efficient compliance checking of RDF data. J. Log. Comput. **33**(8), 1753–1776 (2023)
27. Robaldo, L.: Towards compliance checking in reified I/O logic via SHACL. In: Maranhão, J., Wyner, A.Z. (eds.) Proceedings of 18th International Conference for Artificial Intelligence and Law (ICAIL 2021). ACM (2021)
28. Robaldo, L., Bartolini, C., Palmirani, M., Rossi, A., Martoni, M., Lenzini, G.: Formalizing GDPR provisions in reified I/O logic: the DAPRECO knowledge base. J. Log. Lang. Inf. **29**(4), 401–449 (2020)
29. Sasu, D.: Oil and gas sector contribution to GDP in Ghana 2014–2024. Statista (2021). https://www.statista.com/statistics/1235708/gdp-of-the-oil-and-gas-industry-in-ghana
30. Sun, X., Robaldo, L.: On the complexity of input/output logic. J. Appl. Log. **25**, 69–88 (2017)
31. Zhang, R., El-Gohary, N.: A machine learning approach for compliance checking-specific semantic role labeling of building code sentences. In: Mutis, I., Hartmann, T. (eds.) Advances in Informatics and Computing in Civil and Construction Engineering, pp. 561–568. Springer, Cham (2019). https://doi.org/10.1007/978-3-030-00220-6_67

Programming Contract Amending

Cosimo Laneve[1]📖, Alessandro Parenti[2](✉)📖, and Giovanni Sartor[2]📖

[1] Department of Computer Science and Engineering, University of Bologna,
Bologna, Italy
[2] Department of Legal Studies, University of Bologna, Bologna, Italy
alessandro.parenti3@unibo.it

Abstract. Legal contracts can be generally amended either because
real-world events require an adaptation of the contract to new circumstances or because new agreements between the parties take place. When
legal contracts are defined by a programming language, amendments
likely entail runtime modifications to the contract code. In this paper,
we present a law-derived framework for amending contract codes that are
written in *Stipula*, a programming language for legal contracts. The full
language, called *higher-order Stipula*, is applied to modelling real-world
examples of contract amendments, where modifications may add new
clauses or may rewrite (part of) old ones. We also discuss the prototype
implementation of the language and its graphical user interface.

1 Introduction

The use of computer code to represent, monitor or execute a legal agreement
between parties has been studied and employed in various forms since the 1970s
[20]. The coding of contracts can bring several benefits: lower costs of digital
transactions, the monitoring of business procedures, or the avoidance of litigation
because of an *ex-ante* automatic assessment of compliance [21].

Stipula [6] is a domain-specific language for drafting computable legal contracts. It was designed under the guiding principle of having an abstraction level
as close as possible to contractual practice, to facilitate its use by legal professionals. For this reason, it is based on a small set of primitives that reflect the
basic elements of legal contracts (*permissions, obligations*, etc.).

Current *Stipula* contracts are immutable, *i.e.*, they cannot be modified at runtime once the execution has been started. However, there may be several reasons
to modify a contract, ranging from the fact that that parties have changed their
mind, to the occurrence of an unexpected event that affects the contractual relationship. The latter case is usually dealt with in contracts by *hardship* clauses,
and represents a crucial issue, especially in long-term commercial agreements.
In Sect. 3, we analyse the most common scenarios requiring amendments, and
discuss the legal basis for amending contracts in legal systems.

Because of the immutability of *Stipula*, in order to model contract amendments, one would have to anticipate the potential modifications causes at the
time of contract formation, and provide for them accordingly, in the contract

M. Bono et al. (Eds.): JSAI-isAI 2023 Workshops, LNAI 14644, pp. 19–34, 2024.
https://doi.org/10.1007/978-3-031-60511-6_2

code. Besides being hardly feasible, such a practice would significantly raise the drafting costs, thus nullifying one of the main purposes for digitalizing legal contracts. Therefore, in the present work, we discuss the addition of a new feature to *Stipula* in order to support for future amendments during contract execution. Up to our knowledge, no other programming language for legal contracts has yet addressed this issue.

Our full language, called *higher-order Stipula* features functions that may carry computer code as an input parameter. The code is run when the function is invoked, thus possibly modifying the original contract protocol. This solution allows us to manage situations where the amendment affects the whole body of the contract, so that only the new provisions are operational, as well as situations where only some parts are changed, so that the rest of the previous code remains operational. In Sect. 4, we test the new feature on a real-world example directly taken from contract practice. In Sect. 5 we discuss two methods for restricting amendments. The first method requires the parties' agreement. With the second method, parties may pre-define constraints against which future amendments can be verified at run-time. We then explore in Sect. 6 the prototype implementation of *higher-order Stipula* and its graphical user interface. We end our contribution by discussing the state of the art in Sect. 7 and presenting our conclusions in Sect. 8.

2   Background: Modelling Contracts with *Stipula*

Stipula is a domain-specific language for modelling legal contracts that has been designed to be more concrete and execution-oriented than a specification language and, at the same time, more abstract than a full-fledged programming language [6]. *Stipula* consists of a small set of primitives that reflect some key features of legal contracts:

- A contract enters into force at the moment of the 'meeting of the minds' of the parties. This is represented by the *agreement* operator through which parties are called to agree on the terms of the contract. For example, the following script

```
agreement (Supplier, Buyer, PriceProvider) {
        Supplier, Buyer : formula
} init ⇒ @Start
```

defines a contracts whose parties are `Supplier`, `Buyer` and `PriceProvider`, where `Supplier` and `Buyer` *must initially agree* on the value of the field `formula`;
- legal contracts may create, extinguish or regulate the parties' normative positions such as permissions, prohibitions, obligations or powers. *Stipula* uses *states* to model and automatically enforce prohibitions and permissions. In each state only certain functions may be invoked while others are precluded. States are indicated by an "@" in front. In the foregoing code, the state enabling the invocation of the `update_price` function is @Start. *Functions*

are used to express actions of parties and may correspond to contract clauses. For example, in the state @Start the PriceProvider updates the price and sends the new value to the Supplier and the Buyer.

```
@Start PriceProvider: update_price(p)[] {
        p → price
        p → Supplier, Buyer
} ⇒ @Waiting_order
```

– Legal contracts are usually required to manage currencies or digital goods. In *Stipula* these entities are called *assets* and operations involving them (transfers, escrows, etc.) are characterised by ad hoc syntactical specifications, thus separating them from other data types. For example, an asset transfer is expressed by

```
w —o wallet
```

that *empties* the asset w and *moves* its value into wallet (that is, the value of wallet *is augmented* by the value of w). In contrast to assets, fields hold standard values (e.g., price, deadline) and are not diminished by the transferred value. For example, p → price updates the value of price to p, but p is not emptied;

– *events* are used to check the fulfilment of obligations at a certain time and eventually to issue a penalty. The operation

```
now + time_due >> @Inactive{
    "the contract ends" → Buyer
} ⇒ @End
```

triggers a transition at time now+time_due. The transition, which may only take place in the state @Inactive, informs the Buyer that the contract is terminated;

– in most cases, contracts' execution may depend on external events, such as updates of timetables, sporting event results, mortgage rates, etc., whose data need to be fed into the contract. This need is satisfied by involving a trusted intermediary party, who participates in the contract and is only allowed to call specific functions. The same solution may be used to solve disputes and establish non-automatically verifiable (e.g. open-ended) circumstances, such as *force majeure*, serious damage, etc.

The formal semantics of *Stipula*, as well as the definition of techniques for verifying legal contracts and the design of the prototype, are fully reported in [6]. Here we only provide a simplified description of the syntax, so as to allow the comprehension of the examples presented.

As an example of *Stipula* code, consider the following real-world scenario directly derived from a contractual dispute which arose before the Court of Arbitration of the International Chamber of Commerce[1]. The dispute concerned

---

[1] ICC case n. 10351/2001.

```
1    stipula GasSupply {
2        parties: Supplier, Buyer, PriceProvider
3        fields: price, formula, order
4        assets: wallet
5
6        agreement (Supplier, Buyer, PriceProvider) {
7            Supplier, Buyer : formula
8        } init ➡ @Start
9
10       @Start,@Waiting_order PriceProvider: update_price(p)[] {
11           p → price
12           p → Supplier, Buyer
13       } ➡ @Waiting_order
14
15       @Waiting_order Buyer: place_order()[w] {
16           w/(price×formula) → order
17           order → Supplier
18           w ⊸ wallet
19       } ➡ @Order
20
21       @Order Supplier: send_gas()[g] (g == order){
22           g ⊸ Buyer
23           wallet ⊸ Supplier
24       } ➡ @Waiting_order
25
26       @Waiting_order Supplier,Buyer: formula_revision(f)[] {
27           f → formula
28       } ➡ @Waiting_order
29   }
```

Fig. 1. The Gas Supply contract in *Stipula*

a long-term contract for the purchase of liquid natural gas. In order to set the cost of oil, parties define a price formula (that, in our case, for simplicity, is a multiplicative factor) and agree to refer to a specific pricing agency's publications to retrieve the necessary parameters (the market price, in our case). They also provide for a price revision clause regulating the procedures and conditions for updating the formula. Table 1 presents a simplified version of the agreement in its main points. The contract could be represented in *Stipula* as shown in Fig. 1.

Lines 1–4 define parties, fields, and assets of the contract called GasSupply. The contract includes the third party PriceProvider representing the reporting agency to which Supplier and Buyer refer to retrieve the necessary market data

Table 1. The Gas Supply contract in natural language

1. Agreement. *Supplier* and *Buyer* stipulate a long term agreement for the supply of liquified natural gas. Parties indicate *Price Provider* as the reference price agency and fix a *price formula*.

2. Price. Gas price is calculated by applying the *price formula* to the price provided by *Price Provider*.

3. Purchase. *Buyer* can place an order for gas by paying in advance the corresponding price, as resulting from the *price formula*. *Supplier* shall deliver the gas ordered and payed without undue delay.

4. Formula Revision. Parties can, upon agreement, decide to revise the *price formula*, in order to match market needs.

to calculate the (discounted) price. The `formula` stores the multiplicative factor to be applied to the market price; the field `order` stores the gas order made by the buyer each time.

Through the `agreement` clause (lines 6–8) parties set the field `formula` and express their binding acceptance of contract terms (*meeting of the minds*). The contract is initialised in the state `@Start` (line 8) where the only action admitted is the setting of `price` by the reporting agency `PriceProvider` – lines 10–13. [Line 10 specifies that `update_price` may be also invoked in the state `@Waiting_order`.] Then the contract transits in the state `@Waiting_order`. In this state, the Buyer purchases gas by means of the function `place_order`. This function takes `w` representing the currency sent for the purchase (the square brackets identify the parameters that are assets). The corresponding amount of gas, *i.e.* `w/(price×formula)`, is stored into `order` (line 16) and communicated to the `Supplier` (line 17); then `w` is escrowed by the contract and stored in `wallet` (line 18). At this point, the contract transits to the `@Order` state, enabling the `Supplier` to call the `send_gas` function. Through this, the gas (`g`) is sent to the `Buyer` (line 22) and the money stored in `wallet` sent to the `Supplier` (line 25). We remark that `send_gas` can be invoked provided the gas `g` is exactly what has been ordered by the `Buyer` (that has been stored in `order`). Finally, Lines 26–28 define the price determination formula. It can be called by both parties and allow them to update `formula` with a new one.

Further transpositions of legal contracts in *Stipula* can be found in [5]. The basic definition of *Stipula* does not admit the management of *exceptional behaviours*, *i.e.* all those behaviours that cannot be anticipated due to the occurrence of unforeseeable and extraordinary events, which, in legal contracts, are usually dealt with amendments. The extension of the language with a feature for modelling amendments is discussed in the following sections.

3   Amending Contracts

The principle of *freedom of contract* allows parties to modify contracts at their will, provided that there is an agreement and that the new content is not against the law. Occasionally, one party may yield to the other the power to change some parts of the agreement unilaterally [2]. This is a common practice for consumer contracts and standard terms of service, where the right to modify is usually tied to certain requirements, such as notifying the other party of the change and giving them the possibility to withdraw. In specific cases, the right to unilateral modification (*jus variandi*) may be directly conferred by the legislator (e.g., in Italian law, the employer's right to change employees'ì tasks[2]).

The modification to contract may also originate externally to the parties, such as when a court declares a contract partially void due to formal or substantial flaws or when unexpected events outside the control of parties affect the contractual relationship. These last cases are particularly relevant in long-term contracts and require legal solutions in order to deal with occurrences that couldn't be anticipated by the parties.

---

[2] Art. 2103 Codice Civile.

Contracts are entered into with the expectation that both parties will fulfil their obligations as agreed upon. The roman brocard *pacta sunt servanda* (agreement have to be respected), constitutes a foundational principle of contract theory: the contract is a mutual promise in which each party can hold the other one to the promised performance However, parties accepted to be bound by those promises under the particular set of circumstances standing at the time of stipulation: if these circumstances change, this commitment may need to be revised. For example, the beginning of a war could drastically raise the price of commodities needed for production or the outbreak of a pandemic could halt factories' activity. Such changes of circumstances may make performance of contractual obligations impossible, excessively onerous or even deprive the performance of its original utility for the counterparty. To address these situations, a legal basis to justify non-performance or to legitimately request an amendment of the contract is provided by the principle of *clausola rebus sic stantibus*: a contract is binding only as far as the relevant circumstances remain the same as they were at the time of conclusion of the agreement [22].

The matter is known to most legal systems but it is addressed in different ways. In common law systems, courts have elaborated the doctrine of *frustration*[3]. Frustration represents an excuse when an unforeseen change in circumstances deprives the contract of all utility for one party, even though the material capacity to perform the obligation is not affected. In the United States, one can also find the notion of *impracticability* which, recognised by the Uniform Commercial Code (§ 2-615), offers a defense in case performance became impractical due to a contingency that the parties, at the time of stipulation, assumed would not take place. Unlike under *frustration*, impracticability also applies where performance has become extremely difficult or onerous for one party [18].

In civil law countries, the issue is often addressed by national legislation. For example, in France and Italy, the respective civil codes include a provision dealing with supervening events that render the performance excessively onerous for one party (Art. 1195 Code Civil, art. 1467 Codice Civile). These norms give to the burdened party the possibility to request an amendment of the contract in order to recover the original contractual balance.

In contract practice, especially in international context, the eventuality of unexpected changes in circumstances that might affect the agreement is usually dealt with by specific clauses defining the conditions and procedures to be followed in such cases. By writing such clauses, parties can avoid the uncertainty of being at the mercy of the relevant national legislation and adjudication [10]. The main examples in this sense are *force majeure* and hardship clauses. While force majeure occurs when performance becomes impossible and usually leads to suspension or termination, hardship cases take place where the equilibrium of a

---

[3] The *frustration* doctrine was originally developed by English courts as a consequence to the famous *Coronation* cases in 1902–1904. The cancellation of King Edward VII's coronation frustrated the purpose of the defendants who leased apartments to witness the procession from a privileged spot. See *Krell v Henry* (1903).

contract is altered making compliance significantly more onerous for one party[4].
In these cases, the burdened party is usually entitled to request an amendment
of the contract, or its termination.

The contract defined in the language of Sect. 2 do not provide ways to deal
directly with modifications during its execution. Therefore, in order to model
either *force majeure* or hardship, one should anticipate all the appropriate
amendments for each possible circumstance at the time of first drafting. While
this is easy for termination clauses (it is enough to include a transition to a
final state), it is clearly impossible for other kinds of amendments [16]. Even an
attempt to do that would raise drafting costs and introduce huge complexities
in the contract, thus nullifying one of the main objectives of *Stipula*, which is
to have a simple and intelligible code. For these reasons, in the next section, we
discuss an extension of the language with a feature that allows parties to remove
or amend the effects of a contract in a direct and intelligible way.

4 *Stipula* with Amendments

Switching to the programming perspective, contract amendments entail a modification of the contract protocol. However, we notice that different kinds of
amendment produce different effects on the code. Some cases may only require
the addition of a new function or the removal of an old one, while others may
affect the whole existing protocol. Moreover, old and new codes will often have to
be operational at the same time, potentially giving rise to invocation conflicts.
In order to implement amendments, it is necessary to handle these situations
effectively.

Technically, amendments are runtime adjustments to the contract's behavior.
In programming languages, these runtime adjustment are usually expressed by
higher-order functions that may also take code as an input parameter. This code
is run when such a function is invoked, thus possibly modifying the function's
behaviour. A *higher-order* function in *Stipula* is

@Q Party: amendment $(\!|X,Y,Z|\!)$ {remove X add Y run Z}

This function carries three parameters in brackets $(\!|\cdot|\!)$, whose roles are indicated
by the directives remove X add Y run Z. X is a sequence of function names that
will be removed from the contract (the terms of the sequence may be either f or
A:f or Q A:f); Y represents the new code added and may include declarations of
new parties, fields, assets as well as new functions that will amend the contract;
Z is the body of the higher-order functions. Therefore Z is defined in the form
$\{..\} \Rightarrow$ @Q, and may also include the new elements defined in Y. It is worth
mentioning that, while X and Y are potentially empty sequences (i.e., optional
parameters), Z is mandatory (it is, in fact, necessary to at least define the state
that the contract will transit to after the function invocation).

The formal semantics of *higher-order Stipula* has been defined in [15]; the
purpose of this paper is rather to discuss the underlying legal basis to the new

---

[4] Art. 6.2.2 UNIDROIT Principles.

higher-order feature and to provide practical design patterns. We will do this by presenting real-world cases of contract amendments.

We build on the example presented in Sect. 2, drawing from the dispute arose in case n. 10351 of the ICC Court of Arbitration (hereinafter, "the dispute"). In addition to the contract code in Fig. 1, parties provide an amendment clause which is represented by the *higher-order* function

```
@Waiting_order Seller,Buyer: amendment(X, Y, Z){remove X add Y run Z}
```

that can be called by `Seller` and `Buyer` to introduce a modification. For the purposes of this section, we assume that parties find an agreement on the amendment outside the contract. We discuss in Sect. 5 how to constrain amendments in *higher-order Stipula*.

4.1   Additive Amendment

From the history of the dispute[5] we can see that parties included in their contract a so-called take-or-pay clause. A *take-or-pay* clause is a provision in a contract stating that a buyer has the obligation of either taking delivery of goods from a Supplier or paying a specified penalty amount to the Supplier for not taking them. This kind of provision benefits both parties because reduces the risk of the investment on the supplier side, and allows the buyer to negotiate a lower price[6] For the purposes of our example, we can assume that an external event (*e.g.*, a war) affected the gas market as to increase the contractual risk on all market participants. Therefore, parties agree to introduce a take-or-pay clause to reduce their exposure for the following two years of their business relationship, providing a penalty in case the purchase threshold is not reached. To do so, `Supplier` invokes the `amendment` function as shown in Fig. 2 from the top.

At this stage, all the function's parameters (`remove` X `add` Y `run` Z) are instantiated. The first parameter ε specifies that there are no functions to be removed from the old code. The second parameter, $\mathbb{D}$, defines a list of new functions. They generally reflect the original code presented in Fig. 1 but with some additions necessary to implement the *take-or-pay* clause.

Two fields – `threshold` and `t_thre` – as well as the asset `penalty` are introduced. The fields respectively represent the amount of gas that the buyer committed to buy and the time span within which the parties have committed to do it (two years), while the asset will be used to store the escrowed money for the penalty.

Being the *take-or-pay* clause essentially an obligation (on the buyer), *Stipula* uses *events* to model it (see Sect. 2). In particular, the function `take_or_pay` is used to escrow the penalty fee (line 5) and to schedule an event (lines 6–8) that can be read as follows: if, after two years, in whatever state `@X` of the contract, the threshold amount of gas to be purchased will not be reached yet, then the penalty fee will automatically be sent to `Supplier`. Otherwise, the penalty fee is returned to the `Buyer`.

---

[5] Available at https://tinyurl.com/Case10351.

[6] investopedia.com, available at https://tinyurl.com/5xxjp997.

```
1        Supplier: amendment(ε, 𝔻, {2y → t_thre  100 → threshold} ⇒ @Restart)
```

where 𝔻 is:

```
1     fields: threshold, t_thre
2     asset: penalty
3
4     @Restart Buyer: take_or_pay()[t] (t==1000){
5            t —∘ penalty
6            now + t_thre >> @X {
7                 (threshold>0) penalty —∘ Supplier  ;  penalty —∘ Buyer
8            } ⇒ @X
9     } ⇒ @New_Start
10
11    @New_Start, @New_Waiting PriceProvider: update_price(p)[] {
12               p → price
13               p → Supplier
14               price → Buyer
15         } ⇒ @New_Waiting
16
17    @New_Waiting Buyer: place_order()[w] {
18               w / (price×formula) → order
19               order → Supplier
20               w —∘ wallet
21    } ⇒ @New_Order
22
23    @New_Order Supplier: send_gas()[g] (g == order){
24               g —∘ Buyer
25               wallet —∘ Supplier
26               threshold−order → threshold
27    } ⇒ @New_Waiting
28
29    @New_Waiting Supplier,Buyer: amendment(X, Y, Z)  {remove X add Y run Z}
```

Fig. 2. Take-or-pay amendment

After the execution of this function is over, the contract transits to the new state @New_Waiting. Both the update_price and the place_order function mirror the ones present in the old version of the contract, while send_gas features an important difference. After the Supplier has received the payment for the gas sold, the threshold field is updated by subtracting to it the value of gas just purchased by the buyer (line 25). This allows the automatic assessment of obligation compliance made by the event in lines 6–8.

Finally, the third parameter of the amendment defines its body. The newly introduced fields are instantiated with the values agreed by the parties and the contract moves to the new state @Restart. In this state, the buyer can invoke the take_or_pay function to actually implement the amendment.

Notice that 𝔻 introduces a whole new set of contract states and none of the new functions provide transitions to previous states from Fig. 1. This means that the old code is completely deactivated, even though it is not definitively removed. In fact, it will be enough to invoke again the amendment function and make a transition to an old state to render it operational again. For example, after the two years negotiated by parties, they will be able to get to the old version of the contract. We call this kind of amendment *additive*: it introduces a whole new piece of protocol replacing the old one, and the two never overlap.

```
Supplier,Buyer: amendment(ε, D, {"Provider_revision"→~} ⇒ @Waiting_Order)
```

Where $\mathbb{D}$ is:

```
1    @Waiting_Order Supplier,Buyer: price_revision(x)[] (x=="dispute_provider")
     {
2          x → Supplier, Buyer
3    } ⇒ @Meeting
4
5    @Meeting Supplier,Buyer: define_Provider(X, Y, Z)    {remove X add Y run Z}
```

Fig. 3. Price revision clause amendment

4.2   Overriding Amendment

Along the course of the contractual relationship, parties from the dispute frequently modified the contract, particularly in relation to the determination of price. With one of these amendments, in 1981, parties introduced a modification to the price revision clause, providing for the possibility to replace the price reporting agency where this had stopped publishing reliable data necessary to the price determination. Should one party dispute the publications, they would meet to negotiate a new trusted source.

In order to introduce such a possibility, the amendment function is invoked by either party as shown in the first line of Fig. 3. Also in this case, there is no function to remove (the first argument is ε). The short body of the amendment function, the third parameter, is indicated directly in the first line. It simply communicates the title of the modification to all parties and makes a transition to the Waiting_Order state, already existing in the original contract.

In contrast to the previous example, here the new code $\mathbb{D}$ does not substitute completely the old set of states, therefore old functions are kept operational. $\mathbb{D}$ introduces a new version of the price_revision function from Fig. 1 and implements the possibility of calling a parties meeting in case the provider becomes unreliable. Having the two functions the same name, the same callers and same state, the new and the old price_revision function clearly overlap with each other and enter into conflict once they are invoked. *Higher-order Stipula* handles conflicts though priorities and by leveraging constraints. As a general rule, conflicts are resolved by giving priority to functions of the newest code. However, this can be handled more smoothly by providing specific constraints that have to be satisfied. In this case, the newest price_revision requires the input x to be equal to the string "dispute_provider" (line 1). This means that, whether parties want to use that function to change provider, they will have to fulfill that condition, otherwise they will just call the old version from Fig. 1 and simply modify the price formula. Once the contract has transited to the @Meeting state (line 3), parties are enabled to call the define_provider function. This is modeled as a *higher-order* one in that it is necessary to modify the code to add a new party to the contract.

We call this kind of amendment *overriding*: old and new codes are both operational at the same time and are linked with each other. Potential conflicts are solved through priorities and constraint management.

```
Buyer: define_Provider(update_price, D', {"New_Price_Provider" →˜} ⇒ @Waiting_order)
```

where $\mathbb{D}'$ is:

```
1    parties: NewPriceProvider = NewPriceProvider
2
3    @Waiting_order NewPriceProvider: update_price(p)[] {
4         p → price
5         p → Supplier,Buyer
6    } ⇒ @Waiting_order
```

Fig. 4. Substitution of Provider

After some time, according to parties' opinion, the data published by the reporting agency stop being truly representative of the market situation and therefore they decide to change provider by triggering the newly added clause. To implement this kind of amendment, the intervention needed is two-folded: on the one hand, a new party has to be introduced into the contract, while, on the other, the old price provider has to be prevented from interacting with the contract. Once in the @Meeting state, this can be obtained by invoking define_Provider.

As shown in Fig. 4, the first parameter of define_Provider indicates update_price, meaning that the function is removed from the old code of Fig. 1. At the same time, $\mathbb{D}'$ introduces the new price provider as a party to the contract and defines a new update_price function that can be only accessed by the new provider. Lastly, the body of the function in line 1 communicates the name of the new provider to all parties and moves the contract to @Waiting_Order.

At this stage, the provisions regulating the parties' relationship results from the combination of the original agreement, plus the two following amendments. This is represented by the code from Fig. 1, the code $\mathbb{D}$ from Fig. 3 and $\mathbb{D}'$ from Fig. 4, which are all operational at the same time. Just like the previous one, this amendment does not introduce a new set of states: old and new code uptimes are preserved simultaneously. However, no overlaps occur. The old and new update_price differ as to the party that is able to invoke it. For this reason, the removal of the old function is necessary to prevent the old provider form interacting with the contract. We call this type of amendment *overriding with removal*.

5 Amendment Supplements: Agreements and Constraints

The purpose of the present work was to discuss how to technically define amendments in *higher-order Stipula*. One basic condition for modifying a legal contract was left out of the representation: the *mutual consent of the parties*. In fact, excluding the cases where the legislator confers to one party the power to modify the contract unilaterally, in all other cases, the manifestation of mutual agreement is required[7]. In order to deal with this principle within the contract, it is necessary to allow parties to express the consent to amendments at runtime.

---

[7] Art. 2.1.1 UNIDROIT Principles.

```
constraints [ (parties: fixed;)?   (fields: z̄ constant;)?
                  (assets: k̄ not-decrease;)?   (reachable states: @Q‾)? ]
```

Fig. 5. Static constraints on Amendments

The *Stipula* language already features an agreement clause which is triggered at the deployment of the contract and that corresponds to the "meeting of the minds": every one must accept the terms of the contract in order for the legal bound to arise. By following the same pattern, the *higher-order Stipula* prototype [7] already provides an agreement clause that occurs in correspondence of every amendment that requires the consent of every party.

In addition, it is possible for parties to set specific boundaries to contract amending. In fact, there may be several factors providing limitations to parties freedom in amending an agreement. Beside the general limit represented by legal systems' mandatory rules (*cf.* the principle in Art. 1418 of the Italian Civil Code, the Art. 1:103 of PECL – the European Principle of Contract Law – and the Art. 1.4 of the international Unidroit Principles) legislators can also provide for more domain specific boundaries such as limits to prices for basic commodities, employees' salary or loan interest rates. Moreover, parties themselves may want to limit their behaviour.

In order to specify and implement such possibilities, in [15] we have studied a technique for defining amendments that are mandatorily accepted by parties. That is, the technique allow parties to agree on the type of amendments they might accept in the future when a contract is stipulated. To this aim, we extend *higher-order Stipula* with the syntactic clause in Fig. 5. This clause allows us to define an amendment verifier that automatically checks whether amendments comply or not with the restrictions in the clause.

Every constraint in the clause may be missing (when all the constraints are empty then "constraints [ ]" is omitted and we are back to the basic syntax). The constraint "parties: fixed" specifies that amendments cannot modify the set of parties. If this constraint was present in the *gas supply* contract, then the amendment $\mathbb{D}'$ of Fig. 4 would have been rejected. The constraint "fields: z̄ constant" disables updates of fields in z̄. The constraint "assets: k̄ not-decrease" protects private assets to be drained by unauthorised parties. Finally, the constraint "reachable states: Q‾" guarantees that, whatever contract update is performed, the states in Q‾ can be reached from the ending state of the amendment. This is because, for example, the corresponding functionalities cannot be disallowed forever. The foregoing clause has not yet been integrated in [7]: the prototyping work is ongoing.

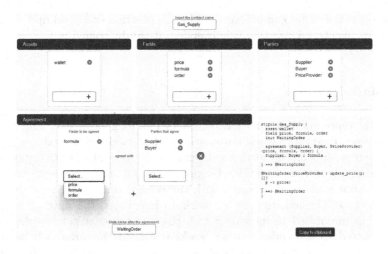

Fig. 6. The *Stipula* editor - Heading and Agreement

6   The *Stipula* Prototype and its Graphical Interface

Stipula has been prototyped, therefore one can experiment enforcement of contractual conditions, traceability, and outcome certainty. The prototype is a Java application that is available on the github website of the project, together with a number of sample contracts [7]. The development has taken three months and ~3000 lines of Java code. In order to use it, it is necessary to clone the repository and install the prototype following the instructions provided on the website. Once installed, it is possible to write a brand new contract and run it to test its execution.

The prototype is also provided with the *higher-order Stipula* extension, supporting runtime amendments. At the implementation level, this functionality is achieved by updating the contract instance with changes contained in the *higher order*. Once the changes are overwritten, the new version is deployed. A technical explanation of the prototype design is contained in [6].

Although *Stipula* features an intuitive syntax, the project is provided with a user-friendly graphical interface to guide the drafting. This is clearly useful for first-time users as well as for users that are already familiar with the language in that avoids potential syntactic mistakes. Figure 6 shows how the interface is presented. For the heading of the contract, the user has to fill in the contract name, the parties, assets and fields in their corresponding windows. For the agreement clause, it is necessary to choose among the already declared fields and parties that are going to comply with the fields' values. As the editor is filled in, the corresponding *Stipula* code is automatically created and updated real-time in the box on the bottom-right. Similarly, writing functions requires declaring both the starting and ending states, the parties entitled to call it and the input parameters needed. Afterwards, the user can choose from a list of possible operations that can be executed by the function call (field update, asset transfer, event, etc.). Once the code is ended, it can be copied in the prototype and executed.

7 Related Works

The digital representation of legal contracts has long been explored, for the main purpose of monitoring and automating contract-related procedures [11,17]. In this context, substantial work has been done in the wake of 'Ricardian Contracts', originally introduced by Ian Grigg in 1996 [13]. This approach consists in linking written contract documents with the related computer executable code via *parameters*. Through the use of mark-up languages, the natural language document is annotated to indicate which parts of the contract are the values to be inputted to the code. Further works extended this approach by building a template model for contracts [4] and providing specifications to increase contract's intelligibility [19]. However, the capability of capturing the semantics of an agreement by annotating natural language documents is limited to the input that is provided by the tagged data. Moreover, operational code may still remain opaque to legal professionals, thus preventing the validation of whether it is faithful to the actual agreement [3].

A different approach to express contracts is represented by Domain-Specific languages (DSL). A well-designed, relatively understandable DSL for legal contracts has the advantage of keeping code and agreement (or a straightforward representation of it), within a single artefact. With a single artefact to deal with, it is simpler to check whether the meaning of the agreement and its code implementation match [3]. Such a contract can still be coupled with natural language explanations of the meaning of the code, but the code, rather than these explanations would provide the binding formulation of the contract. Different formalism and approaches have been studied in the literature. For instance Flood and Goodenough have described a loan agreement (in the financial domain) as a particular kind of finite state machine [9]. These machines are mathematical entities used to describe systems with finite set of states and transitions, where transitions allow movements from a state to another in response to given inputs (*events*). While this approach is interesting when the contract is simple enough, it becomes cryptic when the contract is more complex. In particular, it becomes hard to connect the machine to the standard formulation of the contract in natural languages.

Another interesting technique is based on Controlled Natural languages (CNL) [1,8]. A CNL resembles natural language in wording, but is based on formally defined syntax that is automatically converted to a programming language. As a consequence, the code is easily readable. However, due to the constrains imposed by the CNL, it may result harder to write the contract (with respect to natural language) because the formalism may miss computational constructs. It has also been argued that a CNL might represent a "false friend" for the user [14], i.e., it might induce the user to assume that a CNL-expression has the same meaning as natural language expression, which might not always be the case.

Declarative specifications could provide advantages in formally representing legal contracts and reasoning upon them. For example, they can be more compact than other paradigms, therefore easier to draft and to verify, as well as easier to understand by parties [12]. *Stipula* commits to an imperative paradigm that allows one to represent in a more direct way the stages of contracts' life-cycle by means of a state-aware programming style. Additionally, the pretty straightforward syntax should hopefully make *Stipula* as intuitive as the declarative specifications for legal professionals. The formal semantics defined in [6,15] should allow one to define automatic analyzers that verify legal contract correctness.

Higher-order Stipula is a DSL that is based on state-oriented programming with explicit management of assets and with higher-order to express runtime modifications of the code. In our formalism, states are not finitely many because the contracts have memories that store settings and assets. Rather, states are used to express permissions and prohibition of invoking functionalities by contract parties.

8   Conclusions

The present work showcased an extension of *Stipula* for amending legal contracts at run-time. The extension relies on higher-order functions and allows one to program situations were the old code is completely replaced by new one as well as situations where old and new code are both operative and coexist. Overall, we believe that the higher-order mechanism is a simple and intelligible feature that may assist legal practitioners in programming contract amendments.

Up-to our knowledge, *higher-order Stipula* is the first legal contract language natively integrating amendments in its syntax. From a legal perspective, we believe this technique to reflect contractual practice, where contracts include clauses that allow for future amendments. In our context this is done though the higher-order predicate that enables the revision of the contract, i.e., the removal of old clauses and the insertion of new ones. Simply terminating an instance of the contract and deploying a new version of it would depart legal practice, possibly resulting less intuitive for legal professionals. From the programming perspective, the *higher-order* has the advantage that amendments may be analysed using the same techniques on which the first-order language is based. The compliance assessment of the types of the amendments with respect to the types of the original code is done by using the same original type inference system. By exploiting this property, for example, one can design techniques for constraining amendments at the moment of the drafting, as shown in Sect. 5. Adding a runtime extension to some existing tool that copes with amendments is not the same as it would be unconstrained.

References

1. Lexon language (2022). http://lexon.org/. Accessed 13 Apr 2023
2. Caldarelli, G.: Unilateral modification of long term contracts: American change of terms clauses and Italian Ius Variandi from a 'relational' point of view. Eur. Rev. Contract Law **17**(1), 37–53 (2021)
3. Clack, C.D.: Languages for smart and computable contracts. CoRR abs/2104.03764 (2021). https://arxiv.org/abs/2104.03764
4. Clack, C.D., Bakshi, V.A., Braine, L.: Smart contract templates: foundations, design landscape and research directions. CoRR abs/1608.00771 (2016). http://arxiv.org/abs/1608.00771
5. Crafa, S., Laneve, C.: Programming legal contracts – a beginners guide to *Stipula*. In: Ahrendt, W., Beckert, B., Bubel, R., Johnsen, E.B. (eds.) The Logic of Software. A Tasting Menu of Formal Methods. LNCS, vol. 13360, pp. 129–146. Springer, Cham (2022). https://doi.org/10.1007/978-3-031-08166-8_7
6. Crafa, S., Laneve, C., Sartor, G., Veschetti, A.: Pacta sunt servanda: legal contracts in *Stipula*. Sci. Comput. Program. **225**, 102911 (2023)
7. Crafa, S., Laneve, C., Veschetti, A.: The Stipula prototype. https://github.com/stipula-language/stipula. Accessed 31 Mar 2023
8. Datoo, A., Kowalski, R.: Logical English meets legal English for swaps and derivatives. Artif. Intell. Law **30**(2), 163–197 (2022)
9. Flood, M.D., Goodenough, O.R.: Contract as automaton: representing a simple financial agreement in computational form. Artif. Intell. Law **30**(3), 391–416 (2022)
10. Fontaine, M., De Ly, F.: Drafting international contracts. BRILL (2006)
11. Governatori, G.: Representing business contracts in RuleML. Int. J. Coop. Inf. Syst. **14**(02n03), 181–216 (2005)
12. Governatori, G., Idelberger, F., Milosevic, Z., Riveret, R., Sartor, G., Xu, X.: On legal contracts, imperative and declarative smart contracts, and blockchain systems. Artif. Intell. Law **26**, 377–409 (2018)
13. Grigg, I.: The Ricardian Contract (1996). https://iang.org/papers/ricardian_contract.html. Accessed 13 Apr 2023
14. Idelberger, F.: The uncanny valley of computable contracts: analysis of computable contract formalisms with a focus towards controlled natural languages. Ph.D. thesis, European University Institute (2022)
15. Laneve, C., Parenti, A., Sartor, G.: Legal contracts amending with *Stipula*. In: Jongmans, S.S., Lopes, A. (eds.) COORDINATION 2023. LNCS, vol. 13908, pp. 253–270. Springer, Cham (2023). https://doi.org/10.1007/978-3-031-35361-1_14
16. Mik, E.: Smart contracts: terminology, technical limitations and real world complexity. Law Innov. Technol. **9**(2), 269–300 (2017)
17. Milosevic, Z., Gibson, S., Linington, P., Cole, J., Kulkarni, S.: On design and implementation of a contract monitoring facility. In: Proceedings of the First IEEE International Workshop on Electronic Contracting, pp. 62–70 (2004)
18. Palmer, V.V.: Excused performances: force majeure, impracticability, and frustration of contracts. Am. J. Comput. Law **70**(Supplement_1), i70–i88 (2022)
19. Palmirani, M., Cervone, L., Vitali, F.: Intelligible contracts. In: 53rd Hawaii International Conference on System Sciences, pp. 1780–1789 (2020)
20. Pfeiffer, H.K.: The Diffusion of Electronic Data Interchange. Springer, Cham (2012). https://doi.org/10.1007/978-3-642-51559-0
21. Surden, H.: Computable contracts. UCDL Rev. **46**, 629 (2012)
22. Zimmermann, R.: The Law of Obligations: Roman Foundations of the Civilian Tradition. Juta and Company Ltd. (1990)

Modeling Medical Data Access with Prova

Theodoros Mitsikas[1,2(✉)], Ralph Schäfermeier[3], and Adrian Paschke[1,4]

[1] Institut für Angewandte Informatik, Leipzig, Germany
mitsikas@central.ntua.gr
[2] National Technical University of Athens, Zografou, Greece
[3] Leipzig University, Leipzig, Germany
[4] Freie Universität Berlin and Fraunhofer FOKUS, Berlin, Germany
adrian.paschke@fokus.fraunhofer.de

Abstract. We present a medical data access use case compliant to GDPR legal rules and its implementation in the rule language Prova. The use case demonstrates a typical scenario of a patient consenting to medical data sharing for specified purposes such as treatment, as well as cases where the typical rules are overridden, modifying the access rights. This requires a representation capable of expressing the interaction between parties, and state transitions caused by this interaction. We discuss the Prova implementation which utilizes non-monotonic state transitions and reactive messaging to model the interaction between the parties, which are represented as agents.

Keywords: GDPR · Knowledge Representation · Prova · Legal Reasoning

1 Introduction

Legislation such as the European GDPR (General Data Protection Regulation) sets guidelines for personal data protection. These include sensitive data such as medical records. Medical record handling and usage require reliable procedures adhering to the legislation, as various stakeholders should have access to the data, while their ownership belongs to the patient.

Systems that store and provide access to medical data must comply with the rules in place and incorporate the concepts defined in the legislation. Ideally, such a system should implement the legislation using a high-level specification of the policies. This high-level specification should be able to represent a range of complexity ranging from simple rules, to cases where rules are overridden under specific circumstances establishing a hierarchy prioritizing rules over others, depending on the environment. This makes frameworks that can represent non-monotonic states ideal for modeling such systems. For example, in [11] the authors implement a system that models the relevant legislation of an EU country relating to medical data access. Their implementation is based on the argumentation framework Gorgias that allows for a high-level declarative representation of the policies, and is able to capture contextual-based exceptional

M. Bono et al. (Eds.): JSAI-isAI 2023 Workshops, LNAI 14644, pp. 35–48, 2024.
https://doi.org/10.1007/978-3-031-60511-6_3

decisions via priority rules. However, this declarative approach is limited to the decision policy module, and it is not used for the interaction between stakeholders. This limitation serves as a motivation for implementing a similar use case using a declarative approach both for decision making and for the stakeholder interaction, as well as compare these approaches in terms of expressiveness, code readability, and extendability.

To this end we present a use case for medical data access that has been modeled using the rule language Prova which also supports reaction rule based workflows, event processing, and reactive agent programming. The use case includes typical stakeholders such as a patient, doctors, data controller and others. The access control is realized using the concepts of consent of the patient, the purpose of access, and the role of the party requesting access. As in [11], we define exceptions to the access rules e.g., in emergency situations. Prova has been used in the medical domain [2], as well as for modeling GDPR-compliant data wallet applications [9].

The remainder of this paper is organized as follows: Sect. 2 provides an overview of the Prova language. The use case is presented in Sect. 3, while its Prova implementation in Sect. 4. Section 5 discusses the results and presents related work. Finally, Sect. 6 concludes the paper and proposes future work.

2   Prova Basics

Prova is both a (Semantic) Web rule language and a distributed (Semantic) Web rule engine. It supports reaction rule based workflows, event processing, and reactive agent programming. It integrates Java scripting with derivation and reaction rules, and message exchange with various communication frameworks [2, 4,6]. The message exchange mechanism of Prova is discussed in Sect. 4.

Syntactically, Prova builds upon the ISO Prolog syntax and extends it, notably with the integration of Java objects, typed variables, F-Logic-style slots, and SPARQL and SQL queries. Prolog-like compound terms can be represented as generic Prova lists (e.g., a standard Prolog-like compound term $f(t_1, ..., t_N)$ is a syntactic equivalent of the Prova list $[f, t_1, ..., t_N]$). Slotted terms in Prova are implemented using the arrow expression syntax '->'as in RIF and RuleML, and can be used as sole arguments of predicates. They correspond to a Java HashMap, with the keys limited to Stings [3].

Semantically, Prova provides the expressiveness of serial Horn logic with a linear resolution for extended logic programs (SLE resolution) [7], extending the linear SLDNF resolution with goal memoization and loop prevention. Negation as failure support in the rule body can be added to a Knowledge Base (KB) by implementing it using the cut-fail test as follows:

```
not(A)  :- derive(A), !, fail().
not(_).
```

Notice the Prova syntax for `fail` that requires parentheses, as well as the built-in meta-predicate `derive` that allows to define (sub) goals dynamically with the predicate symbol unknown until run-time [6].

Prova implements an inference extension called literal *guards*, specified using brackets. By using guards, we can ensure that during unification, even if the target rule matches the source literal, further evaluation is delayed unless a guard condition evaluates to true. Guards can include arbitrary lists of Prova literals including Java calls, arithmetic expressions, relations, and even the cut operator. Prova guards play even a more important role in message and event processing as they allow the received messages to be examined before they are irrevocably accepted. The guards are tested right after pattern matching but before a message is fully accepted, so that the net effect of the guard is to serve as an extension of pattern matching for literals [3, 8]. Moreover, guard constraints can be also used to define additional constraints on metadata scopes, i.e. they can be used to define constructive views on the knowledge base by constraining the reasoning to certain selected knowledge axioms, which are selected by scoped literals on the basis of their metadata annotations (e.g., temporal, spatial, legal metadata).

3   Use Case

In this section, we present a concrete use case from the medical domain, which involves actors having to comply with established legal rules for patient data access and a situation in which the latter are overridden in the presence of an emergency situation.

The use case is built around a distributed data wallet scenario, in which a patient owns and controls a secured storage space containing sensitive personal medical data. The data wallet infrastructure allows the patient to share the data with other parties, such as doctors and hospitals.

Sharing data is accomplished by granting appropriate permissions (such as "read" and "write") and binding each permission to a particular purpose (for example, "diagnosis/treatment", "research", "emergency handling", etc.). In this scenario, the entity storing the data and providing controlled access to it by the owner as well as selected third parties, is referred to as the *data controller*, which is a term from the European General Data Protection Regulation (GDPR) [1], as are several concepts employed in this use case, such as *consent* and *purpose of consent*. For a more detailed example of a personal data wallet scenario in the context of GDPR and an in-depth introduction to the concepts and terminology involved, we refer the reader to [9].

Usually, distributed data wallet infrastructures require a complex interworking of a variety of entities, such as identity providers and multiple data controllers for each party involved. For the sake of understandability, we abstract from this degree of complexity and assume that a single data controller provides all the necessary infrastructure for data storage and access, permission handling, and authentication.

The use case description captures the dynamic behavior of the system. It consists of two interlinked parts: a description of a sequence of actions/message exchanges between actors and a description of states the system can be in, and state transitions as a consequence of an action/message. We illustrate the use case by a series of sequence diagrams, as well as a state diagram. Linking between the two is accomplished as follows: Actions that trigger a state change are marked in bold in the sequence diagrams, and state transitions carry the corresponding action names in the state diagram.

In the first part of our use case, a patient consults a doctor. They both log in to the data controller, and the doctor admits the patient to a hospital, where a medical health record of the patient is created. Figure 1 shows a sequence diagram of the above actions.

- A patient *Patient* authenticates with the data controller.
- A doctor *Doctor1* logs in to the data controller.
- Patient is admitted to a clinic by Doctor1.
- Patient demonstrates consent for health data sharing with clinical doctors at the hospital for diagnostic/treatment purposes.
- Doctor1 uploads clinical data of patient.
- Doctor1 uploads more clinical data of patient.
- Doctor1 requests all patient history.

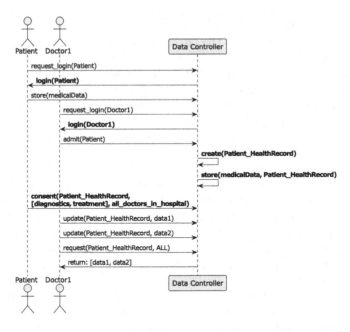

Fig. 1. The first part of the interaction of our use case

In the second part, a researcher is interested in the patient's data for a medical study. The patient consents to the use of her anonymized data for research purposes. The doctor or the researcher can prompt the hospital to produce an anonymized version of the patient's health record for research purposes, as depicted in Fig. 2.

- Patient demonstrates consent for anonymized health data sharing with researchers for research purposes.
- A researcher logs in.
- The researcher requests all patient files.
- The researcher realizes that no anonymized data exist so proceeds with requesting anonymized data generation.
- Researcher requests again all patient files in her department.
- Doctor1 requests anonymized data.

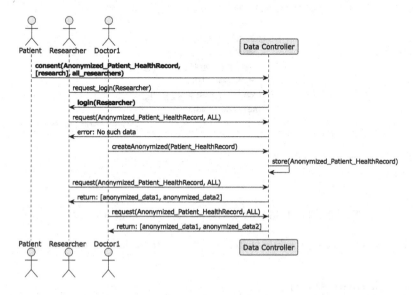

Fig. 2. The second part of the interaction of our use case

The third part describes a possible sequence of actions in an emergency situation, which temporarily overrides the existing rules for data access. During the emergency of the patient, all doctors of the hospital who are logged in to the data controller can view the patient's data for the purpose of handling the emergency. As soon as the emergency is lifted, all access permissions are reset to their previous state, as seen in Fig. 3.

- Patient is cured and discharged from the clinic by Doctor1
- Doctor1 requests again all patient history
- Patient is feeling unwell and calls the emergency services
- Nearby researcher sees him in distress and requests all patient data for providing emergency assistance
- Emergency doctor *Doctor2* also comes in to help and logs in to the data controller
- Doctor2 requests all patient history for treating the patient
- Doctor2 uploads new clinical data of the patient
- Patient is now treated and Doctor2 lifts the emergency for the patient

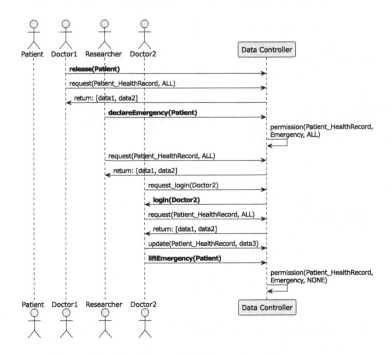

Fig. 3. The third part of the interaction of our use case

Figure 4 shows the possible states and state transitions of our use case.

4   Implementation

The implementation[1] utilizes Prova's features such as message exchange, reactive agent messaging with assertions and retractions, and guards.

Prova's reactive agents are instances of running rulebases that include message passing primitives. In the presented use case, the following agents are defined: the `patient`, `doctor1` and `doctor2`, the `researcher`, the `dataController` and the identity provider `idp`. Both `doctor1` and `doctor2` are instances of the rulebase `doctor`, while all other agents have a dedicated rulebase.

All agent rulebases are utilizing the built-in message passing primitives to communicate, which are the predicates `sendMsg/5`, `rcvMsg/5`, as well as their variants `sendMsgSync/5`, `rcvMult/5`. The position-based arguments for the above predicates are [3]:

1. *XID* - conversation id of the message
2. *Protocol* - name of the message passing protocol
3. *Destination* or *Sender* - the agent name of the receiver/sender
4. *Performative* - the message type characterizing the meaning of the message
5. *Payload* - a Prova list containing the actual content of the message

---

[1] The source code is available at https://github.com/tmitsi/recomp-usecases.

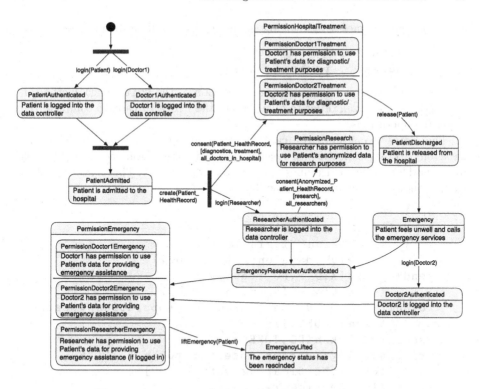

Fig. 4. The states and state transitions of our use case

Prova defines the Java interface `ProvaService` and its default implementation `ProvaServiceImpl` that allows for a runner Java class – depending on the modularization (mapping each agent to a separate bundle vs. multiple agents in a bundle) – to embed one or more agents communicating with each other via messaging. The fundamental method is the method `send`, as follows:

```
send(String xid, String destination, String sender,
        String performative, Object payload, EPService callback)
```

The arguments have a direct correspondence with the message passing primitives, while `EPService` is a superclass of the `ProvaService` interface. Also, the message passing protocol can be selected automatically if not specified (in our use case, the `osgi`[2] protocol is selected).

Agent actions are initiated from a Java runner class that sends a message to the agent. For example, to instruct the agent `doctor1` to log in, we first prepare the HashMap `payload`. Each key-value HashMap element corresponds to a slot (specifically, to the slot name and filler):

```
Map<String, String> payload = new HashMap<>();
payload.put("operation", "login");
payload.put("idp", "idp");
payload.put("dataController", "dataController");
```

---

[2] https://www.osgi.org/.

Then we send the message, invoking the method **send**, described above:

```
service.send("xid", "doctor1", "javaRunner",
    ↪ "request", payload, this);
```

The above message is followed by an invocation of the **wait(long)** method in the service's thread, in order to give time to the Prova threads to complete the requested operations.

The Prova agent **doctor1** captures the message and forwards it to the **dataController**, expecting to receive back a message from **idp** containing a token used for subsequent requests to the **dataController**. This is accomplished by the following inline reaction rule [3]:

```
doctor() :-
    rcvMult(XID,P,javaRunner,request,
        ↪ {operation->login,
        ↪ idp->IDP,dataController->DC}),
    sendMsgSync(XID,P,DC,request,
        ↪ {operation->login,idp->IDP}),
    rcvMult(XID,P,IDP,data_exchange,{operation->assert,
        ↪ token->TOKEN}),
    assert(useToken(DC,TOKEN)),
    println(["log: doctor asserted token ", TOKEN, "
        ↪ for authenticating with ", DC]),
    spawn(XID,$Service,resume,[]).
```

Note that in the above rule the assertion happens only if **doctor1** receives back from the **idp** a message containing the generated token, as **dataController** checks if the agent is already logged in (see also Table 1). If **doctor1** receives such a message, the received token is asserted to the KB. This constitutes a positive update transition, i.e., a fact assertion [6] (retractions are similarly also called negative update transitions).

The last evaluated predicate **spawn/4** is a Prova built-in that invokes a Java method. In our case, it results in a **notifyAll()** call, signaling that the operation is complete and all threads can resume. The argument **$Service** is a global constant [3] defined in the Java runner class and in this case corresponds to the instance of the runner class.

For demonstrating consent for data sharing, the **patient** receives a message from the **javaRunner**, and makes a request to the **dataController**, specifying the operation, purpose, and parties that will be allowed to access the data. The **dataController** captures the message with the following inline reaction rule:

```
dataController() :-
    rcvMult(XID,P,A,request,
        ↪ {operation->demonstrateConsent,
        ↪ purpose->PU,parties->PA,token->T})
        ↪ [token_check(A,T)],
    assert(consent(A,PU,PA)),
```

```
println(["log: DC asserted consent for sharing
    ↪ data with ", PA, "s for ", PU, "
    ↪ purpose(s)", " for ", A]),
spawn(XID,$Service,resume,[]).
```

The message is accepted only if the guard [token_check(A,T)] succeeds. It checks if dataController has an agent A associated with the token T, while also checking if the variable T is bounded (otherwise an agent would be able to log in by sending unbounded token).

In the presented use case, the patient provides consent for both medical data sharing for treatment purposes with clinical doctors, as well as for anonymized medical data sharing for research purposes with researchers and doctors.

Medical data of consenting patients can be added by clinical doctors for patients admitted in their departments. In this implementation, we are using just a representation of data (a filename). Then data can be accessed by clinical doctors of the department treating the patient:

```
dataController() :-
    rcvMult(XID,P,A,request,{operation->retrieveAllData,
        ↪ token->T, subject->S, purpose->PU})
        ↪ [token_check(A,T),
        ↪ staffDB(A,clinical_doctor,DEPT),
        ↪ patient(S,DEPT)],
    findall(Data,data(S,PU,Data,ANON),L),
    sendMsgSync(XID,P,A,data_exchange,{data->L}).
```

The built-in predicate findall/3 accumulates all solutions of a goal specified in the second argument, and returns them as a Prova list in the third argument. The first argument provides the pattern specifying the actually desired elements to be added to a list given the current goal solution [3]. As in many Prolog implementations, it does not fail if no solutions are found, instead returning an empty list.

In emergency situations, the criteria of medical data access change. In our use case, we assume that every medical personnel can request access to the medical data of a person in an emergency situation. The corresponding rule of the dataController capturing requests for data access in emergency situations is as follows:

```
dataController() :-
    rcvMult(X,P,A,request,{operation->retrieveAllData,
        ↪ token->T, subject->S, purpose->PU})
        ↪ [bound(S), emergency(S), token_check(A,T),
        ↪ staffDB(A, Role, DEPT)],
    findall(Data,data(S,PU,Data,ANON),L),
    sendMsgSync(X,P,A,data_exchange,{data->L}).
```

The above two rules differ only in the guarded constrains of the receiving message. The first rule allows access only for clinical doctors in the department in which the patient is admitted: staffDB(A,clinical_doctor,DEPT), `patient(S,DEPT)`. The second rule, for emergency situations, has less restrictions on the role and department of the sender (`staffDB(A, Role, DEPT)`) constituting a more general context, but also a stricter context that defines the emergency situation (`bound(S), emergency(S)`). Thus, if patient S is in emergency, the default access is overridden, allowing more roles to access the data.

Additional anonymized medical data of patients that provided consent for anonymized data sharing for research purposes can be generated. They can then be accessed for research purposes by researchers and doctors.

Similarly, inline reaction rules exist for operations such as data access for research purposes, asserting an emergency, and accessing data under emergency.

Table 1 provides a high-level description of the operations defined for the agent `dataController`. The first column describes the operation (which is specified in the payload), the resulting KB update ("+" for a positive update transition, "−" for negative), and the rule functionality, while the second column specifies the sender. The third column contains the additional message payload slots. The slot `subject` is describing the patient, and the slot `parties` is defining the role. The last column provides a high-level description of the guard constrains applied to the received messages.

Table 1. High-level description of inline reaction rules of `dataController`

	Operation	Sender	Slot Names	Guard Constraints
+	login	any	idp	sender not logged in
	login (displays error message)	any	idp	sender logged in
+	admit patient	clinical doctor	token, subject	doctor id verification, patient not already admitted
	admit patient (displays error message)	clinical doctor	token, subject	doctor id verification, patient already admitted
−	discharge patient	clinical doctor	token, subject	doctor id verification, patient already admitted
+	demonstrate consent	patient	purpose, parties (roles)	patient id verification
+	assert patient data	clinical doctor	data, token, subject	doctor id verification, patient consent
	retrieve patient data (rule accumulates all data with consent)	any	token, subject, purpose	sender id and role verification, patient admitted
+	generate patient anonymized data (rule anonymizes all data with consent for research)	any	token, purpose	sender id and role verification

(continued)

Table 1. (*continued*)

	Operation	Sender	Slot Names	Guard Constraints
	retrieve anonymized data (rule accumulates all anonymized data with consent)	any	token, purpose	sender id and role verification, patient consent
+	declare patient emergency	any	token, subject	sender id verification
	retrieve patient data in an emergency situation (rule accumulates all data with consent)	any	token, subject, purpose	patient in emergency, sender id verification, sender has medical training
+	assert patient data	emergency doctor	data, token, subject	emergency doctor id verification, patient in emergency, patient consent
−	lift patient emergency status	emergency doctor	token, subject	sender id and role verification
	retrieve patient data (displays error message)	any	token, subject, purpose	sender id and role verification, patient not provided consent
	any (displays error message)	any	token	failed id verification

5   Discussion and Related Work

The agent-based Prova implementation with the message passing primitives was able to model all key parts of the workflow. The reactive rules, combined with positive and negative update transitions were adequate to model the possible states of the use case. As shown in Sect. 4, the state transitions are non-monotonic, and Prova is able to express exceptions to general rules. For example, in an emergency situation, agents that under normal circumstances would not have access to a patient's medical data are provided with access.

Medical data access modeling includes the work presented in [11] using the Argumentation framework Gorgias and the tool Gorgias-B, based on the SoDA methodology. The authors model various data access levels to a patient's medical record depending on concepts such as medical service providers, patients, controllers, and consent. The access type depends on three main contexts, namely who is asking to get access, the purpose of the access, and possible specific circumstances. Although this decision policy module is able to model the domain under consideration, the stakeholder interaction relies on external components.

Comparing our approach with the argumentation-based approach presented in [11], Prova's reactive messaging with positive or negative update transitions leads in to a sequence of states of the KB, under which the guard constraints succeed or fail. The argumentation approach, defines a contextual hierarchy of the various application scenarios from the most general to the most specific. As the presented use case does not exhibit a deep multi-level context hierarchy, Prova's guards are providing the necessary expressiveness with a relatively limited use of negation as failure mainly for printing error messages, while the use of the cut operator is avoided. Thus, both approaches are avoiding the use of red cuts [12]. Negation as failure is not used in the argumentation-based approach. Comparing the readability of the source code of the two approaches, Prova provides a better readability and is more intuitive than the pure Gorgias source code. However, Gorgias code can be generated from tools that offer similar readability levels, such as Gorgias-B or the scenario-based formalism presented in [5].

Extending the Prova implementation to a (web) application is feasible using any Java (web) framework or using the Java Message Service, where the actions will be triggered from the Java part of the implementation, providing seamless integration. An the other hand, the argumentation approach relies on the JPL library for exposing the Prolog- and Gorgias-based decision policy module to the web application. However, Prova does not provide a Prolog-like web server which is available for the SWI-Prolog-based Gorgias argumentation system (but not used in [11]).

6   Conclusions and Future Work

We described a use case for medical data access and we presented its implementation in the rule language Prova. The use case focuses on medical data access, where actors such as a patient, doctors, researchers, and data controller act according to established legal rules. We also included an emergency situation, where actors can gain access, overriding their default access rights.

The implementation, realized in the rule language Prova, utilizes the concepts of consent and purpose, which are defined in the GDPR and similar legislations. These key concepts are imprinted in the Prova rules, providing a transcription of legal norms into an executable rule-based specification.

Specifically, the Prova implementation models the interaction of different parties (such as patients, doctors, and data controller), represented as agents that exchange messages with requests that can possibly assert or retract facts, resulting in different states. The reactive messaging capabilities, and the non-monotonic state transition semantics can model all possible states of the use case. The use of Prova guards provides a mechanism of defining preconditions before the acceptance of messages. This creates clear pointcuts, which are human-readable and also have the benefit that the cut operator is no longer necessary in operations with assertions and retractions.

Future work will consist in extending the implementation to a broader set of use cases. Specifically, representing legal and ethical rules side-by-side and having a reasoning procedure for deciding when an ethical rule overrides a legal rule might be of particular interest.

Furthermore, a formal evaluation of the approach using evaluation criteria of rule-based legal systems from the literature will be conducted.

As a further line of future work we plan to implement the present and possible future use cases using different representation formalisms and/or execution/reasoning environments and compare the current and future implementations as part of the evaluation. An implementation of the representational part in AspectOWL[3] [10] should be feasible and might prove advantageous wrt. usability of the modeling paradigm. In particular, AspectOWL provides mechanisms for naturally representing combinations of state and deontic knowledge that changes with state transitions (rules that apply in one state but are overridden in another state, such as an emergency). State and deontic axioms may be represented using aspects, whereas the AspectSWRL built-ins[4] permit the representation of state transitions using SWRL[5] rules. An additional advantage of AspectOWL is that it comes along with OWL's classification system[6], which can be used as a typing system for different domain concepts (such as clinical vs. legal concepts). We expect that the combination of AspectOWL as a representation/typing formalism and Prova as a message based runtime and rule execution environment might yield the best results.

Acknowledgments. This work has been partially funded by the Deutsche Forschungsgemeinschaft (DFG, German Research Foundation) project RECOMP (DFG - GZ: PA 1820/5-1). We also thank Gerhard Kober for the insightful discussions.

References

1. European Commission: Regulation (EU) 2016/679 of the European Parliament and of the Council (2016). http://data.europa.eu/eli/reg/2016/679/oj
2. Kober, G., Robaldo, L., Paschke, A.: Modeling medical guidelines by Prova and SHACL accessing FHIR/RDF. Use case: the medical ABCDE approach. In: dHealth 2022, pp. 59–66. IOS Press (2022)
3. Kozlenkov, A.: Prova Rule Language version 3.0 User's Guide (2010). https://github.com/prova/prova/tree/master/doc
4. Kozlenkov, A., Penaloza, R., Nigam, V., Royer, L., Dawelbait, G., Schroeder, M.: Prova: rule-based Java scripting for distributed web applications: a case study in bioinformatics. In: Grust, T., et al. (eds.) EDBT 2006. LNCS, vol. 4254, pp. 899–908. Springer, Heidelberg (2006). https://doi.org/10.1007/11896548_68
5. Mitsikas, T., Spanoudakis, N.I., Stefaneas, P.S., Kakas, A.C.: From natural language to argumentation and cognitive systems. In: Proceedings of the 13th International Symposium on Commonsense Reasoning. CEUR.org (2017). https://ceur-ws.org/Vol-2052/
6. Paschke, A.: Rules and logic programming for the web. In: Polleres, A., et al. (eds.) Reasoning Web 2011. LNCS, vol. 6848, pp. 326–381. Springer, Heidelberg (2011). https://doi.org/10.1007/978-3-642-23032-5_6
7. Paschke, A., Bichler, M.: Knowledge representation concepts for automated SLA management. Decis. Support Syst. **46**(1), 187–205 (2008). https://doi.org/10.1016/j.dss.2008.06.008

---

[3] http://aspectowl.xyz/syntax.
[4] https://github.com/RalphBln/aspect-swrl-builtins.
[5] https://www.w3.org/Submission/SWRL/.
[6] https://www.w3.org/TR/owl2-overview/.

8. Paschke, A., Boley, H.: Reaction RuleML 1.0 for distributed rule-based agents in rule responder. In: Proceedings of the RuleML 2014 Challenge and the RuleML 2014 Doctoral Consortium, hosted by the 8th International Web Rule Symposium (RuleML 2014). CEUR.org (2014)

9. Schäfermeier, R., Mitsikas, T., Paschke, A.: Modeling a GDPR compliant data wallet application in Prova and AspectOWL. In: Proceedings of the 16th International Rule Challenge and 6th Doctoral Consortium @ RuleML+RR 2022, part of Declarative AI 2022. CEUR.org (2022). https://ceur-ws.org/Vol-3229/

10. Schäfermeier, R., Paschke, A.: Aspect-oriented ontologies: dynamic modularization using ontological metamodeling. In: Garbacz, P., Kutz, O. (eds.) Proceedings of the 8th International Conference on Formal Ontology in Information Systems (FOIS 2014). Frontiers in Artificial Intelligence and Applications, vol. 267, pp. 199 – 212. IOS Press (2014)

11. Spanoudakis, N.I., Constantinou, E., Koumi, A., Kakas, A.C.: Modeling data access legislation with Gorgias. In: Benferhat, S., Tabia, K., Ali, M. (eds.) IEA/AIE 2017. LNCS (LNAI), vol. 10351, pp. 317–327. Springer, Cham (2017). https://doi.org/10.1007/978-3-319-60045-1_34

12. Sterling, L., Shapiro, E.Y.: The Art of Prolog: Advanced Programming Techniques. MIT Press, Cambridge (1994)

Improving Vietnamese Legal Question–Answering System Based on Automatic Data Enrichment

Thi-Hai-Yen Vuong[1]([✉]), Ha-Thanh Nguyen[2], Quang-Huy Nguyen[1],
Le-Minh Nguyen[3], and Xuan-Hieu Phan[1]

[1] VNU University of Engineering and Technology, Hanoi, Vietnam
{yenvth,19020011,hieupx}@vnu.edu.vn
[2] National Institute of Informatics, Tokyo, Japan
nguyenhathanh@nii.ac.jp
[3] Japan Advanced Institute of Science and Technology, Ishikawa, Japan
nguyenml@jaist.ac.jp

Abstract. Question answering (QA) in law presents a significant challenge, as legal documents are often complex in terms of terminology, structure, and temporal and logical relationships. This is particularly difficult for low-resource languages like Vietnamese, where labelled data are scarce and pre-trained language models remain limited. In this paper, we address these limitations by developing a Vietnamese, article-level retrieval-based legal QA system and introducing a novel approach to enhancing language model performance through data quality improvement via weak labelling. We hypothesize that, in contexts where labelled data are limited, effective data enrichment can boost overall performance. Our experimental design evaluates multiple aspects and demonstrates the efficacy of the proposed technique.

Keywords: Vietnamese Legal QA · Low-resource Languages · Data Enrichment · Legal Retrieval · Weak Labelling

1 Introduction

The performance of question-answering (QA) systems has improved significantly due to the rapid progress and recent breakthroughs in natural language processing. These advancements have led to the active implementation of QA solutions across various business domains, aiming to reduce human labor, increase automation, and enhance user experience. Among these application areas, the legal domain has garnered considerable interest from both the research community and industry professionals, including legal practitioners, experts, law firms, and government agencies. Legal QA systems have the potential to assist these stakeholders in swiftly, accurately, and reliably locating relevant legal information.

M. Bono et al. (Eds.): JSAI-isAI 2023 Workshops, LNAI 14644, pp. 49–65, 2024.
https://doi.org/10.1007/978-3-031-60511-6_4

Technically, the legal retrieval-based QA problem can be simply stated as follows: given a query q and a text corpus $D = \{d_1, d_2, \ldots, d_n\}$, the retrieval-based QA aims to find the most likely document d^* that maximizes the relevance score R:

$$d^* = \arg \max_{d \in D} R(q, d) \tag{1}$$

where $R(q, d)$ represents the relevance score of the query q and document d.

Traditionally, lexical weighting and ranking approaches like TF-IDF or BM25 are used to find the relevant documents based on the match of vocabulary terms. Despite their limited accuracy and simplicity, these techniques are normally cost-effective. Meanwhile, representation and deep learning-based models are likely to give better results, but they are much more expensive in terms of large training data, computing power, storage, and deployment. Various deep learning models have been introduced to enhance the representation of queries and documents, such as CNN [4], RNN and LSTM [11,17]. Pre-trained language models (BERT [2], GPTs [1]) also significantly improve text representation in retrieval tasks.

Developing a reliable legal QA system is challenging due to the complexity of legal documents and the difficulties in data annotation. To address these issues without relying on large deep-learning models, we apply a heuristic method presented by Vuong et al. [20] for creating weak label datasets and enhancing relationship representation models in case law retrieval, ultimately improving data quality and quantity without increasing model parameters.

Technically, our focus lies on article-level retrieval-based legal QA. We utilize the Vietnamese civil law QA dataset introduced by Nguyen et al. [10] to conduct an empirical study of the proposed methods. Table 1 demonstrates an example of a legal query along with its expected response. Representing, retrieving, and determining correct answers are challenging due to the length and complexity of the articles. Additionally, this dataset is characterized by each article having a title that functions as a concise summary.

Our work has two primary contributions. Firstly, we developed an end-to-end article retrieval system for tackling the legal QA task. Secondly, we demonstrated the efficiency of automated data enrichment and performed various experiments to compare our model with the state-of-the-art approaches in this domain.

2 Related Work

In natural language processing, question answering (QA) typically refers to systems and models designed to provide information in response to a given question. Depending on the task's specifics, it can be categorized into various classifications. Factoid QA [6] represents a problem class where the answer tends to be simple and can be derived from the provided question or context. Such problems can often be addressed using generation models or sequence tagging methods. Retrieval-based QA [3], another problem class, requires the answer to be obtained from a vast candidate pool based on relevance and the ability to answer

Table 1. A sample in the dataset

Question	Hợp đồng ủy quyền có hiệu lực khi đáp ứng tiêu chí nào? *(An authorization contract is effective when it meets what criteria?)*
Answer	Article 117 form Document 91/2015/QH13
Article Title	Điều kiện có hiệu lực của giao dịch dân sự *(Valid conditions of civil transactions)*
Article Content	Giao dịch dân sự có hiệu lực khi có đủ các điều kiện sau đây: a) Chủ thể có năng lực pháp luật dân sự, năng lực hành vi dân sự phù hợp với giao dịch dân sự được xác lập; b) Chủ thể tham gia giao dịch dân sự hoàn toàn tự nguyện; c) Mục đích và nội dung của giao dịch dân sự không vi phạm điều cấm của luật, không trái đạo đức xã hội. Hình thức của giao dịch dân sự là điều kiện có hiệu lực của giao dịch dân sự trong trường hợp luật có quy định. *(A civil transaction takes effect when the following conditions are satisfied:* *a) The subject has civil legal capacity and civil act capacity suitable to the established civil transactions;* *b) Entities participating in civil transactions completely voluntarily;* *c) The purpose and content of the civil transaction do not violate the prohibition of the law and do not violate social ethics. The form of a civil transaction is the effective condition of a civil transaction in case it is provided for by law.)*

the query, also known as List QA. Confirmation QA [15] is a problem class in which systems or models must determine whether a statement is true or false, typically employing end-to-end deep learning models, knowledge-based systems, or neuro-symbolic systems.

In the legal field, question-answering has been posed in the research community for many years [12]. The main challenges of this problem on the rule language include fragmented training data, complex language, and long text. With the emergence of transformer-based [19] language models as well as transfer learning and data representation techniques, the performance of systems on tasks is significantly improved. In legal information retrieval, a number of neural approaches are also introduced to address the problem of word differences and characteristics of complex relationships [5,10,16,18].

3   Dataset

Original dataset: the corpus is collected from Vietnamese civil law. The labelled dataset was introduced by Nguyen et al. [10]. Table 2 and 3 give a statistical summary of the corpus and dataset. There are 8,587 documents in the corpus. Vietnamese civil law documents have a long and intricate structure. The longest document contains up to 689 articles, and the average number of articles per document is also comparatively high at 13.69. The average title length in this dataset is 13.28 words, whereas the average content length is 281.83 words.

Table 2. Corpus of Vietnamese legal documents statistics

Attribute	Value
Number of legal documents	8,587
Number of legal articles	117,557
Number of articles missing title	1,895
The average number of articles per document	13.69
Maximum number of articles per document	689
The average length of article title	13.28
The average length of article content	281.83

This is also worth noting because one of the challenges and restrictions is the presentation of long texts. On average, the questions are less than 40 words long. Because of the similarity in their distributions, it is expected that the model trained on the training set will yield good performance on the test set.

Table 3. Original dataset statistics

	Train set	Test set
Number of samples	5329	593
Minimum length of question	4	5
Maximum length of question	45	43
Average length of question	17.33	17.10
Minimum number of articles per query	1	1
Maximum number of articles per query	11	9
Average number of articles per query	1.58	1.60

Weak Labelled Dataset: Vuong et al. have the assumption that the sentences in a legal article will support a topic sentence [20]. On the basis of this supposition, the weak labelled dataset is created. There is also a similar relationship in this dataset. The title serves as a brief summary of the article, so the sentences in the article content support to title. We apply this assumption to our method. By considering the title to be the same as the question, we will produce a dataset with weak labels. A title and content pair would be a positive example equivalent to a question and related articles pair. We randomly generated negative examples at a ratio of 1:4 to positive labels and obtained a weak label dataset consisting of 551,225 examples.

4   Methods

For a legal question-answering system at the article level, given a question q, and a corpus of Civil Law $CL = \{D_1, D_2, ..., D_n\}$, the system should return a list of related articles $A = \{a_i | a_i \in D_j, D_j \in CL\}$. The following section provides a detailed description of the phases involved in resolving the problem.

4.1   General Architecture

Our proposed end-to-end article retrieval-based question-answering system architecture is demonstrated in Fig. 1. The system comprises three primary phases: preprocessing, training, and inference phase, which work together to provide accurate and efficient responses to user queries.

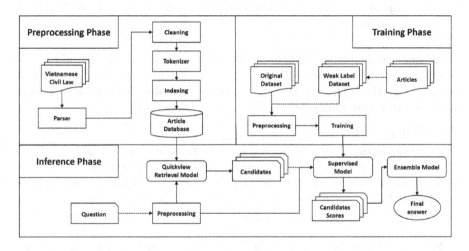

Fig. 1. Pipeline in the end-to-end article retrieval-base question answering system

Preprocessing phase: a database consisting of individual articles is generated by processing the original Vietnamese civil law documents. The resulting article-level database enables easy access and retrieval of specific information contained within the documents.

- *Vietnamese Civil law* is a corpus of Vietnamese legal documents.
- *Parser* segment legal documents into list of articles.
- *Cleaning* will filter out documents with metadata. Special symbol characters are also removed from the article. Numbers and vocabulary are retained and converted to lowercase.
- *Tokenizer* is crucial to the processing of Vietnamese natural language. Vietnamese word structure is quite complicated, a word might contain one or more tokens.

– *Indexing* is a task to represent and put articles into the database. Given a query, the search engine will return the response quickly and accurately.

Training phase: a supervised machine learning model is developed to rank the articles related to the input question. This model uses training data to learn patterns and relationships within the articles and applies this knowledge to provide accurate rankings of relevant articles.

– *Original dataset* is a legal question answering dataset provided by Nguyen et al. [10].
– *Articles* is result of the preprocessing phase.
– *Weak label dataset* was create by our heuristic method.
– *Preprocessing* includes tasks similar to the preprocessing phase for question processing.
– *Training*, we will construct a deep learning model to rank the texts related to the question.

Inference phase: refers to the process of generating a response for a new input question. This phase typically involves applying a trained machine learning model to the input question and selecting the most appropriate response from a set of potential answers.

– *Question* is use's query in natural language.
– *Preprocessing* is same as previous phases to process input question.
– *Quickview retrieval model* matches questions and texts using unsupervised machine learning techniques. The processing speed of this model is typically fast.
– *Candidates* are a list of limited candidates returned from quickview retrieval model.
– *Supervised model* is result of the training phase. Its inputs are the question and the article candidates.
– *Candicate scores* are outputs of Supervised model.
– *Ensemble model* will combine the scores of the quickview retrieval model and the supervised model to make a final decision.

4.2   Indexing

There are numerous methods for indexing text into a database; in this work, we conduct experiments in two ways: word indexing and dense indexing.

Word Indexing: During the indexing process, the words in the text will be analyzed, normalized, and assigned a corresponding index. When given a query, the system searches the index the most related. Word indexing helps to find and look up information in the text faster and more accurately.

Dense Vector Indexing: In addition to word indexing, word-to-vec and sequence-to-vec are both common methods for representing text semantically.

These dense vectors can be used to represent text and index the database for search purposes. We apply two ways of representing text as dense vector according to w2v (FastText [7]) and contextual embedding (BERT [2]) to encode the given question and the legal articles. FastText is a model that converts each word into a dense vector of 300 dimensions. To construct a vector representation of a text, we average over the word vectors to form a single representation vector. Sentence-BERT converte the text into a dense vector with 768 dimensions that can represent the contextual semantics of the document by the Sentence-BERT model [13].

Table 2 shows that the length of articles is often large, which is a limitation of the text representation by FastText and BERT. On the other hand, most questions just partially match articles, we overcome this long presentation weakness by splitting the legal article into a list of sentences and then generating dense vectors before indexing them into the database.

4.3 Quickview Retrieval Model

There are 117,575 legal articles in this corpus. This is a huge number, so in order to ensure the effectiveness of the QA system, we build a so-called Quickview Retrieval model using unsupervised machine learning techniques in order to rapidly return a limited candidate set. In this Quickview Retrieval Model, I have used 2 way of matching techniques: word matching and dense vector matching.

Word matching: to compare questions and articles in the word indexing database, we use the BM25 algorithm [14]. The bag-of-words retrieval function BM25 estimates the relevance of a document to a given search query by ranking documents according to the query terms that appear in each document.

Given a question Q, containing tokens $\{t_1, t_2, ..., t_n\}$, the BM25 score of a article A is:

$$BM25S(Q, A) = \sum_{i=1}^{n} IDF(t_i) \cdot \frac{f(t_i, A) \cdot (k_1 + 1)}{f(t_i, A) + k_1 \cdot (1 - b + b \cdot \frac{|A|}{avgdl})} \qquad (2)$$

in which:

- $f(t_i, A)$: t_i's term frequency in the legal article A
- $|A|$: a number of word in in the legal article A in terms
- $avgdl$: the average article length in the legal corpus.
- k_1: a saturation curve parameter of term frequency.
- b: the importance of document length.
- $IDF(t_i)$ is the inverse document frequency weight of the given question t_i, follow as: $IDF(t_i) = \ln(1 + \frac{N - n(t_i + 0.5)}{n(t_i) + 0.5})$. N is amount of articles in the legal corpus, and $n(q_i)$ is amount of articles containing q_i.

While the content of the article is intense with full meaning, the title contains a significant meaning and carries key information. An assumption is made that the similarity between the query and the title is more important than the content of the article. We use additional weights in calculating quickview retrieval scores as follows:

$$QS(Q, A) = \alpha * BM25S(Q, TA) + \beta * BM25S(Q, CA) \qquad (3)$$

in which, α and β are boosting weights. TA and CA are the titles and content of the article.

Dense vector matching: to estimate the semantic similarity between questions and legal articles in the dense indexing database, we use cosine similarity to calculate quickview retrieval score in two ways:

Article level:

$$QS(Q, A) = Cosine(VQ, VSA) = \frac{VQ^T \cdot VSA}{||VQ|| \cdot ||VSA||} \qquad (4)$$

in which,

– VSA is the presentation vector of the legal article.

Sentence level:

$$Cosine(VQ, VSA) = \frac{VQ^T \cdot VSA}{||VQ|| \cdot ||VSA||} \qquad (5)$$

$$QS(Q, A) = \max_{1 \le j \le n} (Cosine(VQ, VSA_j)) \qquad (6)$$

in which,

– VSA_j is presentation vectors of the jth sentence in the legal article.
– n is the number of sentences in the legal article.

Finally, We use minmaxscaler to normalize scores and generate a list of ranked candidates.

4.4 Supervised Model

Pre-trained language models have proven useful for natural language processing tasks. Particularly, BERT significantly enhanced common language representation [2]. We use the BERT pre-training model and adjust all its parameters to build the related classifier model. We use the first token's final hidden state h as the presentation for the question-article pair. The last layer is a single fully connected added on the top of BERT. The output of the model is a binary classification. Cross-entropy loss is applied to the loss function. Adam [9] is used to optimize all model parameters during the training phase with a learning rate of e^{-5}. The supervised score between the question and the legal article is the classification probability of label 1:

$$SS(Q, A) = P_{label=1}(Q, A) \qquad (7)$$

Lastly, we also use minmaxscaler to normalize scores and reranking a list of candidates. In this model, we proceed to build a related classification model based on two training datasets: the original dataset and a full dataset (original and weak label dataset). In the training process with the full dataset, we fit the model on weak label data first. Then use the best model to fine-tune with the original dataset.

4.5 Ensemble Model

We utilize the quickview retrieval model to generate a list of the $top - k$ candidates. These candidates are then refined using a supervised ensemble model, which provides higher precision but is slower. The quickview model serves as a preliminary selection step due to its fast computation despite its lower precision.

We use a variety of measures of similarity, including lexical similarity (the quickview retrieval model) and semantic similarity (the supervised model). Despite the fact that lexical and semantic similarities are very different from one another, they can work in tandem and are complementary. The combined score of the question Q and the candidate article CA_i is calculated as follows:

$$CombineS(Q, CA_i) = \gamma * QS(Q, CA_i) + (1 - \gamma) * SS(Q, CA_i) \qquad (8)$$

where $\gamma \in [0, 1]$.

Table 2 indicates that each question can have one or more related articles (the average is about 1.6). The most relevant article $MRCA$ is returned by default, to determine a set of candidates to return, we would normalize the combined score and use the threshold parameter: a final returned articles set $FRA = \{CA_i | CombineS(Q, MRCA) - CombineS(Q, CA_i) < threshold\}$.

5 Experimental Results and Discussion

To ensure fairness in the training process and selection of hyperparameters, we divided the training dataset into training and validation with a ratio of 9:1. In the quickview retrieval phase, we utilize the $Recall@k$ measure to assess the list of returned candidates. Recall@k is (Number of correctly predicted articles in the $top - k$ results)/(Total number of gold articles). Macro-F2 is a metric to evaluate the end-to-end question-answering system. Precision, recall, and average response time per question are also used to evaluate the system's performance.

The processing phase and the quickview retrieval model are carried out on CPU Intel core i5 10500 and 32 Gb ram. The supervised model is trained and inference on NVIDIA Tesla P100 GPU 15 Gb. In the indexing step and the quickview retrieval model, we use Elasticsearch[1] with the configuration setting 8 Gb heap size. Besides, during the experiment with some pre-trained BERT models, the BERT multilingual model produces the best results, so it is used to generate vector representation for the given question and the articles in the dense vector indexing and is used in a supervised model.

---

[1] https://www.elastic.co/.

5.1   Quickview Retrieval Result

In order to evaluate the impact of each component of the law article of the word matching method outcome, we carried out experiments using various combinations used of the article title, and article body. As shown in Table 4, several noteworthy aspects can be observed.

Initially, it can be observed that by using solely the article title, we still get a very considerate score compared to using only the article body, this reinforces our observation that the article title can serve as a brief summary of the article body and it alone can carry out most of the ideas presented in the article body. Secondly, using combinations of the law article components could boost the score significantly, to nearly 0.90 of Recall@1000. Additionally, it demonstrates that although the article title significantly contributed to the retrieval recall score, the document title was found to be relatively ineffective. Eventually, we decided to carry on my experiments with the combinations of article title and article body.

Table 4. *Recall@k* of Word matching method in quickview retrieval model

Top-k	20	50	100	200	500	1000
Time per Q (ms)	11.60	14.43	20,32	31.32	63.21	115,63
Training set						
article title only	0.4898	0.5674	0.6169	0.6644	0.7172	0.7536
article body only	0.4966	0.6169	0.6941	0.7586	0.8220	0.8659
article title and article body	0.5676	0.6739	0.7478	0.8060	0.8651	0.8998
boosting article title by 1.2	0.5930	0.6913	0.7598	0.8168	0.8719	0.9046
boosting article title by 1.5	**0.5979**	**0.6942**	**0.7612**	**0.8169**	**0.8740**	**0.9063**
boosting article title by 2.0	0.5492	0.6506	0.7193	0.7850	0.8557	0.8959
Testing set						
article title only	0.5079	0.5743	0.6282	0.6792	0.7259	0.7611
article body only	0.5171	0.6309	0.7103	0.7709	0.8368	0.8747
article title and article body	0.5802	0.6943	0.7728	0.8261	0.8798	0.9080
boosting article title by 1.2	0.6172	0.7208	0.7972	0.8442	0.8848	0.9124
boosting article title by 1.5	**0.6420**	**0.7214**	**0.7973**	**0.8453**	**0.8863**	**0.9128**
boosting article title by 2.0	0.5785	0.6830	0.7486	0.8106	0.8767	0.8979

To determine an optimal boosting weight α for the article title, we performed experiments using various α values of range from 1.0 to 2.5 with a step of 0.1 in the ElasticSearch query. Some of the results obtained from the experiments are presented in Table 4, indicating that by boosting the article title weight by 1.5 achieve the highest score of Recall@1000 on the train set of 0.9063 and on the test set of 0.9128. In addition, the test set achieved commendable scores of *Recall@k* for the values of 100 and 200, which were 0.7973 and 0.8453, respectively. Overall, the word-matching technique has shown its undeniable strength in its simplicity while obtaining a high score and an efficient processing speed. As referring to Table 4, this method can generate a list of 100 potential matches with an average processing time of 20.32 ms, while a list of 1000 candidates can be produced with an average processing time of 115.63 ms (with an approximate Recall score of 0.91).

The experimental result of the dense vector matching method is illustrated in Table 5.

At the document level, we utilize the FastText, with unfine-tuned PhoBERT and bert-base-multilingual-uncased pre-trained models to encode the entire article into a single vector. From the results of the experiments, our experiments revealed that the length of the article body, combined with the vast number of legal articles in my civil law corpus, have made this approach unfeasible. This is evident from the fact that the Recall@1000 even failed to reach the 0.2 thresholds. There are two factors that can explain this result. Firstly, the relatively long article length made it challenging for the vector representation to encapsulate the entire meaning of the article. Secondly, the high number of law articles in the corpus may have contributed to the poor performance, since the length of the vector representation is not enough to distinguish the difference between the two articles in the corpus.

Table 5. *Recall@k* of quickview retrieval model on the dense vector indexing

k	Embedding Method	R@k	Time(ms)
1000	FastText(D = 300)	0.40	203
	BERT(D = 768)	0.38	755
2000	FastText(D = 300)	0.48	384
	BERT(D = 768)	0.45	1,059
5000	FastText(D = 300)	0.56	896
	BERT(D = 768)	0.60	2,433
10000	FastText(D = 300)	0.61	1,757
	BERT(D = 768)	0.67	5,204

On the sentence level approach, we first split the article body into a number of sentences, and use FastText, PhoBERT unfine-tune pre-trained models for vector encoding. Based on the results of the experiment in Table 5, it is clear that both BERT and FastText have significantly longer execution times compared to the term frequency matching method. However, their Recall@k scores are only average. This lower performance can be attributed to the fact that when using the dense vector indexing method at the sentence level, remarkably more records need to be returned compared to the term frequency matching approach at the article level. Furthermore, computing similarity between vectors with significant dimensions presents a challenge, which leads to longer execution times. It is also simple to understand these scores. The advantage of FastText is a semantic representation at the word level. Whereas BERT is known for its powerful contextual representation of paragraphs, splitting the article into sentences loses this contextual property. With the performance of retrieving 10000 sentences that take 1.7 and 5,2 s with a low Recall score of 0.61 for the FastText and 0.67 for BERT, which consider this approach is not possibly applied in a real-time question-answering system.

Based on the aforementioned experiment results, we decided to build the quickview retrieval model using BM25 with the $\alpha = 1.5$ and $\beta = 1$. For the real-time response, we obtain respectable $Recall@k$ scores of 0.7214, 0.7973 and 0.8453 for the k values in (50, 100, 200), which indicates that the number of candidates will be returned following this phase.

5.2 Supervised Model Results

In order to ensure fairness due to the relatively small dataset, we employed K-fold cross-validation. (In this experiment, we worked with K = 3). To select the optimal threshold parameter for determining the set of candidates returned by the ranking model, we utilized 90% of the training dataset for training and allocated 10% of the training dataset as a validation set. As a result, Table 6 displays our results of the threshold parameter.

Table 6. The list of threshold

Top-k	20	50	100	200	500	1000
Threshold	0.38	0.28	0.26	0.26	0.25	0.2

Based on the information presented in Table 7, the supervised model achieves a pretty promising F2 score of around 0.50 when re-ranking the top-20, top-50, and top-100 candidates from the Quick-view Retrieval Model. However, with top-200 and higher, the model f2-score start decreases when the precision score is much lower, even when the recall score is higher. Furthermore, the table illustrates that the weak-labelled dataset has significantly improved the results, with F2 Scores increasing by an average of roughly 0.02 points, which is approximately 4% improvement compared to training on original data, thereby supporting my hypothesis of using the article title as a question to create more data automatically. However, at top k = 1000, the model train with full data has a lower F2 score compared to the model train with the original data, although the Recall score is still higher, this can be explained by the fact that the model is having difficulty selecting an answer due to a large number of candidates.

Table 7. Supervised Model 3 Folds Average Results

	Top_k	20	50	100	200	500	1000
Original data	Recall	0.5333	0.5648	0.6002	0.6237	0.6497	0.6355
	Precision	0.3830	0.3278	0.2636	0.1883	0.1116	0.0751
	F2	0.4944	0.4932	0.4775	0.4255	0.3294	0.2535
Full data	Recall	0.5429	0.5817	0.6244	0.6578	**0.6927**	0.6903
	Precision	**0.4003**	0.3420	0.2756	0.1973	0.1096	0.0645
	F2	0.5067	**0.5100**	0.4981	0.4483	0.3351	0.2341

5.3   End-to-End Question Answering System Result

Table 8 indicates the *first-Fold* experimental results of the end-to-end question answering system result with a top 200 candidates from the quickview retrieval model. The word-matching model with BM25 and the supervised model built from the original data gives F2 score is about 0.38. The ensemble model outperforms the other models in F2 score with 0.6007, which is 22% higher than the single models. As was pointed out in the previous section, lexical and semantic similarity are highly dissimilar. But we believe they can cooperate and support one another. Results certainly support that. Table 8 also clearly illustrates the contribution of the weak label dataset. It improved the supervised machine learning model's F2 score by 8%. The weak label data continues to have an impact on the F2 score when the lexical and semantic matching models are combined. The ensemble model that used the weak label data had a 1% increase in F2 scores.

Table 8. The *first-Fold* experimental result of end-to-end QA system result with $top_k = 200$

Model	R	P	F2
Quickview Model(1.5,1)	0.4454	0.2399	0.3803
Supervised Model (original data)	0.6165	0.1461	0.3750
Supervised Model (full data)	0.6651	0.1998	0.4538
Ensemble Model (original data)	**0.6681**	0.4080	0.5925
Ensemble Model (full data)	0.6651	**0.4331**	**0.6007**

Additionally, there is a sizeable distinction between precision and recall. The recall is given more consideration because of its great impact on F2 score. We discovered that similarity in lexical and semantics has the same effect during the experimental and evaluation phases. Consequently, γ is set at 0.5. Infer time is also a remarkable point in the construction of the question-answering system, which shows the feasibility of the system when applied in practice.

Table 9 illustrate the results with the computational resources in the experimental environment, we can use the model with the top 50—100 candidates with an execution time of 1 s and 1.7 s per question. Their F2 scores are also only 2–5% lower than the best model.

Table 9. The result of end-to-end QA system result with ensemble model

Ensemble Model	R	P	F2	Time(s)
(full data, k = 20)	0.5677	0.4034	0.5252	0.5
(full data, k = 50)	0.5842	0.4428	0.5491	1
(full data, k = 100)	0.6222	**0.4475**	0.5771	1.7
(full data, k = 200)	0.6651	0.4331	**0.6007**	3.4
(full data, k = 500)	**0.6793**	0.4015	0.5967	8.5
(full data, k = 1000)	0.6583	0.4261	0.5936	17

Table 10 shows that our recall and F2 scores are incredibly high when compared to the Attentive CNN [8] and the Paraformer [10] models (0.6651 and 0.6007). Their models return small amounts of related articles, while our system is designed to return flexible amounts of articles with *threshold*. This explains why their precision is great, about 0.5987, whereas our precision is only 0.4331.

Table 10. The result compared with other research groups

Systems	R	P	F2
Attentive CNN [8]	0.4660	0.5919	0.4774
Paraformer [10]	0.4769	**0.5987**	0.4882
Our model (k = 50)	0.5842	0.4428	0.5491
Our model (k = 100)	0.6222	0.4475	0.5771
Our model (k = 200)	**0.6651**	0.4331	**0.6007**

Table 11 describes an example of our legal question-answering system, compared with Paraformer [10]. A small number of related articles are frequently returned by Paraformer models. Our system is more flexible with 3 returned related articles. While the gold label number is 2. As an outcome, a paragraph model like Paraformer is produced that has great precision but low recall, whereas our method leans in the opposite direction. Since recall has a greater impact on F2 scores, our model has a significantly higher F2 score of 11%.

Our model predicts that "Article 466 from Doc 91/2015/QH13" is relevant to the given query but the gold label is 0. Considering this article, we believe the article is pertinent to the given question but it seems that the annotator's point of view is different. In addition, we discovered some similar cases in our error analysis.

Table 11. An output example of ours System, compared with Paraformer [10].

Question: Vay tiền để kinh doanh nhưng không còn khả năng chi trả phải trả lãi suất thì như thế nào? *(In the case of insolvency, how does one address the issue of paying the interest on a business loan?)*	Ours	Para-former	Gold
Candidate 1: Id: Article 357 from Doc 91/2015/QH13 **Title:** Trách nhiệm do chậm thực hiện nghĩa vụ trả tiền *(Liability for late performance of the obligation to pay)* **Content:** 1. Trường hợp bên có nghĩa vụ chậm trả tiền thì bên đó phải trả lãi đối với số tiền chậm trả tương ứng với thời gian chậm trả. 2. Lãi suất phát sinh do chậm trả tiền được xác định theo thỏa thuận của các bên nhưng không được vượt quá mức lãi suất được quy định tại khoản 1 Điều 468; nếu không có thỏa thuận thì thực hiện theo quy định tại khoản 2 Điều 468. *(1. Where the obligor makes late payment, then it must pay interest on the unpaid amount corresponding to the late period.* *2. Interest arising from late payments shall be determined by agreement of the parties, but may not exceed the interest rate specified in paragraph 1 of Article 468 of this Code; if there no agreement mentioned above, the Clause 2 of Article 468 of this Code shall apply.)*	1	1	1
Candidate 2: Id: Article 466 from Doc 91/2015/QH13 **Title:** Nghĩa vụ trả nợ của bên vay *(Obligations of borrowers to repay loans)* **Content:** [...]5. Trường hợp vay có lãi mà khi đến hạn bên vay không trả hoặc trả không đầy đủ thì bên vay phải trả lãi như sau: a) Lãi trên nợ gốc theo lãi suất thỏa thuận trong hợp đồng tương ứng với thời hạn vay mà đến hạn chưa trả; trường hợp chậm trả thì còn phải trả lãi theo mức lãi suất quy định tại khoản 2 Điều 468 của Bộ luật này; b) Lãi trên nợ gốc quá hạn chưa trả bằng 150% lãi suất vay theo hợp đồng tương ứng với thời gian chậm trả, trừ trường hợp có thỏa thuận khác. *([...] 5. If a borrower fails to repay, in whole or in part, a loan with interest, the borrower must pay:* *a) Interest on the principal as agreed in proportion to the overdue loan term and interest at the rate prescribed in Clause 2 Article 468 in case of late payment;* *b) Overdue interest on the principal equals one hundred and fifty (150) per cent of the interest rate in proportion to the late payment period, unless otherwise agreed.)*	1	0	0
Candidate 3: Id: Article 468 from Doc 91/2015/QH13 **Title:** Lãi suất *(Interest rates)* **Content:** 1. Lãi suất vay do các bên thỏa thuận.[...] 2. Trường hợp các bên có thỏa thuận về việc trả lãi, nhưng không xác định rõ lãi suất và có tranh chấp về lãi suất thì lãi suất được xác định bằng 50% mức lãi suất giới hạn quy định tại khoản 1 Điều này tại thời điểm trả nợ. *(1. The rate of interest for a loan shall be as agreed by the parties.[...]* *2. Where parties agree that interest will be payable but fail to specify the interest rate, or where there is a dispute as to the interest rate, the interest rate for the duration of the loan shall equal 50% of the maximum interest prescribed in Clause 1 of this Article at the repayment time.)*	1	0	1

Defining and agreeing on a measure of relevance is an important research question that needs the participation of the AI and Law community in its research. This not only benefits the development of automated methods but also makes legal judgments and decisions more reliable and accurate.

6   Conclusions

In this paper, we present a method to improve performance in the task of legal question answering for Vietnamese using language models through weak labelling. By demonstrating the effectiveness of this method through experiments, we verify the hypothesis that improving the quality and quantity of datasets is the right approach for this problem, especially in low-resource languages like Vietnamese. The results of our work can provide valuable insights and serve as a reference for future attempts to tackle similar challenges in low-resource legal question-answering.

Acknowledgement. This work was supported by VNU University of Engineering and Technology under project number CN22.09.

References

1. Brown, T., et al.: Language models are few-shot learners. In: Advances in Neural Information Processing Systems, vol. 33, pp. 1877–1901 (2020)
2. Devlin, J., Chang, M.W., Lee, K., Toutanova, K.: BERT: pre-training of deep bidirectional transformers for language understanding. In: NAACL, pp. 4171–4186 (2019)
3. Feldman, Y., El-Yaniv, R.: Multi-hop paragraph retrieval for open-domain question answering. In: Proceedings of the 57th Annual Meeting of the Association for Computational Linguistics, pp. 2296–2309 (2019)
4. Hu, B., Lu, Z., Li, H., Chen, Q.: Convolutional neural network architectures for matching natural language sentences. In: Advances in Neural Information Processing Systems, pp. 2042–2050 (2014)
5. Huang, P.S., He, X., Gao, J., Deng, L., Acero, A., Heck, L.: Learning deep structured semantic models for web search using clickthrough data. In: Proceedings of the 22nd ACM International Conference on Information & Knowledge Management, pp. 2333–2338 (2013)
6. Iyyer, M., Boyd-Graber, J., Claudino, L., Socher, R., Daumé, H., III.: A neural network for factoid question answering over paragraphs. In: Proceedings of the 2014 Conference on Empirical Methods in Natural Language Processing (EMNLP), pp. 633–644 (2014)
7. Joulin, A., Grave, E., Bojanowski, P., Mikolov, T.: Bag of tricks for efficient text classification. In: Proceedings of the 15th Conference of the European Chapter of the Association for Computational Linguistics: Volume 2, Short Papers, pp. 427–431. Association for Computational Linguistics (2017)
8. Kien, P.M., Nguyen, H.T., Bach, N.X., Tran, V., Le Nguyen, M., Phuong, T.M.: Answering legal questions by learning neural attentive text representation. In: Proceedings of the 28th International Conference on Computational Linguistics, pp. 988–998 (2020)
9. Kingma, D., Ba, J.: Adam: a method for stochastic optimization. In: International Conference on Learning Representations (2014)
10. Nguyen, H.T., Phi, M.K., Ngo, X.B., Tran, V., Nguyen, L.M., Tu, M.P.: Attentive deep neural networks for legal document retrieval. Artif. Intell. Law 1–30 (2022)
11. Palangi, H., et al.: Deep sentence embedding using long short-term memory networks: analysis and application to information retrieval. IEEE/ACM Trans. Audio Speech Lang. Process. **24**(4), 694–707 (2016)
12. Rabelo, J., Goebel, R., Kim, M.Y., Kano, Y., Yoshioka, M., Satoh, K.: Overview and discussion of the competition on legal information extraction/entailment (Coliee) 2021. Rev. Socionetwork Strategies **16**(1), 111–133 (2022)
13. Reimers, N., Gurevych, I.: Sentence-BERT: sentence embeddings using Siamese BERT-networks. In: Proceedings of the 2019 Conference on Empirical Methods in Natural Language Processing and the 9th International Joint Conference on Natural Language Processing (EMNLP-IJCNLP), pp. 3982–3992 (2019)

14. Robertson, S.E., Walker, S.: Some simple effective approximations to the 2-Poisson model for probabilistic weighted retrieval. In: Croft, B.W., van Rijsbergen, C.J. (eds.) SIGIR 1994, pp. 232–241. Springer, London (1994). https://doi.org/10.1007/978-1-4471-2099-5_24

15. Sanagavarapu, K., et al.: Disentangling indirect answers to yes-no questions in real conversations. In: Proceedings of the 2022 Conference of the North American Chapter of the Association for Computational Linguistics: Human Language Technologies, pp. 4677–4695 (2022)

16. Sugathadasa, K., et al.: Legal document retrieval using document vector embeddings and deep learning. In: Arai, K., Kapoor, S., Bhatia, R. (eds.) SAI 2018. AISC, vol. 857, pp. 160–175. Springer, Cham (2019). https://doi.org/10.1007/978-3-030-01177-2_12

17. Tai, K.S., Socher, R., Manning, C.D.: Improved semantic representations from tree-structured long short-term memory networks. In: Proceedings of the 53rd Annual Meeting of the Association for Computational Linguistics and the 7th International Joint Conference on Natural Language Processing (Volume 1: Long Papers), Beijing, China, pp. 1556–1566. Association for Computational Linguistics (2015)

18. Tran, V., Le Nguyen, M., Tojo, S., Satoh, K.: Encoded summarization: summarizing documents into continuous vector space for legal case retrieval. Artif. Intell. Law **28**, 441–467 (2020)

19. Vaswani, A., et al.: Attention is all you need. In: Advances in Neural Information Processing Systems, vol. 30 (2017)

20. Vuong, Y.T.H., et al.: SM-BERT-CR: a deep learning approach for case law retrieval with supporting model. Artif. Intell. Law 1–28 (2022)

Modeling the Judgments of Civil Cases of Support for the Elderly at the District Courts in Taiwan

Chao-Lin Liu[1]([✉]), Wei-Zhi Liu[1], Po-Hsien Wu[1], Wei-Jie Li[1], Sieh-chuen Huang[3], and Ho-Chien Huang[2]

[1] Department of Computer Science, National Chengchi University, Taipei City, Taiwan
`{chaolin,109753157,111753120,110753128}@nccu.edu.tw`
[2] College of Law, National Chengchi University, Taipei City, Taiwan
`110601014@nccu.edu.tw`
[3] College of Law, National Taiwan University, Taipei City, Taiwan
`schhuang@ntu.edu.tw`

Abstract. The problem of legal judgment prediction (LJP) has attracted substantial attention from researchers of both the law and computer science communities in recent years. The majority of the previous LJP work is for criminal cases. We report our attempt to predict the judgments for the cases about the support for the elderly, which is an instance of the civil cases. We investigated the effects of choosing different design parameters in our decision models, which adopted traditional machine learning and deep learning concepts. The results of the empirical evaluations showed some encouraging results, but some others uncovered the challenges that remain to be tackled.

Keywords: Legal Informatics · Artificial Intelligence · Machine Learning · Deep Learning · Modeling Court Decisions · Legal Judgment Prediction

1 Introduction

With the accelerated advancement and increasing affordability of computing technology, the technology has been applied to many areas, including legal informatics. Yamakoshi et al. discussed the translation of Japanese law articles for foreign readers [16], Rabelo et al. reported their studies on text entailment between legal statements [13], and Komamizu et al. shared their experience in identifying relevant parts between legal documents [5] in recent JURISIN workshops.

The work reported in this article is an instance of legal judgment prediction (**LJP**) [2]. Due to the recent expedited advancement in artificial intelligence and machine learning, the problem of predicting judges' judgments based on information about criminal activities or legal disputes has attracted the attention of more and more legal experts and computer science researchers [1].

Most current research activities in LJP are about criminal cases, partially because specific criminal activities must be reported to establish the conditions for starting a

M. Bono et al. (Eds.): JSAI-isAI 2023 Workshops, LNAI 14644, pp. 66–84, 2024.
https://doi.org/10.1007/978-3-031-60511-6_5

criminal case. Suppose one may identify the criminal activities sufficiently and explicitly. In that case, a computer system can recommend the types of sentences and even the lengths of imprisonment for some criminal cases based on the results of the statistical analysis of the previous cases. The Judicial Yuan of Taiwan provides a legal judgment recommender system for eight types of criminal crimes online[1]. The primary users of such a public service might be something other than human judges. Such a recommender is both educational and helpful for ordinary civilians and lawyers.

Some researchers have started to explore the domain of civil cases. It is relatively harder to interpret and understand the intentions and functions of statements in civil cases, and researchers are working on more fundamental issues. Wu et al. attempted to predict courts' views based on plaintiffs' claims [15]. Liu et al. aimed at identifying and differentiating the statements of the plaintiffs and the defendants in judgment documents [9]. Zhao et al. overviewed the sub-tasks for the predictions of civil cases [17].

We report the results of our modeling of the court decisions for cases of support for the elderly. Muhlenbach et al. worked on the alimony issues for divorce cases [12]. Their interests included the jurisdictional factors and the economic consequences. They applied tree-based methods for classification and regression models for predicting the amount of alimony. The structures of our problems are similar, but we report our experience of applying technically more complex models in this paper.

We discuss the data source in Sect. 2 and define our goals in Sect. 3. Section 4 presents the preliminary results of the predictions of whether the judges would accept or dismiss the plaintiffs' requests. Sections 5 and 6 delineate the applications of a model-tree model for estimating the granted amount of funds. Section 7 offers short concluding remarks. The Appendix provides information about finetuning the SBERT.

2 Data Source

2.1 Open Data of Taiwan Judicial Yuan (TWJY)

The Judicial Yuan is the highest official agency for governing the judicial system in Taiwan. By law, the judgment documents of the courts should be published, except those that are not allowed to be published by law. The website for the open documents (TWJY, henceforth) is in Chinese, and is publicly accessible on the Internet[2].

TWJY contains judgment documents for lawsuits since January 1996, and has accumulated 18.70 million documents as of July 2023. The available data were limited in the first four years, mostly from special courts. Since 2000, the documents of the three layers of courts, i.e., district, high, and supreme courts, started to become available. The Judicial Yuan updates the contents of TWJY monthly, with a three-month lag. Namely, the judgment documents of January will be published in April. New judgment documents from different types and levels of courts will be published and can be downloaded as a compressed file. Sometimes, the published documents may be retracted due to legal

---

[1] 量刑趨勢建議系統 (Legal Judgment Recommender): https://sen.judicial.gov.tw/pub_pla tform/sugg/index.html (in Chinese), last accessed 2023/nov/09.

[2] Open data of Taiwan Judicial Yuan: https://opendata.judicial.gov.tw/, last accessed 2023/11/09.

reasons, so the number of available documents does not remain highly stable. The published documents are also anonymized according to the law, and it is the government's responsibility to protect the privacy of the individuals involved in the lawsuits.

2.2 Selecting Relevant Documents

Although there are about 18 million judgment documents, typical research usually focuses on one or some special categories of lawsuits, and does not need to use all of those documents. Our current work focuses on the issues regarding support for the elderly, which are related to family support problems and belong to civil cases. To this end, we select the judgment documents that meet a special set of criteria.

Each of the judgment documents in TWJY is a JSON file and follows a top-level structure, including the long identification number (JID), the year when the lawsuit started in terms of the Taiwan calendar (JYEAR), the abbreviated code for the type of the lawsuit (JCASE), the short identification number for the lawsuit (JNO), the date for the current judgment in terms of the Western calendar (JDATE), the category of the lawsuit (JTITLE), and the full text for the judgment document (JFULL).

To find specific types of judgments from TWJY, we can select the documents based on whether or not the JCASE and the JTITLE of the documents contain specific keywords. As a preliminary step, we extracted documents whose JTITLE has the word "扶養費" (amount of fund for support) while ignoring documents whose JTITLE is either "請求扶養費代墊" or "請求扶養費代墊款" because they were not related to our research goals[3]. The contents of the JCASE may indicate more subtleties about the judgments. If the JCASE contains the characters in {審, 調, 補, 促, 抗, 消, 更, 上, 續, 救,, 他, 高等, 最高, 婚} [8], they are not directly about the judgments about whether to grant money or the amount of granted fund to the plaintiffs at the district courts. It is difficult to explain each of these legal exclusions in this paper. By adopting this list, we can exclude cases for appeals to the high courts and the Supreme Court, for instance. In this study, we want to focus on the judgments of the district courts.

Furthermore, we dropped documents that passed the above filtering steps if they were about transferring the jurisdiction from one court to another. This could also be achieved by detecting keywords like "本件移送" in the JFULL.

Between January 2000 and December 2021, we identified only 1930 judgment documents from TWJY that satisfied these criteria. The judges granted the plaintiffs a certain amount of funds in 938 cases and dismissed 992 cases.

2.3 A Relevant Social Factor and Mediation

It might be surprising that we obtained only 1930 documents from TWJY, which claims to have about 18 million documents. We can offer two factors for this phenomenon.

The documents included in TWJY are for all administrative, criminal, and civil courts in Taiwan from 1996 to the present. Among them, the cases of support for the elderly are not the most frequent.

---

[3] "請求扶養費代墊" and "請求扶養費代墊款" refer to situations when the plaintiffs had paid to support the elderly, and the plaintiffs are requesting the courts to order those who should be responsible to support the elderly to reimburse the plaintiffs.

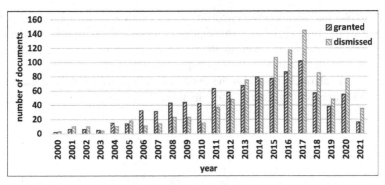

Fig. 1. The distribution of the selected judgment documents for the cases of support for the elderly between 2000 and 2021

More specifically, in Taiwan, an Asian country, it is uncommon for family members to bring family issues to the courts. In the old days, family problems should be resolved within the family, and they should not even let any outsiders know. Otherwise, that would become a shame for the whole family.

In addition, the courts will offer mediation between the plaintiffs and the defendants. Hence, not all litigations would result in the final court decisions. Therefore, the number of judgment documents we could use may be smaller than expected. Huang, a professor in Law, also reported a similar amount of judgment documents in an unpublished conference presentation [4].

Table 1. Regular expressions for extracting claims of the plaintiffs and of the defendants

	regular expressions
plaintiffs	(聲請|聲請人|原告).{0,10}(主張|略以|意旨)
defendants	(相對人|被告).{0,10}(主張|略以|意旨|則以|抗辯)

We show the distributions of the number of the selected cases over the years, including "granted" and "dismissed," in Fig. 1. We can observe increasing trends, but the total number of cases remains low.

3 Problem Definitions and Data Preprocessing

3.1 Judgment and Grant Predictions

Given a selected document, there are two tasks we can do. The first is to predict whether the plaintiffs' requests can be granted, and the second is to predict the amount granted monthly for support.

We treat the first task as a classification problem, as indicated in Fig. 1. We need to extract the claims of the plaintiffs and of the defendants from the JFULL field of the documents, and must not use any other parts that may shed light on the final judgments, e.g., paragraphs that mention the cited law articles may indicate the opinions of the judges and so the final decisions. This can be achieved by observing the regularities of the statements of how the documents recorded the claims of the plaintiffs and of the defendants. Table 1 shows the regular expressions (mixed with Chinese words) that can catch the regularities. Based on the extracted statements, we trained classifiers to categorize the cases into **"granted"** and **"dismissed"** categories.

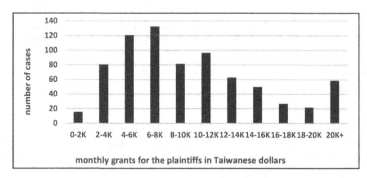

Fig. 2. The distributions of monthly grants to the plaintiffs

We treat the second task as a regression problem. A relatively more common approach for the LJP problems is to discretize the range of the penalties, and treat the LJP problems as a classification task. We will identify the features for building the regression models with both manual and algorithmic methods, and details will be provided in Sect. 5.1. We show the monthly grants distribution to plaintiffs who won their cases in Fig. 2. The amounts of the granted funds for support are small, partially because there are social programs that could support those in need in Taiwan. The distribution range is not tiny, so achieving precise prediction is not a trivial goal. We will discuss more details in Sects. 5 and 6.

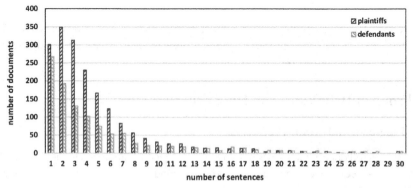

Fig. 3. The distributions of the number of sentences in the claims of the plaintiffs and of the defendants

3.2   Preprocessing: Word Segmentation and the Blurring Procedure

Due to the size of our data, we would like to compare the effectiveness of traditional machine-learning methods and deep-learning models. Hence, we need to do word segmentation for Chinese strings when building some classifiers. We adopted the CKIP classifier that Academia Sinica maintained[4].

The Judicial Yuan anonymized the documents in TWJY by replacing the given names with circles. For instance, a person name in Chinese, "劉昭麟" will be substituted by "劉○○". In our current study, we will replace an anonymized name with "某人" ("somebody"). This is because we do not think it is necessary to consider the surnames of the plaintiffs or of the defendants in our classification models. Similarly, we may replace the street names with "somewhere" ("某地") and time expressions with "a point of time" ("某時") unless it is necessary to consider the locations and the information about time in the lawsuit (to be explained in Sect. 5). This **blurring** procedure can be achieved by regular expressions and sometimes by small functions that consider the contexts. Here is a concrete example of the effects of the blurring step: changing "被告丁○○答辯略以：㈠92年間被告丁○○在中壢市上班" into "被告某人答辯略以：㈠某時間被告某人在某地上班".

We may identify person names, place names, and time expressions with two possible methods. When we use the CKIP to do Chinese word segmentation, we will also obtain information about the part-of-speech (POS) of the words. The words about person names, locations, and time expressions have specific POS labels. We can also employ tools for named entity recognition (written as **NER** in the literature) for this task.

4   The Grant and Dismiss Decisions

4.1   Vectorizations of the Texts: TF-IDF and Sentence-BERT

We vectorized the claims of the plaintiffs and of the defendants with two methods: (1) TF-IDF [11] and (2) with the help of the Sentence-BERT (**SBERT**, henceforth) [14]. TF-IDF is a well-known method for vectorizing text, and there are many variants. We used the CKIP to segment the Chinese strings and relied on the tool **TfidfVectorizer** in the **scikit learn**[5] to build the TF-IDF models for classifying individual judgments as "granted" or "dismissed." We selected the sentence-transformers/distiluse-base-multilingual-cased-v1 model as the pretrained BERT.

We also relied on SBERT to provide BERT-style sentence vectors for the claims of the plaintiffs and of the defendants. Since there are no strict standards for splitting Chinese statements in "sentences", we chose to split Chinese strings by four punctuation marks: "。！？；". After this sentence-splitting step, we can find the distributions of the number of sentences in the claims of the plaintiffs and of the defendants. Figure 3 shows the distribution of the number of sentences (horizontal axis) in the claims of the plaintiffs and of the defendants. Due to the width of the page, we do not show the complete distribution. The claims can have as many as 50 sentences. On average, there are six and seven sentences in the claims of the plaintiffs and of the defendants, respectively.

---

[4] CKIP: https://github.com/ckiplab/ckiptagger, last accessed 2023/nov/09.

[5] Scikit learn: https://scikit-learn.org/stable/, last accessed 2023/nov/09.

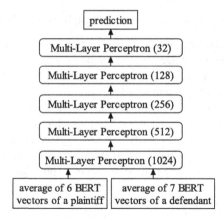

Fig. 4. A model for the SBERT experiment

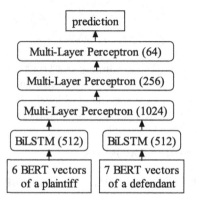

Fig. 5. Another model for the SBERT

After splitting the sentences, we could calculate the number of Chinese characters in the sentences in the claims of the plaintiffs and of the defendants, and observe their distributions, which is analogous to how we created Fig. 3. We could not include the chart due to page limits for the JURISIN submissions. The average number of characters in the sentences of the plaintiffs and of the defendants are 88 and 83, respectively. Less than 0.2% of the sentences have more than 512 characters that a typical BERT model will accept. Hence, we would do more padding than truncation. We have to feed the same number of sentences for each plaintiff and the same number of sentences for the defendants to the classifiers, as shown in Fig. 4, and we chose to use the average number of sentences in the claims that we reported above.

4.2 Classification of the Judgment Documents

Recall that we had only 1930 documents. Nevertheless, we still had to split these documents for training and testing at the 8:2 ratio. Then, 20% of the training data would be used for validation. We fed the TF-IDF vectors to a naïve Bayes (**NB**) model and a logistic regression (**LR**) model, and we tried two different flows with the SBERT, shown in Figs. 4 and 5. The numbers in the parentheses in the rounded boxes were the numbers of output units. In Fig. 5, the BiLSTM symbol denotes two BiLSTM layers.

On top of these four combinations, we tried to compare how whether we did the blurring procedure or not would influence the classification results. When we conducted the blurring procedure, the resulting vocabulary size in the TF-IDF model was about 18000. If not, the vocabulary size increased to about 24000. In both cases, stop words were ignored, but we had yet to try to reduce the dimensionality by SVD.

When we trained these models in Figs. 4 and 5, we chose Adam as the optimizer, set the initial learning rate to 0.002, used the binary cross entropy as the loss function, and let the batch size be 128. Training would stop if the loss for the validation data did not improve for two consecutive epochs. Moreover, we repeated each of these experiments 100 times by re-splitting the data to gather the statistics about the observed distributions of the accuracy and F_1 measure.

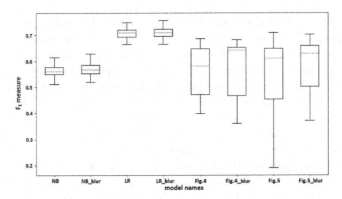

Fig. 6. The boxplots for the F_1 measures for the eight classifiers [10]

Table 2 shows the results. The "vectorizer+model" column summarizes the methods for vectorization and the classification models. Doing the blurring step led to better performance than not constantly. It might be surprising that using TF-IDF with logistic regression (LR) performed the best. We note that we have not finetuned the SBERT due to insufficient data. This is also one of the possible reasons we observed that the F_1 measures in the boxplots in Fig. 6 that the neural network models achieved dispersed relatively wider in the 100 experiments. At the time of writing, we have figured out where to find the extra data to finetune the SBERT, and will do so soon. We have also published some preliminary results for another approach that considers the semantic functions of statements in the judgment documents [9], and the results of some extended experiments have validated the potential of using the pretrained BERT models.

Table 2. The averages of the performance measures of the eight classifiers

vectorizer + model	blur	accuracy	F_1
TF-IDF+NB	no	0.5603	0.5593
TF-IDF+NB	yes	0.5709	0.5695
TF-IDF+LR	no	0.7057	0.7070
TF-IDF+LR	**yes**	**0.7147**	**0.7152**
Figure 4	no	0.5806	0.5601
Figure 4	yes	0.5907	0.5695
Figure 5	no	0.5994	0.5204
Figure 5	yes	0.5998	0.5257

5 A Model-Tree Approach for Predicting the Grants

If the judges do not dismiss the plaintiffs' requests, the judges will then determine the amount of grants. There are two types of common decisions. The grants may be stated in an annual or a monthly amount. We would convert all the grants to a monthly scale for building our models. There might be multiple defendants in an individual lawsuit, e.g., the plaintiffs had more than one child. In such cases, the defendants would have their shares to pay the grant to the plaintiffs, and the shares might be different. In such cases, we would sum up the shares of the defendants and use the total as the grant for the lawsuit. Our goal was to predict the total monthly amounts that were granted to the plaintiffs, whose distribution was depicted in Fig. 2.

We do not aim to predict all types of solutions for support for the elderly. Predicting the shares of individual defendants is a challenging and interesting goal. Sometimes, the court will grant a one-time lump sum to the plaintiffs because the life expectance is short. In other cases, the lawsuits might be interrupted due to the success of the mediation process. We may tackle these special topics in the future.

As we wish to predict the grants from the regression perspective, rather than classification, we need to identify the factors that may influence the grant amount. At this stage, we rely on legal knowledge, e.g., [4, 7], and our observations from reading the documents to select the factors.

5.1 Factors Influencing the Grants

The factors which influence the amounts of the grants may be categorized into two main sources: financial and social factors.

It is easy to understand that the **cost-of-living index** is an important factor. This is one example when we need to know the exact places where the plaintiffs live. In Taiwan, the needy, including the qualified elderly, may receive **a social allowance** from the central and local governments. In a lawsuit, the plaintiffs must **request an amount of grant**, which may include their **special needs**. By law, there may be a certain number of persons who should be responsible for the support of the plaintiff(s), and among these groups, some or all are listed as the defendants. Notice that it is possible that not all of the **responsible persons** are to be included in the defendants. Knowing this key difference, we try to find information about the total monthly incomes and the total (estimated) values of the estate of the responsible persons and of the defendants that are recorded in the judgment documents. Table 3 summarizes these items.

Table 3. Financial factors

code	summary
C	cost-of-living index
G	social allowance
O	special needs
A	requested amount
P	number of defendants
N	number of responsible persons
I	total monthly income of P
E	total estate of P
NI	total monthly income of N
NE	total estate of N

Table 4. Social factors influencing the grants

code	summary
S1	Do plaintiffs have bad records?
S2	defendants domestically abuse?
S3	plaintiffs domestically abuse?
S4	Are plaintiffs responsible?
S5	Are defendants disabled?
S6	monthly incomes above the median?
S7	monthly incomes below minimum salary?
RI	(I/P)/(NI/N)
RE	(E/P)/(NE/N)

According to [7] and our own observations, the courts will consider some behavioral factors of the litigants. These factors include (1) whether the plaintiffs have some bad records, e.g., a drunkard, a frequent gambler, debt-loaded, etc.; (2) whether the plaintiffs were domestically abused by the defendants; (3) whether the defendants were domestically abused by the plaintiffs; (4) whether the plaintiffs took care of the family responsibly in the past; (5) whether the defendants were physically or mentally disabled; (6) whether the average monthly income of the defendants is above the national median monthly income; (7) whether the average monthly income of the defendants is below the minimum monthly salary (that is required by law). We summarize these factors in Table 4. The last two factors measure the relative economic conditions between the responsible persons and the defendants from both the perspective of the monthly incomes (RI) and their estates (RE).

$$\text{average request} = (C - G + O) \times \frac{P}{N} \tag{1}$$

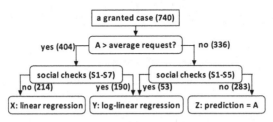

Fig. 7. The main flow of our model tree

5.2 Using a Model-Tree Model for Prediction

We show the main flow of our model tree in Fig. 7. Note that although the judges awarded plaintiffs in 938 cases among the 1930 cases that we found useful from TWJY, only 740 among them remain useful for the study of predicting the monthly support.

We define the **average request** in Eq. (1). Based on the definitions of C, G, and O in Table 3, we consider that $C - G + O$ is the amount the plaintiff needs to maintain an ordinary living. The ratio $\frac{P}{N}$ is the proportion that the plaintiff can request the defendants to support among the responsible persons.

Among the 740 cases which the judges would award grants to the plaintiffs, the requested amounts (A in Table 3) of 404 cases were larger than the average request. 336 cases were smaller. We then checked different subsets of the social factors (Table 4) for these two branches. Of those 336 cases that had lower requests, 283 of them did not have any of the conditions from S1 to S5, so our model would predict that the judges would award the requested amount (A). For those 404 cases that had higher requests, 214 of them did not have any of the conditions from S1 to S7, so we used them to train and test a linear regression model, which we shall explain next.

In the lower middle of Fig. 7, we can see that 53 cases that had lower requests and 190 cases that had higher requests would be used to train and test a log-linear regression model because these cases satisfied at least one special social factor from S1 to S7. We shall explain the log-linear model below.

5.3 The Linear and Log-Linear Regression Models

We used the 214 cases (lower left corner of Fig. 7) to train and test a linear regression model. We relied on the **LinearRegression** of the scikit learn for this task, and used the default settings. We employed the features listed in Table 3 in the experiments, and used 80% of the 214 cases for training and 20% for tests.

There are 243 cases ($190 + 53$, in the lower middle part of Fig. 7) that we would use to train the log-linear regression model. The main purpose was to use the average request as the basis and to adjust the basis based on the factors we listed in Table 4. Notice that factors S1 to S7 are Boolean and that RE and RI are ratios. When the Boolean factors are true and false, they will be converted to **2** and **1**, respectively. Hence, if the results at the step of "social checks" are [True, True, False, False, True, True, False, 1.2, 1.1], we will obtain a **feature vector** of [2, 2, 1, 1, 2, 2, 1, 1.2, 1.1].

Let us denote the feature vector that we obtain at the "social checks" as $F = \{f_1, f_2, \ldots, f_9\}$. We assume that the grants can be modeled by Eq. (2), where A is defined in Table 3. The average request was defined in Eq. (1), and it would vary with each different case. Notice that when a Boolean feature is false, it is converted to

$$\text{grant} = \min(\text{A}, \text{average\_request}) \times \prod_{i=1}^{i=9} f_i^{w_i} \tag{2}$$

$$\log(\text{grant}) = \log(\min(\text{A}, \text{average\_request})) + w_i \sum_{i=1}^{i=9} f_i \tag{3}$$

1. When an f_i is 1, the power of f_i will also be 1, independent of the value of w_i. Hence, when a social factor is false, that feature will **not** influence the calculated grant.

Table 5. The average MAE of 1000 experiments, using manual input

test group	only linear regression	linear+log-linear	Figure 7
X	–	1968.96	1968.96
Y	–	3132.69	3112.20
Z	–	1605.41	1048.71
All (740)	2390.27	2212.59	1992.88

We can convert the exponential form in (2) by taking the logarithm of both sides. Equation (2) will turn into a form of linear regression in Eq. (3), and we could still rely on the LogisticRegression of scikit learn to train and test our models. Again, we split the data into the ratio of 8:2 for training and test, respectively.

5.4 Results of Empirical Evaluations and Ablation Study

We used the mean absolute error (MAE) to measure the quality of the predictions for the grants. Let g_i and p_i denote the actual monthly grant and the predicted grant for case i, , respectively; the MAE is defined in (4), where n denotes the number of test cases in an experiment. We reported the results of measuring the quality with other metrics in [10].

$$\text{MAE} = \frac{1}{n} \sum_{i=1}^{i=n} |g_i - p_i| \qquad (4)$$

We repeated the experiments 1000 times, each by re-splitting the training and the test data. Table 5 shows the averages of the MAE values of these 1000 experiments. The unit of these numbers is Taiwanese dollars. The rightmost column shows the results of the average MAEs in the X, Y, and Z in Fig. 7, which is the best-performing model. If we did not include the "social checks (S1-S5)" step, and let the 336 cases be handled by the log-linear model in Fig. 7, we would observe the results listed in the column "linear+log-linear", which are inferior to those that are listed in the column "Fig. 7". In this case, the X and Y groups were used to train and test a log-linear regression model. We could still calculate and show their MAEs separately in Table 5. If we used all of the 740 cases as the training and test data for the linear regression model directly, we would observe the result listed under the column "only linear regression", which is the worst among the three designs.

We compared our results with those reported in [4] and found that the size of our dataset was larger, and our results were also better.

We can look more deeply into the results. Define the **degree of deviation** of the predicted grants from the actual grants in Eq. (5). If a p_i is 10% larger or smaller than the true g_i for a case i, then the deviation will be 0.1.

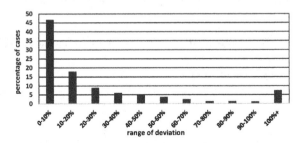

Fig. 8. The distribution of deviations, using manual inputs

Table 6. The results of using NER for factor identification

Feature	C	G	O	A	I	E
F_1	0.915	0.840	0.676	0.821	0.868	0.960

Figure 8 shows the distribution of the deviation. The horizontal axis shows the ranges of the deviation, using 10% for the increments. The vertical axis shows the percentages of cases in the test data. In this small-data test, the predicted grants were within the 10% range of the actual grants for more than 45% of the test cases.

6 Using NER for Factor Identification

The results discussed in the previous section relied on humans to pick the feature values from the judgment documents for the classifiers. We just showed that a prediction system might recommend grants that are fairly close to the judges' decisions, under such favorable preconditions. Although this assumption seems impractical, it is how the online recommender system of the Judicial Yuan works.

The Judicial Yuan started to offer an online legal judgment prediction system for eight categories of criminal crimes many years ago. The system asks human users to enter feature information about criminal activities, and the system will provide a range and a recommended sentence for the provided information (See Footnote 1). If we are holding judgment documents and want to test this system, then our task would be to extract the correct information from the document, enter the information into the system, and see if the recommender will return good recommendations. That is what we did and described in the last section.

In this section, we report our attempt to push the boundary further. We try to identify the values of the key features algorithmically. We employed a tool for named-entity recognition (NER), W2NER [6][6]. With the name entities recognized by the W2NER, we can apply regular expressions to train and learn the functions of the numbers in the plaintiffs' and the defendants' claims. Following are a few sample contexts in which the functions of the numbers before "元" are about the social allowance (Table 3).

$$\text{deviation}_i = \frac{|g_i - p_i|}{g_i} \tag{5}$$

Table 7. The average MAE of 1000 experiments with NER

test group	only linear regression	linear+log-linear	Figure 6
X	–	3044.53	3044.53
Y	–	3533.94	7613.63
Z	–	3080.29	2664.39
All (740)	3415.35	3171.19	3912.93

- 聲請人每月領有榮民就養給與(.{0,15})元
- 每月領有身心障礙者補助(.{0,15})元
- 目前領有托育養護補助每月(.{0,15})元
- 中(.{0,1})低收入戶(.{0,1})補助(.{0,15})元,

With the help of W2NER, we could achieve seemingly good results for the features that we listed in Table 3. Table 6 provides the F_1 measures.

---

[6] W2NER: https://github.com/ljynlp/W2NER, last accessed 2023/nov/09.

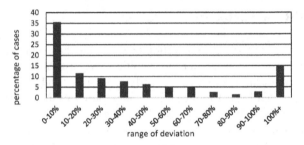

Fig. 9. The distribution of deviations of experiments with NER

Using the recognized feature values, we repeated the experiments that we reported in Sect. 5, and we observed the results in Table 7 and Fig. 9. All of the predictions in Table 7 are much worse than their counterparts in Table 5. We have only about 35% of the cases for which the predicted values were within 10% of the correct answers.

Recognizing some of the feature values correctly is not good enough for predicting the grant. When some of the feature values are wrong or missing, it is still hard to come up with correct or high-quality predictions with a fully automatic procedure.

7 Concluding Remarks

The reported observations in some of the experiments are encouraging, and some others show us more work to do. To provide more precise recommendations for judgments automatically, we need to find ways to identify the relevant factors more precisely from the text of the civil cases (and, of course, of the criminal cases). Gray et al. have just shown an example [3]. We should strengthen the depth of our current work as well [9].

Acknowledgments. We thank the reviewers of JURISIN 2023 and the post-conference LNAI proceedings for their recommendations about how we may improve our work. We could not respond to all suggestions because we always need more pages to do so. We have added information about how we finetuned the SBERT in the Appendix, and will pursue other recommendations in future experiments. This article was based on the thesis of Wei-Zhi Liu, who was co-advised by Sieh-chuen Huang and Chao-Lin Liu [10]. Po-Hsien Wu assisted in the technical part, and Ho-Chien Huang offered comments on the law. Wei-Zhi Liu's research also benefited from the comments of Chi-Yang Lin and Min-Yuh Day of National Taipei University, Taiwan. Chao-Lin Liu is the main author of this article. This research was supported in part by grant 110-2221-E-004-008-MY3 of the National Science and Technology Council of Taiwan.

Appendix: Finetuning the SBERT

This appendix responds to reviewers' comments for completing the finetuning of the pre-trained SBERT that we discussed in Sect. 4.

As we discussed in Sect. 2.3 and in the workshop, the first and most challenging barrier was that we had only 1930 documents for the classification task of predicting the judgments of the cases. This limited amount was partially due to the need to select the documents that meet the requirements for legal studies, as we explained in Sect. 2.2, and partially due to the results of the social pressure and legal mediation factors. Therefore, even in the study led by law experts, the number of selected cases was similar to ours [4]. We show and discuss some possible ways to work around the data size problem.

A.1 Data Preparation

When we did not finetune the pre-trained SBERT, we split these 1930 documents into three parts. We needed data for training the classifiers and for validating the training results. We certainly needed a portion of the data for the final tests.

To put the finetuning task back, we need to allocate data for this task, and, to avoid the potential data leakage problems, the data for finetuning the SBERT cannot be used in the downstream task.

Consequently, we will have less data for the training, validating, and testing the models for the grant/dismiss classification task (cf. Sect. 4).

To this end, we allocate 40% of the 1930 documents for the finetuning task and 60% for training, validating, and testing the classifiers. The finetuning task itself also needs the training and validation steps. Hence, we further split the 772 (1930 × 40%) documents by 8:2, using about 618 and 154 for training and validation, respectively. We would select the best-performing tuned model for the downstream task.

We split the 1158 (1930 × 60%) documents by 8:2, using about 926 documents for training the classifiers and 232 documents for the final tests. These 926 documents will be split for training and validation by 8:2. We repeated this training, validation, and testing procedure 100 times to collect the statistics of the observed quality of the classification with the help of boxplots, as we did in Fig. 6, i.e., we re-split the 926 documents for training and validation 100 times for each repeated experiment.

A.2 Finetuning

There are some conceivable tasks that we may use to finetune the SBERT. In Sect. 4, we discussed that we used six vectors for the plaintiffs and seven vectors for the defendants. If we directly used such a setup for the finetuning task, we would have only 618 training cases. To increase the training cases, we can sample between one to three vectors each from the plaintiff's and the defendant's vectors as the input, and use the vectors in the task of BertForSequenceClassifiction to tune the SBERT parameters. There are $\binom{6}{1} \times$ $\binom{7}{1} + \binom{6}{2} \times \binom{7}{2} + \binom{6}{3} \times \binom{7}{3} = 1057$ such combinations from a set of six and seven vectors. Hence, we can create at most 1057 training instances from one original training instance.

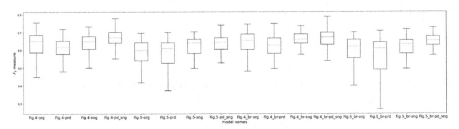

Fig. 10. 16 boxplots for the finetuning experiments

A simplified way to prepare the training instances was to use only one vector each from the plaintiff's and the defendant's vectors to form the input. Again, we would obtain more than 618 training instances.

A more drastic way of finetuning was to create two finetuned SBERT models: one for the plaintiff and one for the defendants. We carried out this exploration by trial using one vector of the plaintiff as the input and using the judgment of the corresponding case as the ground truth to finetune the SBERT for the plaintiffs. We could repeat the same procedure for the plaintiffs to create an SBERT for the defendants. When running the classification with the models in Figs. 4 and 5, we used different models for the plaintiffs and for the defendants.

We followed a typical training procedure to finetune the SBERT models. We created more training instances from the 618 original instances, trained the model for the Bert-ForSequenceClassifiction task, and validated the learned model with the 154 validation instances. We kept track of the validation loss in each epoch for early stopping and selected the best-performing model for the downstream task.

A.3 Results and Discussions

In Fig. 10, we use '**prd**,' '**sng**,' and '**pd-sng**' (in the order of their being mentioned above) to indicate the experimental results of these ways of finetuning. '**br**' stands for blur. For each of the rightmost four boxes in Fig. 6, we have four boxes in Fig. 10, where '**org**' indicates that we used an SBERT that was not finetuned. The statistics of the results for these not-tuned SBERT models varied in Fig. 10 because we resampled the training and test instances.

We tried several possible ways to finetune the SBERT, while producing more training instances, and chose to present these three methods here. The effects of different finetuning methods varied a lot.

Among these three finetuning strategies, **pd-sng** performed best, although it might not be an intuitive method. Usually, people use only one BERT model in a classification task. Using different SBERT models allows us to capture the different language characteristics of the plaintiffs and of the defendants. Using **pd-sng**, we observed both improved F_1 measures and smaller ranges for the [25%, 75%] boxes than using **org**.

The reviewers also recommended other ways to improve our predictions of the judgments, and we will do more work in the near future. Collecting more features is important, and we have reported related work [9].

References

1. Bex, F., Prakken, H.: On the relevance of algorithmic decision predictors for judicial decision making. In: Proceedings of the 2021 International Conference on Artificial Intelligence in Law, pp. 175–179 (2021)
2. Feng, Y., Li, C., Ng, V.: Legal judgment prediction: a survey of the state of the art. In: Proceedings of the 2021 International Joint Conference on Artificial Intelligence, pp. 5461–5469 (2021)
3. Gray, M., Savelka, J., Oliver, W., Ashley, K.: Toward automatically identifying legally relevant factors. In: Proceedings of the Thirty-Fifth International Conference on Legal Knowledge and Information Systems, pp. 53–62 (2022)
4. Huang, S.-C.: An empirical study on the grants for the support for the elderly (老親扶養費酌定裁判之實證研究). Presented in the Conference on Technology for Law and Justice (法律科技與接近正義研討會), National Taiwan University (2022). (in Chinese)
5. Komamizu, T., Fujioka, K., Ogawa, Y., Toyama, K.: Exploring relevant parts between legal documents using substructure matching. In: Proceedings of the 2019 JURISIN, pp. 5–19 (2019)
6. Li, J., et al.: Unified named entity recognition as word-word relation classification. In: Proceedings of 2022 AAAI Conference on Artificial Intelligence, pp. 10965–10973 (2022)
7. Lin, C.-F.: Regulation of the Judicial Discretion in Domestic Property Law: Focusing on the Determination of Maintenance, Living Expenses of the Household, and Alimony, Dissertation of the College of Law, National Chengchi University, Taiwan (2014). (in Chinese)
8. Lin, K.-I.: A Computational Approach to Analyze Court Decisions Regarding Alimony Claims after Divorce, Thesis of the Graduate Institute of Interdisciplinary Legal Studies, National Taiwan University (2018). (in Chinese)
9. Liu, C.-L., Lin, H.-R., Liu, W.-Z., Yang, C.: Functional classification of statements of Chinese judgment documents of civil cases (alimony for the elderly). In: Proceedings of the Thirty-Fifth International Conference on Legal Knowledge and Information Systems, pp. 206–212 (2022)
10. Liu, W.-Z.: Predicting Judgments and Grants for Civil Cases of Alimony for the Elderly, Thesis of the Department of Computer Science, National Chengchi University (2023). (in Chinese)

11. Manning, C.D., Raghavan, P., Schütze, H.: Introduction to Information Retrieval, chap. 6, Cambridge University Press (2008)
12. Muhlenbach, F., Sayn, I., Nguyen-Phuoc, L.: Predicting court decisions for alimony: avoiding extra-legal factors in decision made by judges and not understandable AI models. Presented in ICML 2020 Workshop on Law and Machine Learning (2020). arXiv:2007.04824. Accessed 09 Nov 2023
13. Rabelo, J., Kim, M.-Y., Goebel, R.: The application of text entailment techniques in COLIEE 2020. In: Proceedings of the 2020 JURISIN, pp. 240–253 (2020)
14. Reimers, N., Gurevych, I.: Sentence-BERT: sentence embeddings using Siamese BERT-networks. In: Proceedings of the 2019 Conference on Empirical Methods in Natural Language, Proceedings of the and the 9th International Joint Conference on Natural Language Processing, pp. 3982–3992 (2019)
15. Wu, Y., et al.: De-Biased court's view generation with causality. In: Proceedings of the 2020 Conference on Empirical Methods in Natural Language Processing, pp. 763–780 (2020)
16. Yamakoshi, T., Komamizu, T., Ogawa, Y., Toyama, K.: Differential translation for Japanese partially amended statutory sentences. In: Proceedings of the 2020 JURISIN, pp. 162–178 (2020)
17. Zhao, L., et al.: Legal judgment prediction with multiple perspectives on civil cases. In: Proceedings of 2021 CAAI International Conference on Artificial Intelligence, pp. 712–723 (2021)

Using WikiData for Handling Legal Rule Exceptions: Proof of Concept

Wachara Fungwacharakorn$^{(\boxtimes)}$ (iD), Hideaki Takeda (iD), and Ken Satoh (iD)

National Institute of Informatics, Sokendai University, Tokyo, Japan
{wacharaf,takeda,ksatoh}@nii.ac.jp

Abstract. Since social expectations and circumstances always change, it is challenging to refine formalized legal rules for handling new exceptions driven from cases. Recent research has explored using linked open datasets for handling exceptions. However, most research uses domain-dependent datasets developed by specific authorities. To handle legal rule exceptions, which typically need knowledge from various domains and need to be updated in response to social changes, we present in this paper a framework for handling legal rule exceptions using WIKIDATA. WIKIDATA is a linked open dataset retrieved from various Wikimedia projects with collaborative edits. The framework aims to guide the user to find the boundary of exceptional situation using descendent subclass hierarchies in WIKIDATA. As WIKIDATA cannot always handle the correspondence between legal concepts describing the antecedent of the rule and factors describing the case, the framework also helps guiding the user in revising rules or knowledge bases to restore the correspondence. We demonstrate the framework using cases from the European Court of Human Rights, and discuss possible improvements of this framework by integrating it with large language models such as CHATGPT.

Keywords: Legal reasoning · Linked Open Data · Wikidata

1 Introduction

Researchers have been long interested in representing legal rules using various formalizations, including CATALA [15], Defeasible Logic [20], PROLEG [24], and PROLOG [25–27]. In those formalizations, representations of legal rules are commonly divided into conclusions, antecedents (positive conditions of the rules), and exceptions (negative conditions of the rules). One of the most challenging aspects in formalizing legal rules is to handle new exceptions, which are frequently updated according to changing circumstances and social expectations. Thus, legal reasoning is viewed as moving classification systems [13] as judges may introduce new exceptions to distinguish cases while judging them [4]. The needs of handling new exceptions also occur in Artificial Intelligence (AI) as it is infeasible to express all of the exceptions in the first place [29].

In recent years, there has been a growing interest in using linked open datasets to aid in legal decision systems, including using Privacy Ontology

M. Bono et al. (Eds.): JSAI-isAI 2023 Workshops, LNAI 14644, pp. 85–99, 2024.
https://doi.org/10.1007/978-3-031-60511-6_6

(PRONTO) [19] for making legal decisions in General Data Protection Regulation (GDPR) [22] and using ASAM OPENXONTOLOGY [2] for handling exceptions to traffic rules [31]. However, in several types of cases, judges require board and update knowledge from various domains. For instance, the European Court of Human Rights reiterates that the European Convention on Human Rights must be interpreted and applied in the light of current circumstances [14].

To cope with the requirement of board and updated knowledge in handling exceptions, we investigate a framework using WIKIDATA [30]. WIKIDATA is a domain-independent linked open dataset supported by the Wikimedia Foundation. The dataset is retrieved from several Wikimedia projects and is open for both humans and machines to read and edit it. It shows that WIKIDATA can be used for analogical reasoning, but with manual effort [11]. We expect that using WIKIDATA may open up a possibility for handling legal rule exceptions across various domains and update according to circumstances and social expectations.

In our framework, we assume that antecedent concepts of legal rules and factors in cases are matched with items in WIKIDATA. Following that there must be correspondences between antecedent concepts in legal rules and facts in the cases, the framework guides the user to explore other items in WIKIDATA to facilitate in discovering new exceptional concepts for distinguishing the present case from the general implication of the rule. However, such correspondences may not be held in WIKIDATA. To deal with the problem, the framework helps guiding the user to restore the correspondences by fixing relations of concepts or revising antecedent concepts. We demonstrate the framework using example cases involving the rights to freedom of wearing religious items from the European Court of Human Rights. We discuss several parts of the framework that still depend on manual effort, including matching legal concepts with items, exploring similar cases, inventing exceptional concepts, and restoring correspondences. Then, we explore possibilities of assisting in some parts with large language models.

This paper is structured as follows. Section 2 provides background on interpretation of the European Convention on Human Rights and example cases related to the rights to freedom of wearing religious objects. Section 3 then gives background on the WIKIDATA dataset and the query service. Section 4 presents the framework using WIKIDATA for handling legal rule exceptions. Section 5 demonstrate the framework using the example cases. Section 6 discusses possible improvements for the framework. Finally, Sect. 7 provides a conclusion of this paper.

2   Examples from the European Court of Human Rights

In this paper, we focus on the interpretation of the European Convention on Human Rights (hereafter the *Convention*) and example cases decided by the European Court of Human Rights (hereafter the *Court*). The procedure in the Court can be divided into three phrases. The first phrase is to gather facts of the case, including relevant circumstances such as relevant domestic and international law and practice. The second phrase is to interpret the Convention and to analyze a correspondence between concepts in the Convention and facts of the case. The third phrase is to make a decision based on the correspondence.

In this paper, we account for the concept of wearing religious objects, which corresponds to Article 9 of the Convention, stating that:

Article 9 - Freedom of Thought, Conscience and Religion

1. Everyone has the right to freedom of thought, conscience and religion; this right includes freedom to change her/his religion or belief and freedom, either alone or in community with others and in public or private, to manifest her/his religion or belief, in worship, teaching, practice and observance.
2. Freedom to manifest one's religion or beliefs shall be subject only to such limitations as are prescribed by law and are necessary in a democratic society in the interests of public safety, for the protection of public order, health or morals, or for the protection of the rights and freedoms of others.

Following Article 9, the Court has decided several cases whether the state had failed to protect the rights to the freedom of wearing religious objects, in breach of this article. Example cases are as follows.

Ahmet Arslan and Others v. Turkey (2010). In October 1996, Ahmet Arslan and others wore the distinctive dress of their group and went to the mosque and public places in Turkey. Then, they were arrested and taken into police custody in breach of anti-terrorism legislation. In the hearing and prosecution procedure, they refused to remove their turbans. They were convicted in March 1997 and their appeals were unsuccessful. The Court decided that the state had failed to protect the rights to freedom of religion, in breach of Article 9, with discussions of wearing religious objects as follows [6]:

> ... Accordingly, the Turkish courts' decisions had amounted to interference with the applicants' freedom of conscience and religion, the legal basis for which was not contested (the law on the wearing of headgear and regulations on the wearing of certain clothing in public). In so far as the interference was meant to ensure respect for secular and democratic principles, it pursued a number of legitimate aims: the protection of public safety, the prevention of disorder and the protection of the rights and freedoms of others. However, the applicants were ordinary citizens. Not being representatives of the State engaged in public service, they could not be bound, on account of any official status, by a duty of discretion in the public expression of their religious beliefs. Moreover, the applicants had been punished for wearing particular clothing in public areas that were open to all, such as the public highway. Regulations on the wearing of religious symbols in public establishments, where religious neutrality might take precedence over the right to manifest one's religion, did not therefore apply. In addition, there was nothing in the case file to suggest that the manner in which the applicants had manifested their beliefs by their specific attire represented or might have represented a threat for public order or a form of pressure on others.

Eweida v. UK (2013). In May 2006, Ms Eweida, an employee of British Airways, wore a necklace with a small cross, against the uniform policy of wearing religious jewellery out of sight. The British courts ruled in favor of British Airways. The Court decided that the state had failed to protect the rights to freedom of religion, in breach of Article 9, with discussions of wearing religious objects as follows [7]:

> ... The Court considers that, while this aim was undoubtedly legitimate, the domestic courts accorded it too much weight. Ms Eweida's cross was discreet and cannot have detracted from her professional appearance. There was no evidence that the wearing of other, previously authorised, items of religious clothing, such as turbans and hijabs, by other employees, had any negative impact on British Airways' brand or image. Moreover, the fact that the company was able to amend the uniform code to allow for the visible wearing of religious symbolic jewellery demonstrates that the earlier prohibition was not of crucial importance.

S.A.S. v. France (2014). In 2011, banning full-face veils in public places became effective in France. A Muslim French woman (referred to as S.A.S.) filed a complaint against the French state as the law prevented her from wearing the niqab (a religious full-face veil, leaving the eyes uncovered) in public places. The European Court ruled in favor of France as an exception to Article 9, with discussions of wearing religious objects as follows [8].

> ... The Court is aware of the fact that the impugned ban mainly affects Muslim women who wish to wear the full-face veil. It nevertheless finds it to be of some significance that the ban is not expressly based on the religious connotation of the clothing in question but solely on the fact that it conceals the face. This distinguishes the present case from that in *Ahmet Arslan and Others* (cited above).

3   Wikidata

To facilitate judges with board and up-to-date knowledge, we consider WIKI-DATA [30], which is a domain-independent and collaboratively-created linked open dataset supported by Wikimedia Foundation. The dataset is retrieved from several Wikimedia projects including Wikipedia, Wiktionary, Wikisource, etc. As of March 2023, the dataset contains around 102 million items covering knowledge from various domains.

In WIKIDATA, each item is identified with a prefix `wd:` and a unique identification code to distinguish two items with the same label, for instance Apple (`wd:Q312`) refers to a technology company while Apple (`wd:Q26944932`) refers to a family name. Direct relations between items are identified with a prefix `wdt:`, including general relations like a subclass of (`wdt:P279`) and specific relations like a father of (`wdt:P22`). WIKIDATA provides a query service based on SPARQL.

Below shows an example query for finding all items which are subclasses of religious objects (wd:Q21029893). The query after SERVICE is for retrieving item labels in English. We denote such a query by a function *subclass(i)*, which returns a set of all WIKIDATA items that are subclasses of *i*.

```
SELECT ?item ?itemLabel
WHERE {
    ?item wdt:P279 wd:Q21029893.
    SERVICE wikibase:label {
        bd:serviceParam  wikibase:language "en".}
}
```

Furthermore, WIKIDATA query service allows a query to contain a property path, which is useful for querying multiple and/or recursive relations using asterisks (*). Below shows an example query for extracting a list of descendent subclasses (i.e. subclasses, subclasses of subclasses, ...) from a generic item religious_objects (wd:Q21029893) to a specific item niqab (wd:Q210583). We denote such a query by a function *desclist(i, j)* where *i, j* are items in WIKIDATA. The function returns a list of descendent subclasses from a generic item *i* to a specific item *j*.

```
SELECT ?item ?itemLabel
WHERE {
    ?item wdt:P279* wd:Q21029893.
    wd:Q210583 wdt:P279* ?item.
    SERVICE wikibase:label {
        bd:serviceParam wikibase:language "en".}
}
```

4   Framework

Our framework follows the principle that legal rules can be considered as combinations of legal concepts in the form of conclusions, antecedents, and exceptions [25]. When a case presents to the court, judges need to find correspondences between legal concepts and facts in the case. The conclusion is derived if all antecedents are provable and all exceptions are not provable. If the derivation of the conclusion is not intended, the judge may introduce a new exception that is provable at least in the present case.

Following the principle, we describe the design of our framework using description logic as follows. There are two sets of input from two sources, one from the rule and another from the case, considering one rule and one case each time. For the first set of input, we consider the rule written in description logic of the form:

$$A_1 \sqcap \ldots \sqcap A_n \sqsubseteq B \tag{1}$$

It represent that the intersection of *antecedent concepts* $A_1, \ldots, A_n$ generally implies the consequent concept B. Let $\mathcal{R} = \{A_1, \ldots, A_n\}$. One restriction following the legal principle is that the antecedent concepts within one rule must be independent, that is:

$$\forall A_i, A_j \in \mathcal{R} \ [(A_i \neq A_j) \Rightarrow (A_i \not\sqsubseteq A_j \wedge A_j \not\sqsubseteq A_i)] \tag{2}$$

We also assume that the considering rule is unfolding [28] so the antecedent concepts are not the consequent concepts of the other rules.

To obtain the antecedent concepts, we can reuse antecedent concepts from other legal systems that based on ontologies or linked datasets. Another possibility is that we can consider predicates in formalized legal rules.

For the second set of input, we consider the case as a set of *factors*, as in several classic case-based legal reasoning systems [1,3,21]. The factors are expressed as instances in description logic $f_1, \ldots, f_m$. Let $\mathcal{F} = \{f_1, \ldots, f_m\}$. We call each element of $\mathcal{F}$ a *case factor*. To reflect the correspondence between legal concepts and facts in the case, we assume that for all antecedent concepts, there must be one case factor that is an instance of.

$$\forall A \in \mathcal{R} \ \exists f \in \mathcal{F} \ [f : A] \tag{3}$$

The framework aims to handle legal rule exceptions when we find an exceptional case, of which an outcome should be opposite from the outcome from the general implication of the rule and hence an exception to the rule is needed. The expected output of the framework is *exceptional concepts* $E_1, \ldots, E_k$ to mark the exceptional situation of the case. Let $\mathcal{E} = \{E_1, \ldots, E_k\}$. Following the research on handling exceptions in formalized legal rules [10] as well as in non-monotonic reasoning [23], we expect the following properties:

$$\forall E \in \mathcal{E} \ \exists f \in \mathcal{F} \ [f : E] \tag{4}$$

$$\forall E \in \mathcal{E} \ \forall A \in \mathcal{R} \ [A \not\sqsubseteq E] \tag{5}$$

Property 4 means for all antecedent concepts, there must be one case factor that is an instance of. Property 5 prevents exceptional concepts from overriding the antecedents of the considering rule.

Figure 1 shows the relationship between an antecedent concept (A), a case factor (F), and exceptional concepts (E or E'). A case factor could be an instance of an antecedent concept or an exceptional concept (as well as both or none of them). An exceptional concept can be included in an antecedent concept (such as E) or excluded from an antecedent concept (such as E'), but such exceptional concepts cannot include any antecedent concepts.

To cooperate with WIKIDATA, we assume that antecedent concepts and case factors could be matched with WIKIDATA items, while inclusion relations between concepts can be retrieved by the relation subclass of (wdt:P279). For efficiency, we suggest finding an exceptional concept that is included in an antecedent concept (like E in Fig. 1) because we know the list of descendent subclasses from an antecedent concept to a case factor. The algorithm used in

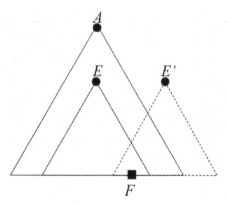

Fig. 1. Relationship between antecedent concept (A), case factor (F), and exceptional concepts $(E$ and $E')$

the framework is then designed as Algorithm 1. The algorithm consists of two main parts. The first part is to find exceptional concepts with a list of descendent subclasses, climbing from a case factor to an antecedent concept. For each step of climbing, the algorithm guides the user to find the boundary of the exceptional situation of the case using *sibling items* – items which share a common parent item. After the boundary is found, the algorithm lets the user invent a new concept that distinguishes exceptional cases from the others.

However, an assumption that items representing antecedent concepts must have items representing case factors as their descendent subclasses, may not hold in WIKIDATA. To solve this issue, we design the second part of the algorithm that additionally guides the user to find a problematic item that we may fix its subclass relations or find a more appropriate item to represent the antecedent concept to make the assumption hold again. After that, the algorithm repeats the first part.

5 Demonstration

Let us demonstrate the algorithm with the example case *S.A.S. v. France (2014)*. Suppose there is a legal rule explaining the wearable objects in public places as follows.

```
religious_objects ⊑ objects_with_the_freedom_to_be_worn_in_public
```

where the concept `religious_objects` in the rule is matched with the WIKIDATA item `religious objects` (`wd:Q21029893`). Meanwhile, a factor in the case is matched with the WIKIDATA item `niqab` (`wd:Q210583`). Fortunately, the item `niqab` is a descendant subclass to the item `religious objects`. With the query mentioned in Sect. 3, a list of descendent subclasses from `religious_objects` (`wd:Q21029893`) to `niqab` (`wd:Q210583`) can be extracted as in Fig. 2.

Algorithm 1. Find exceptional concepts for handling exceptions

---

Input a WIKIDATA item set $I_R = \{I_{A_1}, \ldots, I_{A_m}\}$, each of which represents *antecedent concepts* $A_1, \ldots, A_m$ respectively ($\mathcal{R} = \{A_1, \ldots, A_m\}$), and $I_F = \{I_{f_1}, \ldots, I_{f_n}\}$, each of which represents *case factors* $f_1, \ldots, f_n$ respectively ($\mathcal{F} = \{f_1, \ldots, f_n\}$)
Output a set of *exceptional concepts*

procedure FIND-EXCEPTIONAL-CONCEPTS(I_R, I_F)
    Let $Exc = \emptyset$
    while there is an unmarked item $i_r \in I_R$ **do**
        Find $i_f \in I_F$ and $I_D = desclist(i_r, i_f)$ such that $I_D \neq \emptyset$
        if there exists such $i_f \in I_F$ **then**
            Mark i_r and let $i = i_f$
            while $i \in I_D$ and $i \neq i_r$ **do**
                Find $i_p \in I_D$ such that $i \in subclass(i_p)$ ▷ Find a parent item
                Let $Sim =$ EXPLORE-SIMILAR-CASES-USING-SIBLINGS($i_p, i_f, \mathcal{F}$)
                if $Sim = subclass(i_p)$ and $i_p \neq i_r$ **then**
                    $i = i_p$ ▷ Exceptional concepts not found then climb up
                else if $Sim = subclass(i_p)$ and $i_p = i_r$ **then**
                    $Exc = Exc \cup$ INVENT-NEW-CONCEPT($Sim, \{i_r\}$)
                else
                    $Exc = Exc \cup$ INVENT-NEW-CONCEPT($Sim, subclass(i_p) \setminus Sim$)
    for all unmarked $i_r \in I_R$ **do**
        RESTORE-CORRESPONDENCE(i_r, I_R, I_F)
    return Exc
procedure EXPLORE-SIMILAR-CASES-USING-SIBLINGS($i_p, i_f, \mathcal{F}$)
    Let $Sim = \emptyset$
    for all $i_g \in subclass(i_p)$ **do**
        Let i_f (resp., i_g) represent instances of concepts f (resp., g)
        if $\mathcal{F} \setminus \{f\} \cup \{g\}$ decided in a similar way to $\mathcal{F}$ **then**   ▷ see Section 6
            $Sim = Sim \cup \{i_g\}$
    return Sim
procedure INVENT-NEW-CONCEPT(S_1, S_2)   ▷ see Section 6
    if S_1 is a singleton set $\{i\}$ **then**
        return a singleton set with the concept that i represents
    else return a set of new invented concepts that distinguishes S_1 from S_2
procedure RESTORE-CORRESPONDENCE(i_r, I_R, I_F)   ▷ see Section 6
    Let Q be a priority queue
    Add i_r to Q, mark i_r, and let $i_c = i_r$
    Find $i_f \in I_F$ that is the most relevant to i_r
    while Q is not empty **do**
        Pick and mark an item i within Q that is the most relevant to i_f
        if i_f should be a direct subclass of i **then**   ▷ a problematic item found
            Add i_f as a direct subclass of i (so that the property 3 holds) **return**
        else if there is an item in $subclass(i)$ that is unmarked and relevant **then**
            Add all unmarked and relevant items from $subclass(i)$ to Q
    if i_f should be a direct subclass of i_r **then**
        Add i_f as a subclass of i_r **return**
    else
        Replace $i_r \in I_R$ with a more appropriate item or a new invented item i'_r
        (it requires checking with other antecedent concepts and other cases)
        if there is $i_f \in I_F$ such that $desclist(i_r, i_f) \neq \emptyset$ **then return**
        else RESTORE-CORRESPONDENCE(i'_r, I_R, I_F)

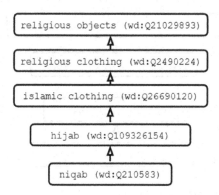

Fig. 2. List of descendent subclasses from `religous_objects` (`wd:Q21029893`) to `niqab` (`wd:Q210583`)

Then, the algorithm guides the user to find an exceptional concept using the sibling items. For example, since `Jilbab` (`wd:Q1248904`) is a sibling item of `niqab` as it shares the common parent `hijab` (`wd:Q109326154`) but jilbab allows to open the whole face, it leads to the question whether a jilbab is included in an exception, i.e. shall we allow to ban an open-faced jilbab, in the similar manner of banning a niqab, which is a closed face covering. Applying the principle from *Ahmet Arslan and Others v. Turkey (2010)*, a jilbab is excluded from the exceptional situation, i.e. we shall not ban a jilbab. Then, the user may invent a new concept `close_face_covering` that is suitable for handling the exception. As a result, we have

$$\text{religious\_objects} \sqsubseteq \text{objects\_with\_the\_freedom\_to\_be\_worn\_in\_public}$$
$$\text{close\_face\_covering} \sqsubseteq \text{exceptions\_of\_objects\_with\_the\_freedom}$$
$$\text{\_to\_be\_worn\_in\_public}$$
$$\text{niqab} : \text{close\_face\_covering}$$

Now, let us demonstrate the problem when an antecedent concept could not find any case factor as its descendent subclass. We demonstrate the problem using the example case *Eweida v. UK (2013)*. We have that a factor in the case is matched with an item `cross necklace` (`wd:Q5188464`) in WIKIDATA. Unfortunately, `cross necklace` (`wd:Q5188464`) is not a descendant subclass to `religious_objects` (`wd:Q21029893`).

Figure 3 shows two disconnected descendant lists, one with `religious objects` (`wd:Q21029893`) and another with `cross necklace` (`wd:Q5188464`). We have that `cross necklace` (`wd:Q5188464`) is a subclass of `crucifix` (`wd:Q20460`) described as a *cross with an image or artwork of Jesus on it* while there is another item labelled `crucifix` (`wd:Q107194653`) described as a *kind of religious object*. The algorithm guides the user to add `cross necklace`

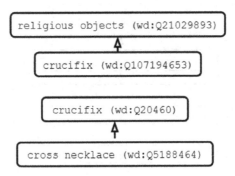

Fig. 3. Two disconnected descendant lists related to `religious_objects` (`wd:Q21029893`) and `cross necklace` (`wd:Q5188464`)

(`wd:Q5188464`) as a subclass of `crucifix` (`wd:Q107194653`), which is then a subclass of `religious objects` (`wd:Q21029893`).

6 Discussion

In this section, we discuss several limitations and possible improvements for this framework by integrating it with large language models (LLMs), such as CHATGPT. The section is structured based on the preprocess and the sub-procedures noted in Algorithm 1. We also discuss the complexity and the validity of the algorithm at the end of the section.

6.1 Matching Legal Concepts with Wikidata Items

Since WIKIDATA contains millions of items covering knowledge from various domain while there are few legal concepts involved in one legal rule, it is manually affordable to match legal concepts with WIKIDATA items. However, as the matching may face several issues on manual knowledge representation, including biases and ambiguities, future research could investigate reducing such issues. In this paper, we investigate one issue that the matched items may not exactly reflect the correspondences between legal concepts and factors in the case. This is probably because WIKIDATA is not designate specifically for legal domains. It may prove to be useful if we can use both domain-independent linked datasets (like WIKIDATA) and domain-dependent linked datasets by matching concepts between those datasets. Future research could explore more effective ways to reflect correspondences between antecedent concepts and case factors in domain-independent linked datasets.

6.2 Exploring Cases Using Sibling Items

In this paper, we suggest guiding the user to consider exceptional situations using sibling items, i.e. items that share common parent items in the descendant list. Since sibling items do not occur in the case presented to the court, our framework seems to be suitable for legislators rather than judges for discussing several concepts outside the case. We expect that sibling items could help the user to consider exceptional situations of the case exhaustively; however, it still depends on the user to decide whether cases made from sibling items is similar to the present case. To assist the task, we tested whether CHATGPT [18] can understand the exceptional concept. For example, we ask CHATGPT "What is an exceptional situation of *S.A.S. v. France (2014)* ?" in a new session of CHATGPT and here is a part of the answer.

> ... One exceptional situation of this case was the argument put forth by the French government that the ban on full-face veils was necessary for public safety and security reasons. ...

We can see that CHATGPT can identify the exceptional situation correctly. However, it is still a question of whether LLMs can consider exceptional situations correctly for a case that has not been decided.

6.3 Inventing Exceptional Concepts

The first attempt of the framework is to use WIKIDATA items for describing exceptional situations of the case. Nevertheless, it turns out the items that exactly describe exceptional situations are rarely found in WIKIDATA. This is probably because, if the items already exist in WIKIDATA, they should be already exceptions of the rule. Hence, mismatches between concepts in rules and in knowledge bases would lead to revisions of the rules and the knowledge bases, as the previous study [12] has suggested.

Currently, inventing exceptional concepts is still handcrafted. To explore CHATGPT for inventing exceptional concepts, we tested whether CHATGPT can invent a term that includes exceptional cases but excludes non-exceptional cases. The test was conducted with the following *filling in the blank* question in a new session of CHATGPT and here is an answer.

> Q: Fill in the blank:
> input: brothers and sisters, but not fathers
> output: siblings
> input: burqa and niqab, but not jilbab
> output: ___
> A: face veils

The answer is close but still incorrect (*full-face veils* is a correct answer). Since the usage of LLMs in this task is still exploratory and questionable, we have not expected LLMs for inventing concepts on their own. They might be able to be integrated to the framework as an assistance for the user. Future research could investigate more techniques to invent exceptional concepts.

6.4 Restoring Correspondences

Since a correspondence between an antecedent concepts and a case factor might not be held in WIKIDATA, the framework guides the user to explore descendant subclasses of such antecedent concepts for find a problematic item that we may fix its subclass relations, in line with the previous work on debugging defects in legal rules [9]. To make effective exploration, we introduce the heuristic search, in line with the previous work on constructing case law theories [5]. The current framework still depends on the user heuristics to find the most relevant item within the subclass items. For this part, it is interesting to use several techniques in natural language processing, such as WORD2VEC [16] word embeddings, as heuristics for searching the most relevant item to the considering case factor.

6.5 Complexity and Validity of Algorithm

To analyze the complexity of the algorithm, we can consider extracting a descendant list from an antecedent concept to a case factor as breadth-first search. Let r be a number of antecedent concepts. If every antecedent concept has a case factor as it is a descendant subclass with the depth at most d and each item has direct subclasses with the size at most n, it runs $O(rn^{d+1})$ in the worst case to extract all descendant lists of antecedent concepts, and it runs $O(rnd)$ in the worst case to consider sibling items in the descendant list for each antecedent concept. However, if an antecedent concepts does not have a case factor as an instance of, it runs $O(rn^{D+1})$ at most, where D is the longest depth of descendent subclasses of the antecedent concept, for finding a problematic item to fix its subclass relations. Hence, the execution time are generally larger if an antecedent concepts does not have a case factor as an instance of. It is interesting to reduce the complexity of the search. One possibility is to use WIKIDATA-LITE [17], which is pruned from WIKIDATA, to reduce the complexity.

Regarding the validity of the algorithm, the algorithm always returns exceptional concepts, which there is a case factor as an instance of and which any antecedent concepts are excluded from, because we explore through the list of descendent subclasses from a case factor to an antecedent concept and the antecedent concepts within one rule are all independent. The algorithm is not complete as the algorithm does not search for an exceptional concept that is excluded from an antecedent concept (like E' in Fig. 1). However, we can partially search for such an exceptional concept by the algorithm as the intersection of such an exceptional concept and an antecedent concept is included in the antecedent concept ($A \sqcap E' \sqsubseteq A$ with respect to Fig. 1), and the user may recall such an intersection of concepts from the list of descendent subclasses. Further research could explore the discovery of exceptional concepts that are not the descendent subclass of antecedent concepts.

7 Conclusion

In this paper, we present a framework for handling legal rule exceptions using WIKIDATA, a collaboratively-edited linked open dataset supported by Wikimedia foundation. The inputs of the framework are a set of *antecedent concepts* and a set of *case factors*, both of which are matched with WIKIDATA items. We assume that every antecedent concept has a case factor as its instance. To find concepts that are suitable for describing exceptional situations, the framework navigates a user to explore a list of descendent subclasses extracted from WIKI-DATA by climbing from a case factor to an antecedent concept. For each step of climbing, the framework guides the user to find the boundary of the exceptional situation of the case using sibling of each item in list of descendent subclasses. After the boundary is found, the algorithm let the user invent a new concept that distinguishes exceptional cases from the others. However, it is possible that an antecedent concepts might not have any case fact as an instance in WIKI-DATA so the framework navigates the user through WIKIDATA to fix subclass relations or find a more appropriate items to represent the antecedent concept. In the future, we are interested in using several technologies, such as WIKIDATA-LITE, WORD2VEC, CHATGPT, for pruning unnecessary navigation as well as inventing new terms for describing exceptional situations.

Acknowledgements. This work was supported by JSPS KAKENHI Grant Numbers, JP17H06103 and JP19H05470 and JST, AIP Trilateral AI Research, Grant Number JPMJCR20G4.

References

1. Aleven, V.: Teaching case-based argumentation through a model and examples. Ph.D. thesis, University of Pittsburgh (1997)
2. ASAM: Asam openxontology. https://www.asam.net/project-detail/asam-openxontology/ Accessed 06 Mar 2023
3. Ashley, K.D.: Modeling Legal Arguments: Reasoning with Cases and Hypotheticals. The MIT Press, Cambridge (1990)
4. Ashley, K.D.: Artificial Intelligence and Legal Analytics: New Tools for Law Practice in the Digital Age. Cambridge University Press, Cambridge (2017)
5. Chorley, A., Bench-Capon, T.: AGATHA: using heuristic search to automate the construction of case law theories. Artif. Intell. Law **13**(1), 9–51 (2005)
6. European Court of Human Rights: Case of Ahmet Arslan and Others v. Turkey (2010). https://hudoc.echr.coe.int/app/conversion/pdf/?library=ECHR&id=002-1131
7. European Court of Human Rights: Case of Eweida and Others v. the United Kingdom (2013). https://www.bailii.org/eu/cases/ECHR/2013/37.html
8. European Court of Human Rights: Case of S.A.S. v. France (2014). https://www.bailii.org/eu/cases/ECHR/2014/695.html
9. Fungwacharakorn, W., Satoh, K.: Legal debugging in propositional legal representation. In: Kojima, K., Sakamoto, M., Mineshima, K., Satoh, K. (eds.) JSAI-isAI 2018. LNCS (LNAI), vol. 11717, pp. 146–159. Springer, Cham (2019). https://doi.org/10.1007/978-3-030-31605-1_12
10. Fungwacharakorn, W., Satoh, K.: Generalizing culprit resolution in legal debugging with background knowledge. In: Legal Knowledge and Information Systems. Frontiers in Artificial Intelligence and Applications, vol. 334, pp. 52–62. IOS Press (2020)

11. Ilievski, F., Pujara, J., Shenoy, K.: Does wikidata support analogical reasoning? In: Villazón-Terrazas, B., Ortiz-Rodriguez, F., Tiwari, S., Sicilia, M.A., Martín-Moncunill, D. (eds.) Knowledge Graphs and Semantic Web. LNCS, vol. 1686, pp. 178–191. Springer, Cham (2022). https://doi.org/10.1007/978-3-031-21422-6_13

12. Kurematsu, M., Tada, M., Yamaguchi, T.: A legal ontology refinement environment using a general ontology. In: Proceedings of Workshop on Basic Ontology Issues in Knowledge Sharing, International Joint Conference on Artificial Intelligence. vol. 95 (1995)

13. Levi, E.H.: An Introduction to Legal Reasoning. University of Chicago Press, Chicago (2013)

14. McBride, J.: The Doctrines and Methodology of Interpretation of The European Convention on Human Rights by The European Court of Human Rights. Council of Europe (2021)

15. Merigoux, D., Chataing, N., Protzenko, J.: Catala: a programming language for the law. In: International Conference on Functional Programming, pp. 1–29. Proceedings of the ACM on Programming Languages, ACM, Virtual, South Korea (Aug 2021)

16. Mikolov, T., Chen, K., Corrado, G., Dean, J.: Efficient estimation of word representations in vector space. arXiv preprint arXiv:1301.3781 (2013)

17. Nguyen, P., Takeda, H.: Wikidata-lite for knowledge extraction and exploration. arXiv preprint arXiv:2211.05416 (2022)

18. OpenAI: Chatgpt. https://chat.openai.com/chat. Accessed 06 Mar 2023

19. Palmirani, M., Martoni, M., Rossi, A., Bartolini, C., Robaldo, L.: PrOnto: privacy ontology for legal reasoning. In: Kő, A., Francesconi, E. (eds.) EGOVIS 2018. LNCS, vol. 11032, pp. 139–152. Springer, Cham (2018). https://doi.org/10.1007/978-3-319-98349-3_11

20. Prakken, H.: Logical Tools for Modelling Legal Argument: A Study of Defeasible Reasoning in Law. Kluwer Academic Publishers, The Netherlands (1997)

21. Rissland, E.L., Ashley, K.D.: A case-based system for trade secrets law. In: Proceedings of the 1st International Conference on Artificial Intelligence and Law, pp. 60–66. Association for Computing Machinery, New York, NY, USA (1987)

22. Robaldo, L., Bartolini, C., Palmirani, M., Rossi, A., Martoni, M., Lenzini, G.: Formalizing GDPR provisions in reified I/O logic: the DAPRECO knowledge base. J. Logic Lang. Inform. **29**, 401–449 (2020)

23. Sakama, C.: Nonmonotomic inductive logic programming. In: Eiter, T., Faber, W., Truszczyński, M. (eds.) LPNMR 2001. LNCS (LNAI), vol. 2173, pp. 62–80. Springer, Heidelberg (2001). https://doi.org/10.1007/3-540-45402-0_5

24. Satoh, K.: PROLEG: an implementation of the presupposed ultimate fact theory of Japanese civil code by PROLOG technology. In: Onada, T., Bekki, D., McCready, E. (eds.) JSAI-isAI 2010. LNCS (LNAI), vol. 6797, pp. 153–164. Springer, Heidelberg (2011). https://doi.org/10.1007/978-3-642-25655-4_14

25. Satoh, K., Kubota, M., Nishigai, Y., Takano, C.: Translating the Japanese presupposed ultimate fact theory into logic programming. In: Proceedings of the 2009 Conference on Legal Knowledge and Information Systems: JURIX 2009: The Twenty-Second Annual Conference, pp. 162–171. IOS Press, Amsterdam, The Netherlands (2009)

26. Sergot, M.J., Sadri, F., Kowalski, R.A., Kriwaczek, F., Hammond, P., Cory, H.T.: The British nationality act as a logic program. Commun. ACM **29**(5), 370–386 (1986)

27. Sherman, D.M.: A prolog model of the income tax act of Canada. In: Proceedings of the 1st International Conference on Artificial Intelligence and Law, pp. 127–136. Association for Computing Machinery, New York, NY, USA (1987)
28. Tamaki, H., Sato, T.: Unfold/fold transformation of logic programs. In: Proceedings of the Second International Conference on Logic Programming, pp. 127–138 (1984)
29. Thielscher, M.: The qualification problem: a solution to the problem of anomalous models. Artif. Intell. **131**(1–2), 1–37 (2001)
30. Vrandečić, D., Krötzsch, M.: Wikidata: a free collaborative knowledgebase. Commun. ACM **57**(10), 78–85 (2014)
31. Wang, Y., Grabowski, M., Paschke, A.: An ontology-based model for handling rule exceptions in traffic scenes. In: Proceedings of the International Workshop on AI Compliance Mechanism (WAICOM 2022), pp. 87–100 (2022)

Constructing and Explaining Case Models: A Case-Based Argumentation Perspective

Wachara Fungwacharakorn[1]([✉]) [ID], Ken Satoh[1] [ID], and Bart Verheij[2] [ID]

[1] National Institute of Informatics and SOKENDAI, Tokyo, Japan
{wacharaf,ksatoh}@nii.ac.jp
[2] Artificial Intelligence, University of Groningen, Groningen, The Netherlands
bart.verheij@rug.nl

Abstract. In this paper, we investigate constructing and explaining case models, which have been proposed as formal models for presumptive reasoning and evaluating arguments from cases. Recent research shows applications of case models and relationships between case models and other computational reasoning models. However, formal methods for constructing and explaining case models have not been investigated yet. Therefore, in this paper, we present methods for constructing and explaining case models based on the formalism of abstract argumentation for case-based reasoning (AA-CBR). The methods are illustrated in this paper with a legal example of paying penalties for a delivery company. With these two methods, we show an intended property that a dispute tree explaining the case model constructed from an AA-CBR case-base is homomorhpic to a dispute tree explaining the case-base itself. Additionally, we analyze that the methods are tractable in terms of number of cases and number of propositions used for representing each case.

Keywords: case-based reasoning · argumentation frameworks · case models

1 Introduction

Artificial Intelligence and Law researchers are interested in explanations of reasons using cases. To explain the reasons, early case-based legal reasoning systems, such as HYPO, use analogical reasoning [4]. Later, argumentation has been shown to be useful for explanation [3], and case-based argumentation has been shown to be useful for explaining case-base reasoning and the development of case law [8,10] as well as explaining legal theories based on hypothetical cases in statute law [16]. Abstract argumentation for case-based reasoning (AA-CBR) [7] is one model for formalizing argumentation in case-based reasoning. In AA-CBR, a case-base is a finite consistent set of case-pairs with a default outcome – which is denoted by a default case-pair with empty situation in the case-base. AA-CBR predicts an outcome for a new situation by considering whether the default case-pair is in the grounded extension of the abstract argumentation framework (AA-framework) [9] corresponding to the case-base. AA-CBR

M. Bono et al. (Eds.): JSAI-isAI 2023 Workshops, LNAI 14644, pp. 100–114, 2024.
https://doi.org/10.1007/978-3-031-60511-6_7

explains the inference using dispute trees, which also inspire explanations in other case-based reasoning models such as in precedential constraint [15,20].

Also, Artificial Intelligence and Law researchers are interested in evaluations of arguments using cases. Case models [18] have been recently developed in order to formally evaluate arguments as incoherent, coherent, presumptively valid, and conclusive. Each case model consists of a set of consistent, mutually incompatible, and different logic formulas representing cases, and a total and transitive preference ordering over the cases. Several applications of case models have been investigated, including evidential reasoning [12,19] and ethical system design [17]. Formalizing case models for case-based reasoning has also been investigated [17,18]. However, the questions of how to formally construct case models from a case-base and how to explain argument moves in case models have not been studied.

In order to address these questions, we investigate a connection between AA-CBR and case models. The connection is presented as a method of constructing case models from case-bases and a method of explaining argument moves in case models using dispute trees. For the construction, we define a new concept of *boundary* and *internal sub-boundary*, intuitively reflecting interpolations of each case-pair. In the generated case models, cases are constructed from internal sub-boundaries of case-pairs in the case-base and preferences are derived from the length of attacks from each case-pair to the default case-pair in the corresponding AA-framework. For the explanation, we define *specificity rebuttal*, intuitively representing contrastive explanations in case models. With specificity rebuttals, we define dispute trees with respect to case models in the same manner of dispute trees with respect to AA-CBR. We show the intended property that a dispute tree explaining case models constructed from an AA-CBR case-base are homomorphic to dispute trees with respect to the AA-framework corresponding to the case-base. Moreover, we analyzed that those two methods run in time $O(m^2 n^3)$ in the worst case where m is the size of propositions used for representing one case and n is the number of cases involved in the models.

This paper is structured as follows. Section 2 describes abstract argumentation for case-based reasoning (AA-CBR). Section 3 describes case models. Section 4 presents the first contribution of formalizing a method for constructing case models from AA-CBR case-bases. Then, Sect. 5 presents the second contribution of developing dispute trees for explanations in case models. Section 6 discusses connections with related research, and provides suggestions for future work. Finally, Sect. 7 provides the conclusion of this paper.

2   Abstract Argumentation for Case-Based Reasoning

In this section, we account for abstract argumentation for case-based reasoning (AA-CBR) [7], which is used as a representative of case-based argumentation in this paper. AA-CBR aims for formalizing reasoning from consistent case-bases with default outcomes. AA-CBR uses Dung's abstract argumentation frameworks [9], which we recap here as follows (cf. [7]).

Definition 1 (AA-framework). *An* AA-framework *is a pair* $\langle AR, attacks \rangle$, *where AR is a set whose elements are called* arguments, *and* $attacks \in AR \times AR$. *For arguments* $x, y \in AR$, *if* $(x, y) \in attacks$, *then we say x attacks y. For a set* $E \subseteq AR$ *and arguments* $x, y \in AR$, *we say E attacks x if some argument* $z \in E$ *attacks x; and we say E defends y if, for all arguments* $x \in AR$ *that attack y, E attacks x. The* grounded extension *of* $\langle AR, attacks \rangle$ *refers to a set* $G \subseteq AR$ *that can be constructed inductively as* $G = \bigcup_{i \geq 0} G_i$, *where* G_0 *is the set of unattacked arguments, and* $\forall i \geq 0$, G_{i+1} *is the set of arguments that* G_i *defends.*

Dispute trees for arguments in an AA-framework are defined as follows [7].

Definition 2 (Dispute Tree). *Let* $\langle AR, attacks \rangle$ *be an AA-framework. A dispute tree for an argument* $x_0 \in AR$, *is a (possibly infinite) tree* T *such that:*

1. *every node of* T *is of the form* $[L : x]$, *with* $L \in \{P, O\}$ *and* $x \in AR$ *where L indicates the status of proponent (P) or opponent (O);*
2. *the root of* T *is* $[P : x_0]$;
3. *for every proponent node* $[P : y]$ *in* T *and for every* $x \in AR$ *such that x attacks y, there exists* $[O : x]$ *as a child of* $[P : y]$;
4. *for every opponent node* $[O : y]$ *in* T, *there exists at most one child of* $[P : x]$ *such that x attacks y;*
5. *there are no other nodes in* T *except those given by 1–4.*

A dispute tree T *is an* admissible *dispute tree if and only if (i) every opponent node* $[O : x]$ *in* T *has a child, and (ii) no* $[P : x]$ *and* $[O : y]$ *in* T *such that* $x = y$. *A dispute tree* T *is a* maximal *dispute tree if and only if for all opponent nodes* $[O : x]$ *which are leaves in* T *there is no argument* $y \in AR$ *such that y attacks x.*

Admissible dispute trees are maximal dispute trees but not vice versa [7] because admissible dispute trees are those maximal dispute trees without opponent leaves while maximal dispute trees with opponent leaves also exist. In other words, admissible dispute trees demonstrate argumentations where the proponent can attack all of the opponent's arguments but maximal dispute trees demonstrate argumentations where the proponent's burden is *complete*, i.e. either the proponent cannot attack some opponent's arguments or the proponent already attacks all of the opponent's arguments.

Recently, researchers [6] have generalized AA-CBR for more general representations of situations and preferences. However, in this paper, we mostly follow definitions from the original work [7]. Let $\mathcal{F}$ be a set of propositions called a *fact-domain*, whose elements are called *fact-propositions*[1]. We call a finite subset of $\mathcal{F}$ a *fact-situation*. Let $o \in \{+, -\}$ be an *outcome*. We denote the opposite of $o \in \{+, -\}$ by $\bar{o}$, namely $\bar{o} = +$ if $o = -$; and $\bar{o} = -$ if $o = +$. A *case-pair* is a pair $(X, o) \in 2^{\mathcal{F}} \times \{+, -\}$. A *case-base* in AA-CBR is then defined as follows [7].

---

[1] In the original work, those elements are called *factors* but we use the new terms in order to distinguish them from factors in CATO [1].

Definition 3 (Case-base in AA-CBR). *A case-base is a finite set* $CB \subseteq 2^{\mathcal{F}} \times \{+, -\}$ *of cases-pairs such that:*

- *(consistent) for* $(X, o_x), (Y, o_y) \in CB$, *if* $X = Y$, *then* $o_x = o_y$
- *(containing a default case-pair)* $(\varnothing, d) \in CB$, $(\varnothing, d)$ *is then called a* default *case-pair and* d *is called a* default *outcome*

Example 1. To illustrate case-based argumentation, we adapt an example of penalties from a delivery company [2] with the following rules.

1. If there is no special situation, the delivery company does not have to pay a penalty.
2. If the delivery was delayed, the delivery company has to pay a penalty.
3. If the items were damaged, the delivery company has to pay a penalty.
4. If the items were damaged but they are fungible and the items were replaced, then the delivery company does not have to pay a penalty.

We represent propositions as follows.

- `delayed`: the delivery was delayed.
- `damaged`: the items were damaged.
- `fungible`: the items are fungible
- `replaced`: the items were replaced.
- `penalty`; the delivery company has to pay a penalty

Considering a conclusion of whether the delivery company has to pay a penalty ($+$ means the company has to pay a penalty; $-$ otherwise), the working example can be represented as a case-base consisting of the following case-pairs.

1. $co_0 = (\varnothing, -)$
2. $co_1 = (\{\texttt{delayed}\}, +)$
3. $co_2 = (\{\texttt{damaged}\}, +)$
4. $co_3 = (\{\texttt{damaged}, \texttt{fungible}, \texttt{replaced}\}, -)$

To infer an outcome for a new fact-situation $N \subseteq \mathcal{F}$, AA-CBR forms an AA-framework and considers whether or not a default case-pair $(\varnothing, d)$ is in the grounded extension of the formed AA-framework.

Definition 4 (AA-framework corresponding to an AA-CBR case-base). *An AA-framework corresponding to a case-base* CB *with a default case-pair* $(\varnothing, d)$ *and a new fact-situation* $N \subseteq \mathcal{F}$ *is* $\langle AR, attacks \rangle$ *satisfying the following conditions:*

- $AR = \{(X, o) \in CB | X \subseteq N\}^2$
- (X, o_x) *attacks* (Y, o_y) *for all case-pairs* $(X, o_x), (Y, o_y) \in AR$ *such that*
  - *(different outcomes)* $o_x \neq o_y$, *and*

---

[2] The original work uses $(N, ?)$ that attacks all case-pairs of which situations are not subsets of N, but, to simplify definitions in the rest of the present paper, we adapt this part of the definition following [2] instead.

- *(specificity)* $Y \subsetneq X$, *and*
- *(concision)* $\nexists(Z, o_x) \in AR$ with $Y \subsetneq Z \subsetneq X$

The AA-outcome of N is d if $(\varnothing, d)$ is in the grounded extension of $\langle AR, attacks \rangle$, otherwise the AA-outcome of N is $\bar{d}$.

Since the subset relation is a partial order, an AA-framework corresponding to an AA-CBR case-base is well-founded or acyclic. Besides that, the framework has another property that: if $(X, o_x) \in CB$ is a unique nearest case-pair to a fact-situation $N \subseteq \mathcal{F}$, then the AA-outcome of N is o_x [8], where the nearest case-pair is defined as follows [8].

Definition 5 (Nearest case-pair). *Let $N \subseteq \mathcal{F}$ be a fact-situation, and CB be a case-base. $(X, o_x) \in CB$ is (possibly not unique) nearest to N if and only if $X \subseteq N$, and $\nexists(Y, o_y) \in CB$ with $Y \subseteq N$ and $X \subsetneq Y$. In other words, X is $\subseteq$-maximal in the case-base.*

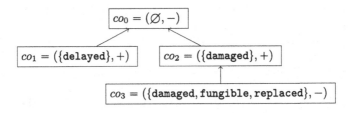

Fig. 1. The AA-framework corresponding to the case-base and N_2 in Example 2

Example 2. From Example 1, suppose we would like to infer an outcome for a situation where items were damaged, the damaged items are fungible, but the delivery company did not replace the items. The situation can be represented as $N_1 = \{\texttt{damaged}, \texttt{fungible}\}$ and the arguments in the AA-framework corresponding to the case-base and N_1 are co_0 and co_2. We have that co_2 is a unique nearest case-pair to N_1 hence the AA-outcome of N_1 is $+$.

Now, suppose we would like to infer an outcome for a situation where items were damaged, the damaged items are fungible, the items were replaced, but the delivery was delayed. The situation can be represented as $N_2 = \{\texttt{damaged}, \texttt{fungible}, \texttt{replaced}, \texttt{delayed}\}$ and the arguments in the AA-framework corresponding to the case-base and N_2 are all case-pairs in the case-base, as depicted in Fig. 1. For this situation, there is no unique nearest case-pair to N_2. To resolve this, we need to consider the grounded extension of the AA-framework. We can see that the default case-pair $co_0 = (\varnothing, -)$ is not in the grounded extension of the AA-framework. Thus, the AA-outcome of N_1 is $+$, i.e. the delivery company has to pay a penalty.

For explanations, AA-CBR uses dispute trees as follows.

Definition 6 (AA-CBR explanation). *Let N be a fact-situation and d be a default outcome. An* explanation *for why the AA-outcome of N is d is any admissible dispute tree for $(\varnothing, d)$. An* explanation *for why the AA-outcome of N is $\bar{d}$ is any maximal dispute tree for $(\varnothing, d)$.*

We refer to a case-pair that can occur in any maximal dispute tree for $(\varnothing, d)$ as a *critical* case-pair (cf. [16]). As a result, $(\varnothing, d)$ is a critical case-pair and any case-pair that attacks a critical case-pair is also a critical case-pair.

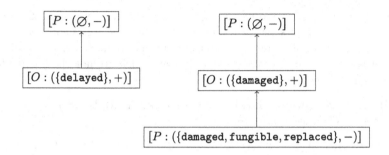

Fig. 2. Two Maximal Dispute Trees for $(\varnothing, -)$ in Example 3

Example 3. From Example 2, two maximal dispute trees can be extracted from the AA- framework, as depicted in Fig. 2. The left tree in the figure is a non-admissible dispute tree which explains why the company has to pay a penalty. The dispute tree on the right in the figure is an admissible dispute tree which explains why the company does not have to pay a penalty.

3 Case Models

Case models [18] aim to formally evaluate arguments from cases. A case in case models is a logical formula, usually a conjunction of literals. A case model consists of a set of cases C, and their preference ordering $\geq$. The cases in a case model must be logically consistent, mutually incompatible, and different. The preference ordering $\geq$ in case models must be total and transitive (hence is what is called a total preorder, corresponding to a numerically representable ordering). Let $\mathcal{L}$ be a classical logical language generated from a set of propositional constants in a standard way. We write $\neg$ for negation, $\wedge$ for conjunction, $\vee$ for disjunction, $\leftrightarrow$ for equivalence, $\top$ for a tautology, and $\bot$ for a contradiction. The associated classical, deductive, monotonic consequence relation is denoted $\models$. A case model is defined as follows.

Definition 7 (Case Model [18]). *A case model is a pair $(C, \geq)$ with finite $C \subseteq \mathcal{L}$, such that the following hold, for all φ , ψ and $\chi \in C$:*

1. $\not\models \neg\varphi$ *(logically consistent, i.e. a negation of of a case cannot be a tautology);*
2. *If* $\not\models \varphi \leftrightarrow \psi$*, then* $\models \neg(\varphi \wedge \psi)$ *(mutually incompatible);*
3. *If* $\models \varphi \leftrightarrow \psi$*, then* $\varphi = \psi$ *(different);*
4. $\varphi \geq \psi$ *or* $\psi \geq \varphi$ *(total);*
5. *If* $\varphi \geq \psi$ *and* $\psi \geq \chi$*, then* $\varphi \geq \chi$ *(transitive).*

The strict weak order $>$ standardly associated with a total preorder $\geq$ is defined as $\varphi > \psi$ if and only if it is not the case that $\psi \geq \varphi$ (for φ and $\psi \in C$). When $\varphi > \psi$, we say that φ is (strictly) preferred to ψ. The associated equivalence relation $\sim$ is defined as $\varphi \sim \psi$ if and only if $\varphi \geq \psi$ and $\psi \geq \varphi$.

An argument in case models is a pair (φ, ψ) with φ and $\psi \in \mathcal{L}$ where φ expresses the argument's premise and ψ expresses the argument's conclusion. There are three types of argument evaluations in case models, which are coherent, presumptively valid, and conclusive (arguments which are not these three types are indeed incoherent).

Definition 8 (Argument Evaluation in Case Models [18]). *Let* $(C, \geq)$ *be a case model. Then we define, for all* φ *and* $\psi \in \mathcal{L}$*:*

- (φ, ψ) *is* coherent *with respect to* $(C, \geq)$ *if and only if* $\exists\omega \in C : \omega \models \varphi \wedge \psi$*.*
- (φ, ψ) *is* presumptively valid *with respect to* $(C, \geq)$ *if and only if* $\exists\omega \in C :$ $\omega \models \varphi \wedge \psi$*; and* $\forall\omega' \in C :$ *if* $\omega' \models \varphi$*, then* $\omega \geq \omega'$*.*
- (φ, ψ) *is* conclusive *with respect to* $(C, \geq)$ *if and only if* $\exists\omega \in C : \omega \models \varphi \wedge \psi$*; and* $\forall\omega \in C :$ *if* $\omega \models \varphi$*, then* $\omega \models \varphi \wedge \psi$*.*

4 Constructing Case Models

In this section, we present our contribution of formalizing a method for constructing a case model from an AA-CBR case-base. The inspiration of the construction is from an observation of classifying possible fact-situations with respect to their unique nearest case-pair, as we demonstrate in Example 4.

Example 4. From Example 2, let the fact-domain be $\mathcal{F} = \{$delayed, damaged, fungible, replaced$\}$, fact-situations can be classified with their unique nearest case-pair as follows.

- $co_0 = (\varnothing, -)$ is unique nearest to:
  $\varnothing$, {fungible},{replaced},{fungible, replaced}
- $co_1 = (\{$delayed$\}, +)$ is unique nearest to:
  {delayed}, {delayed, fungible}, {delayed, replaced},
  {delayed, fungible, replaced}
- $co_2 = (\{$damaged$\}, +)$ is unique nearest to:
  {damaged}, {damaged, fungible}, {damaged, replaced}
- $co_3 = (\{$damaged, , fungible, replaced$\}, -)$ is unique nearest to:
  {damaged, , fungible, replaced}
- No unique nearest case-pair:
  {delayed, damaged}, {delayed, damaged, fungible},
  {delayed, damaged, replaced}, {delayed, damaged, fungible, replaced}

As we can see from the example, a fact-situation can monotonically grow without changing its unique nearest case-pair until it reaches *exceptional* conditions. From this observation, we define the following sets for a case-pair (X, o_x) in a case-base CB.

- $CB_{\to(X,o_x)} = \{(Y, o_y) \in CB | (Y, o_y) \text{ attacks } (X, o_x) \text{ in the AA-framework corresponding to } CB \text{ and } \mathcal{F}\}$
- $F_{\to(X,o_x)} = \bigcup_{(Y,o_y) \in CB_{\to(X,o_x)}} Y$
- $I_{\to(X,o_x)} = \{B \subseteq F_{\to(X,o_x)} | X \subseteq B \land \not\exists (Y, o_y) \in CB_{\to(X,o_x)} Y \subseteq B\}$

We call $F_{\to(X,o_x)}$ a *boundary* of (X, o_x) and a member of $I_{\to(X,o_x)}$ an *internal sub-boundary* of (X, o_x). We have that (X, o_x) is always unique nearest to an internal sub-boundary of (X, o_x).

To define the construction, firstly, we define a naming function *name*. Let $\mathcal{N}$ be a set of propositions called a *name-domain*, distinct from $\mathcal{F}$. Each element of $\mathcal{N}$ is called a *name-proposition*. We define $name : 2^{\mathcal{F}} \times \{+, -\} \mapsto \mathcal{N}$ mapping from every case-pair to a name proposition. For ease of exposition, we use the same symbol for referring to the case-pair and its name proposition.

Then, we define a function *case* based on an informal construction described in [18] for constructing a logical sentence from a case-pair and an internal sub-boundary of the case-pair. Let δ be a proposition called an *outcome-proposition*, which is neither a fact-proposition nor a name-proposition. The literals used for constructing the logical sentence are from five sources: (1) the outcome-proposition (2) the name-domain (3) the internal sub-boundary (4) the fact-propositions inside the boundary but outside the internal sub-boundary (5) the fact-propositions outside the boundary of the default case-pair. The *case* function is formally defined as follows.

Definition 9 (Case construction). *Let CB be a case-base with a default outcome d and a case-pair $(X, o_x) \in CB$, $B_x \in I_{\to(X,o_x)}$, and δ be an outcome-proposition. $case(X, o_x, B_x)$ is a function defined as*

$$case(X, o_x, B_x) = \quad (o_x = d \text{ ? } \delta : \neg\delta) \land \bigwedge_{n \in \mathcal{N}} (n = name(X, o_x) \text{ ? } n : \neg n) \land$$

$$\bigwedge_{p_i \in B_x} p_i \land (I_{\to(X,o_x)} = \{X\} \text{ ? } \top : \bigwedge_{p_k \in F_{\to(X,o_x)} \setminus B_x} \neg p_k) \land$$

$$(X = \varnothing \text{ ? } \bigwedge_{p_l \in \mathcal{F}_{CB} \setminus F_{\to(\varnothing,d)}} p_l : \top)$$

where $(a \text{ ? } b : c)$ expresses a ternary conditional operator, which is interpreted as if a then b otherwise c

Since an internal sub-boundary of (X, o_x) has a unique nearest case, that is (X, o_x), *case* is a one-to-one function, namely given the logical sentence constructed from *case*, we can trace back which case-pair and which internal sub-boundary that the sentence is constructed from.

Secondly, we define a function *depth*, which is a mapping function from any case-pair to an integer, expressing the depth of attacks from the default case-pair to the considered case-pair. This function is used for determining the preference between cases as follows.

Definition 10 (Attack depth). *Let CB be a case-base with a default outcome d and a critical case-pair (X, o_x), and $\langle CB, attacks \rangle$ be the AA-framework corresponding to CB and $\mathcal{F}$. $depth(X, o_x)$ is a function defined as*

$$depth(X, o_x) = \begin{cases} 0 & \text{if } X = \varnothing \\ 1 + \max_{(X,o_x) \text{ attacks } (Y,o_y)} depth(Y, o_y) & \text{otherwise} \end{cases}$$

Using these two functions, we present the following formal method for constructing case models as follows.

Definition 11. *Let CB be a case-base with a default outcome d. We say a case model $(C, \geq)$ is constructed from CB if and only if the following conditions hold.*

1. *for every critical case-pair $(X, o_x) \in CB$ and $B_x \in I_{\rightarrow (X, o_x)}$, there exists $case(X, o_x, B_x) \in C$; and*
2. *for every critical $(X, o_x), (Y, o_y) \in CB$, $B_x \in I_{\rightarrow (X, o_x)}$, and $B_y \in I_{\rightarrow (Y, o_y)}$ such that $c_1 = case(X, o_x, B_x), c_2 = case(Y, o_y, B_y) \in C$, $c_1 \geq c_2$ if and only if $depth(X, o_x) \leq depth(Y, o_y)$; and*
3. *there are no other cases in C except those given by 1.*

Since *case* is a one-to-one function, cases in a constructed case model are different from each other. With the layout of negations in the construction, cases in a constructed case model are mutually incompatible. The preference ordering is total and transitive since it is derived from numeric comparisons.

From Example 1, a case model $(C, \geq)$ is constructed as in Table 1. Case c_0, which is a most preferred case in C, is constructed from the default case-pair co_0. `fungible` and `replaced` are attached to the case since they are not in the boundary of the default case-pair. c_{1a} is constructed from co_1 since it has only one internal sub-boundary. In contrast, c_{1b}, c_{1c}, c_{1d} are constructed from the same case-pair co_2 since it has three internal sub-boundaries. $c_{1a}, c_{1b}, c_{1c}, c_{1d}$ are immediately less preferred than c_0 because they are constructed from the case-pairs that directly attack the default one. Meanwhile, c_2 is constructed from co_3 and c_2 is the least preferred in C.

To analyze computational complexity of the construction method presented, we divide the method into two steps. Let n be the size of the case-base, each of which is a case-pair with the size of the fact situation at most m. The first step is constructing an AA-framework corresponding to a case-base. It runs in time $O(m^2 n^3)$ in the worst case because it runs in time $O(m^2)$ in the worst case to determine whether one fact situation is a subset of another and $O(n^3)$ in the worst case to determine whether the attack is concise. The second step is translating each internal sub-boundary of each case-pair into a case in case

Table 1. Constructing cases in case model from the working example

case-pairs and boundaries	Internal sub-boundary	Cases in case model
$co_0 = (\varnothing, -)$ Boundary = $\{$delayed, damaged$\}$	$\varnothing$	$c_0 : \delta \wedge co_0 \wedge \neg co_1 \wedge \neg co_2 \wedge \neg co_3$ $\wedge$ fungible $\wedge$ replaced
$co_1 = (\{$delayed$\}, +)$ Boundary = $\{$delayed$\}$	$\{$delayed$\}$	$c_{1a} : \neg\delta \wedge \neg co_0 \wedge co_1 \wedge \neg co_2 \wedge \neg co_3$ $\wedge$ delayed
$co_2 =$ $(\{$damaged$\}, +)$ Boundary = $\{$damaged, fungible, replaced$\}$	$\{$damaged$\}$ $\{$damaged, fungible$\}$ $\{$damaged, replaced$\}$	$c_{1b} : \neg\delta \wedge \neg co_0 \wedge \neg co_1 \wedge co_2 \wedge \neg co_3$ $\wedge$ damaged $\wedge$ ¬fungible $\wedge$ ¬replaced $c_{1c} : \neg\delta \wedge \neg co_0 \wedge \neg co_1 \wedge co_2 \wedge \neg co_3$ $\wedge$ damaged $\wedge$ fungible $\wedge$ ¬replaced $c_{1d} : \neg\delta \wedge \neg co_0 \wedge \neg co_1 \wedge co_2 \wedge \neg co_3$ $\wedge$ damaged $\wedge$ ¬fungible $\wedge$ replaced
$co_3 = (\{$damaged, fungible, replaced$\}, -)$ Boundary =$\{$damaged, fungible, replaced$\}$	$\{$damaged, fungible, replaced$\}$	$c_2 : \delta \wedge \neg co_0 \wedge \neg co_1 \wedge \neg co_2 \wedge co_3$ $\wedge$ damaged $\wedge$ fungible $\wedge$ replaced

The preference ordering: $c_0 > c_{1a} \sim c_{1b} \sim c_{1c} \sim c_{1d} > c_2$

models using the function *case*. It runs in time $O(n^2)$ in the worst case to consider the boundary for each case-pair and $O(m^2)$ in the worst case to consider subset relations to interpolate internal sub-boundaries so this step runs in time $O(m^2n^2)$ in the worst case. Therefore, constructing case models runs in time $O(m^2n^3)$ in the worst case due to the first step of constructing a corresponding AA-framework.

5 Explaining Case Models

In this section, we present another contribution of developing dispute trees for explaining case models. To develop the explanation, we first look into the concept of analogy, which is defined as follows [18].

Definition 12. (Analogy). *Let $\mathcal{L}$ be a classical logical language, $(C, \geq)$ be a case model, and $\sigma \in \mathcal{L}$ be a situation. We say $\alpha \in \mathcal{L}$ expresses an analogy of a case $\omega \in C$ and σ if $\omega \models \alpha$ and $\sigma \models \alpha$.*

For any case ω and any situation σ, we have that $\top$ is the most general analogy of ω and σ, and $\omega \vee \sigma$ is the most specific analogy of ω and σ [21]. By extending the concept of specificity from AA-CBR, we introduce a *literal analogy* as an analogy in the form of $\top$ or a conjunction of literals. This makes $\top$ still the most general literal analogy of ω and σ, but $\omega \vee \sigma$ is not always the most specific literal analogy due to the logical or. The exception is that sometimes there is a conjunction of literals that is equivalent to $\omega \vee \sigma$, in that case, such a conjunction is the most specific literal analogy.

Definition 13. (Literal Analogy). *We say an analogy α is a literal analogy of ω and σ if and only if α is $\top$ or a conjunction of literals. and we say a literal analogy α is the most specific literal analogy of ω and σ if and only if for every literal analogy α' of ω and σ, $\alpha \models \alpha'$.*

By the concept of literal analogy, we introduce a new type of rebuttals called *specificity rebuttal*, based on the attack relations in AA-CBR, also inspired by [14]. It intuitively means the rebuttal consists in finding a more specific literal analogy from a most preferred case with the opposite outcome.

Definition 14. (Specificity Rebuttal). *Let $\mathcal{L}$ be a classical logical language, $(C, \geq)$ be a case model, (φ, ψ) be a presumptively valid argument, and $\sigma \in \mathcal{L}$ be a situation. We say a non-tautologous $\chi \in \mathcal{L}$ (i.e. $\chi \neq \top$) is specificity rebutting the argument with respect to σ if and only if*

- $\exists \omega \in C : \omega \models \varphi \wedge \neg\psi;\ \forall\omega' \in C$: *if $\omega' \models \varphi \wedge \neg\psi$, then $\omega \geq \omega'$*
  (ω is a most preferred case in the set of such ω' with respect to $\geq$); and
- *$\varphi \wedge \chi$ is a most specific literal analogy of ω and σ.*

Now, we present dispute trees in case models based on those in AA-CBR as follows.

Definition 15. (Dispute Tree in Case Models). *Let $\sigma \in \mathcal{L}$ be a situation, $(C, \geq)$ be a case model, and ψ_0 be a logic formula such that $(\top, \psi_0)$ is presumptively valid with respect to $(C, \geq)$. A dispute tree for ψ_0 with respect to $(C, \geq)$ and σ is a tree $\mathcal{T}$ such that:*

1. *every node of $\mathcal{T}$ is of the form $[L : (\varphi, \psi)]$ where $L \in \{P, O\}$ and $\varphi, \psi \in \mathcal{L}$.*
2. *the root of $\mathcal{T}$ is $[P : (\top, \psi_0)]$*
3. *for every $[P : (\varphi, \psi)]$ and for every $\chi \in \mathcal{L}$ that is specificity rebutting (φ, ψ) with respect to σ, there exists $[O : (\varphi \wedge \chi, \neg\psi)]$ as a child of $[P : (\varphi, \psi)]$;*
4. *for every $[O : (\varphi, \psi)]$, there exists at most one child $[O : (\varphi \wedge \chi, \neg\psi)]$ such that χ is specificity rebutting (φ, ψ) with respect to σ;*
5. *there are no other nodes in $\mathcal{T}$ except those given by 1–4.*

A dispute tree $\mathcal{T}$ is a maximal dispute tree if and only if for every $[O : (\varphi, \psi)]$ which is a leave in $\mathcal{T}$, no $\chi \in \mathcal{L}$ that is specificity rebutting (φ, ψ) with respect to σ.

We prove a theorem that a maximal dispute tree in the constructed case models is homomorphic to some maximal dispute tree in AA-CBR, i.e. there is a mapping (not always bijective) from nodes in a maximal dispute tree in the constructed case models to nodes in the corresponding maximal dispute tree in AA-CBR such that the parent-child adjacencies are still preserved. Roughly speaking, a maximal dispute tree in the constructed case models can be reduced into a maximal dispute tree in AA-CBR.

Theorem 1. *Given a fact-situation N, a case-base CB with a default case-pair $(\varnothing, d)$; the corresponding AA-framework $\langle AR, attacks \rangle$; and the case model $(C, \geq)$ constructed from CB with respect to a proposition δ. A maximal dispute tree T for δ with respect to $(C, \geq)$ and $\bigwedge_{p_i \in N} p_i$ is homomorphic to some maximal dispute tree T' for $(\varnothing, d)$ with respect to $\langle CB, attacks \rangle$, with a homomorphic mapping from a node $[L : (\varphi, \psi)]$ in T to a node $[L : (X, o)]$ in T' such that a most preferred case in $\{\omega | \omega \models \varphi \wedge \psi\}$ is constructed from (X, o).*

Proof. We prove by induction that T is homomorphic to some maximal dispute tree T' for $(\varnothing, d)$ with respect to $\langle AR, attacks \rangle$.

- **base case:** The root $[P : (\top, \delta)]$ of T corresponds to the root $[P : (\varnothing, d)]$ of T' $(\top, \delta)$ has grounding in a most preferred case in $\{\omega | \omega \models \delta\}$ with respect to $\geq$, which is always constructed from $(\varnothing, d)$.
- **inductive step:** If $[O : (\varphi', \neg\psi)]$ is a child of $[P : (\varphi, \psi)]$ in T and $[P : (\varphi, \psi)]$ corresponds to $[P : (Y, o_y)]$ in T', then there exists a most preferred case ω_x in the set $\{\omega | \omega \models \varphi \wedge \neg\psi\}$ with respect to $\geq$. Since ω_x is constructed from some $(X, o_x) \in CB$, we have that (X, o_x) attacks (Y, o_y) because $o_x \neq o_y$ (as $\omega_x \models \neg\psi$); $Y \subsetneq X$ (as there exists a non-tautologous χ such that $\omega_x \models \varphi \wedge \chi$); and $\nexists(Z, o_x) \in AR$ with $Y \subsetneq Z \subsetneq X$ (as ω_x is a most preferred case in the set, hence (X, o_x) is far from (Y, o_y) by a distance of *attacks* 1). Therefore, $[O : (X, o_x)]$ is a child of $[P : (Y, o_y)]$ (This can be applied analogously for a case that $[P : (\varphi', \neg\psi)]$ is a child of $[O : (\varphi, \psi)]$]).
- If T is maximal, then for all opponent node $[O : (\varphi, \psi)]$ which are leaves in T, no χ is specificity rebutting (φ, ψ) with respect to $\bigwedge_{p_i \in N} p_i$. Hence, there is no $(X, o_x) \in AR$ that attacks (Y, o_y) if $[O : (Y, o_y)]$ corresponds to $[O : (\varphi, \psi)]$, otherwise there is $\chi = \bigwedge_{p_j \in X \setminus Y} p_j$ that is specificity rebutting (φ, ψ) with respect to $\bigwedge_{p_i \in N} p_i$, which leads to the contradiction. Hence, T' is maximal.

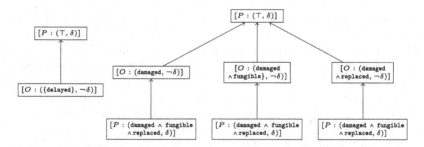

Fig. 3. Examples of maximal dispute trees for δ with respect to the case model constructed from the example

Figure 3 shows examples of maximal dispute trees for δ with respect to the case model in Table 1 and the situation delayed∧damaged∧fungible∧replaced. We have that the dispute trees on the left and the right of the Fig. 3 are homomorphic to the dispute trees on the left and the right of Fig. 2 respectively.

To analyze computational complexity, we divide the explanation of case models into two steps (1) constructing arguments from most specific literal analogies of each case in case models and the situation (2) constructing a dispute tree from the arguments. Let $(C, \geq)$ be a case model with $||C|| = n$ and let a situation σ be a conjunction of m-number of literals. The first step runs in time $O(mn)$ in the worst case to check whether each literal in the situation occurs in each case in the case model. In the second step, constructing a dispute tree from the arguments runs in time $O(m^2n^3)$ in the worst case since it needs to construct an AA-framework. Therefore, explaining argument moves in case models from case bases runs in time $O(m^2n^3)$ in the worst case due to the second step of constructing a dispute tree.

6   Discussion

Although this paper presents the construction of case models from AA-CBR case-bases, we do not expect the constructed case models can replace AA-CBR case-bases in practice. This is because of the complication of evaluating arguments from cases as logical expressions. The construction aims only for gaining insights of case-based argumentation using case models. In this paper, we provide insights of using hypothetical cases (e.g., c_{1a} and c_{1b} in Table 1) and specificity rebutting for supporting case-based argumentation. This aligns with previous works on logical expressions of hypotheticals [5] and contrastive explanation [13] for supporting case-based reasoning. Future research could explore more connections between case models and other case-based reasoning formalisms to gain more insights on other types of rebuttals in case-based reasoning. For example, this paper studied here consider only specificity rebuttals. They do not consider the idea in precedential constraint [11] that a precedent case can defend a decision for a new case with stronger support without using specificity. Therefore, new types of explanations and attack relations in case models might be found if we construct and explain case models from precedential constraint or other perspectives.

There are several differences between the explanation method introduced in this paper and dispute trees in AA-CBR [7,8] and dialogue games in precedential constraint [15,20]. For example, unlike dispute trees in AA-CBR that start with a default case, dispute trees in case models can start with any arbitrary formula ψ such that $(\top, \psi)$ is presumptively valid. Although the formula is originally derived from a proposition representing a default outcome, it is not necessary to be such a proposition. Another difference between our explanation method and dialogue games in precedential constraint is that dispute trees in case models play on hypothetical arguments, i.e. arguments that might not have grounding in real precedent cases, while dialogue games in precedential constraint play on real precedent cases.

Since previous studies [2,16] show that AA-CBR case-bases can be translated into stratified logic programs, it follows immediately from this paper that case models constructed from AA-CBR case-bases can also be translated into stratified logic programs. Unfortunately, not every case model can be translated into stratified logic programs because case models can express indecisiveness (i.e. arguments (φ, ψ) and $(\varphi, \neg\psi)$ can be both presumptively valid in case models), which stratified logic programs cannot express. Future research could investigate whether there is a programming paradigm or a logical framework that every case model can be translated into. Interesting candidates are answer set programming or defeasible logic since they can express indecisiveness.

7 Conclusion

This paper presents a method of constructing case models based on abstract argumentation for case-based reasoning (AA-CBR). The constructed case models consists of cases, each of which is constructed from each internal sub-boundary of each critical case-pair in the case-base, and preferences over cases, which are determined by the distance of attacks between the default case-pair and the considering case-pair in the corresponding argumentation framework in AA-CBR. By connecting AA-CBR to case models, we can derive dispute trees with respect to a case model constructed and a situation. It has been shown that the maximal dispute trees in case models can be reduced into maximal dispute trees in AA-CBR. In future work, it would be interesting to study constructing and explaining case models from other perspectives and to study relations between case models and other programming paradigms or logical frameworks.

Acknowledgements. This work was supported by JSPS KAKENHI Grant Numbers, JP17H06103 and JP19H05470 and JST, AIP Trilateral AI Research, Grant Number JPMJCR20G4.

References

1. Aleven, V.: Teaching case-based argumentation through a model and examples. Ph.D. thesis, University of Pittsburgh (1997)
2. Athakravi, D., Satoh, K., Law, M., Broda, K., Russo, A.: Automated inference of rules with exception from past legal cases using ASP. In: Calimeri, F., Ianni, G., Truszczynski, M. (eds.) LPNMR 2015. LNCS (LNAI), vol. 9345, pp. 83–96. Springer, Cham (2015). https://doi.org/10.1007/978-3-319-23264-5_8
3. Atkinson, K., Bench-Capon, T., Bollegala, D.: Explanation in AI and law: past, present and future. Artif. Intell. **289**, 103387 (2020)
4. Bench-Capon, T.J.: Hypo's legacy: introduction to the virtual special issue. Artif. Intell. Law **25**(2), 205–250 (2017)
5. Bonner, A.J.: A logic for hypothetical reasoning. In: Proceedings of the National Conference on Artificial Intelligence (AAAI), pp. 480–484 (1988)
6. Cocarascu, O., Stylianou, A., Čyras, K., Toni, F.: Data-empowered argumentation for dialectically explainable predictions. In: ECAI 2020, pp. 2449–2456. IOS Press, Amsterdam, The Netherlands (2020)

7. Cyras, K., Satoh, K., Toni, F.: Abstract argumentation for case-based reasoning. In: Fifteenth International Conference on the Principles of Knowledge Representation and Reasoning, pp. 243–254. AAAI Press, CA, USA (2016)
8. Cyras, K., Satoh, K., Toni, F.: Explanation for case-based reasoning via abstract argumentation. In: Computational Models of Argument, pp. 243–254. IOS Press, Amsterdam, The Netherlands (2016)
9. Dung, P.M.: On the acceptability of arguments and its fundamental role in non-monotonic reasoning, logic programming and n-person games. Artif. Intell. **77**(2), 321–357 (1995)
10. Henderson, J., Bench-Capon, T.: Describing the development of case law. In: Proceedings of the Seventeenth International Conference on Artificial Intelligence and Law, pp. 32–41. ICAIL 2019, Association for Computing Machinery, New York, NY, USA (2019)
11. Horty, J.F., Bench-Capon, T.J.: A factor-based definition of precedential constraint. Artif. Intell. Law **20**(2), 181–214 (2012)
12. van Leeuwen, L., Verheij, B.: A comparison of two hybrid methods for analyzing evidential reasoning. In: Legal Knowledge and Information Systems, pp. 53–62. IOS Press, Amsterdam, The Netherlands (2019)
13. Liu, X., Lorini, E., Rotolo, A., Sartor, G.: Modelling and explaining legal case-based reasoners through classifiers. In: Legal Knowledge and Information Systems, pp. 83–92. IOS Press, Amsterdam, The Netherlands (2022)
14. Prakken, H.: A tool in modelling disagreement in law: preferring the most specific argument. In: Proceedings of the 3rd international conference on Artificial intelligence and law, pp. 165–174. Association for Computing Machinery, New York, NY, USA (1991)
15. Prakken, H., Ratsma, R.: A top-level model of case-based argumentation for explanation: formalisation and experiments. Argument Comput. **13**(2), 159–194 (2022)
16. Satoh, K., Kubota, M., Nishigai, Y., Takano, C.: Translating the Japanese presupposed ultimate fact theory into logic programming. In: Proceedings of the 2009 Conference on Legal Knowledge and Information Systems: JURIX 2009: The Twenty-Second Annual Conference, pp. 162–171. IOS Press, Amsterdam, The Netherlands (2009)
17. Verheij, B.: Formalizing value-guided argumentation for ethical systems design. Artif. Intell. Law **24**(4), 387–407 (2016)
18. Verheij, B.: Formalizing arguments, rules and cases. In: Proceedings of the 16th Edition of the International Conference on Artificial Intelligence and Law, pp. 199–208. ICAIL 2017, Association for Computing Machinery, New York, NY, USA (2017)
19. Verheij, B.: Proof with and without probabilities: correct evidential reasoning with presumptive arguments, coherent hypotheses and degrees of uncertainty. Artif. Intell. Law **25**, 127–154 (2017)
20. van Woerkom, W., Grossi, D., Prakken, H., Verheij, B.: Justification in case-based reasoning. In: Proceedings of the First International Workshop on Argumentation for eXplainable AI, pp. 1–13. CEUR Workshop Proceedings, Utrecht University, The Netherlands (2022)
21. Zheng, H., Grossi, D., Verheij, B.: Logical comparison of cases. In: Rodríguez-Doncel, V., Palmirani, M., Araszkiewicz, M., Casanovas, P., Pagallo, U., Sartor, G. (eds.) AICOL/XAILA 2018/2020. LNCS (LNAI), vol. 13048, pp. 125–140. Springer, Cham (2021). https://doi.org/10.1007/978-3-030-89811-3_9

Using Ontological Knowledge and Large Language Model Vector Similarities to Extract Relevant Concepts in VAT-Related Legal Judgments

Davide Liga[1]([✉])[ID], Alessia Fidelangeli[2], and Réka Markovich[1]

[1] University of Luxembourg, Esch-sur-Alzette, Luxembourg
{davide.liga,reka.markovich}@uni.lu
[2] Alma Mater Studiorum - University of Bologna, Bologna, Italy
alessia.fidelangeli2@unibo.it

Abstract. In this paper, we present OntoVAT, a multilingual ontology designed for extracting knowledge in legal judgments related to VAT (Value-Added Tax). This is, to our knowledge, the first extensive ontology in the VAT domain. OntoVAT aims to encapsulate critical concepts in the European VAT area and offers a scalable and reusable knowledge structure to support the automatic identification of VAT-specific concepts in legal texts. Additionally, OntoVAT supports various Artificial Intelligence and Law (AI&Law) tasks, such as extracting legal knowledge, identifying keywords, modeling topics, and extracting semantic relations. Developed using OWL with SKOS lexicalization, OntoVAT's initial version includes ontological patterns and relations. It is available in three languages, marking a collaborative effort between computer scientists and subject matter experts. In this work, we also present an application scenario where the knowledge encoded within OntoVAT is leveraged in combination with several recent Large Language Models (LLMs). For this application, for which we used the most powerful open source LLMs available today (both generative and non-generative, including *legal* LLMs), we show the system's design and some preliminary results.

Keywords: Legal Ontology · VAT · Large Language Models · AI&Law

1 Introduction

The interplay between Artificial Intelligence and Law (AI&Law) is an area that has gained traction, reflecting the potential of technology to transform legal processes. A cornerstone of this evolving field is the use of ontologies. These

This works has been supported by the Analytics for Decision of Legal Cases (ADELE), founded by the European Union's Justice Programme (grant agreement No. 101007420); Davide Liga was supported by the project INDIGO, which is financially supported by the NORFACE Joint Research Programme on Democratic Governance in a Turbulent Age and co-funded by AEI, AKA, DFG and FNR and the European Commission through Horizon 2020 under grant agreement No 822166.

M. Bono et al. (Eds.): JSAI-isAI 2023 Workshops, LNAI 14644, pp. 115–131, 2024.
https://doi.org/10.1007/978-3-031-60511-6_8

structured frameworks of domain-specific knowledge are crucial for machines to make sense of complex legal terminology and concepts. The importance of ontologies becomes especially pronounced when they are combined with sub-symbolic approaches, such as Large Language Models (LLMs), which have recently gained significant momentum. This symbiosis of symbolic and sub-symbolic methods promises a more nuanced and sophisticated handling of legal data, offering both clarity and depth in automated legal reasoning. In this work, we describe Onto-VAT [10], an ontology designed for knowledge extraction from legal judgments related to Value Added Tax (VAT). The ontology serves a dual purpose: firstly, capturing key concepts within the European VAT domain, and secondly, offering an extendable and reusable knowledge representation. This facilitates the extraction and classification of VAT-related concepts in judicial decision analysis.

Such ontologies can facilitate tasks like keyword retrieval, topic modeling, and the extraction of semantic relations. Furthermore, they can be adapted into a visual environment, proving beneficial for lawyers and judges (a visualisation tool implementing OntoVAT can be found at https://adele-tool.eu). Additionally, these ontologies enable the classification of judgments based on their concepts. This aspect is particularly significant in the VAT field, where countries depend on national classifications. The creation of a shared European ontology could, in the short term, ease decision retrieval and, in the long term, promote the adoption of unified terminology and consistent law application - a core principle of European law.

In the next sections, we will describe the few related works and our own contributions (see Sect. 2), the methodology we adopted (see Sect. 3), and the current structure of the ontology (see Sect. 4). In Sect. 5, we will discuss about a current application scenario we are developing using our ontology. Finally, in the last part of the work we will provide some suggestions for future developments in the field (see Sect. 6).

2   Related Works and Motivations

Ontologies hold a notable position in AI&Law research [14] and have seen application across various areas, including privacy law modeling [12] and the forthcoming Artificial Intelligence Act [3]. Despite their widespread use, comprehensive ontological frameworks specifically for Value-Added Tax (VAT) remain largely unexplored. To date, only a handful of efforts have ventured into ontology development in the VAT domain. The most notable of these, dating back two decades, is the work of Kerremans and colleagues [8] [15]. Their exploration was primarily aimed at identifying foundational ontological concepts pertinent to VAT. However, their focus was predominantly on the challenges in crafting complex, multilingual ontologies, especially considering the unique elements of national legal cultures and the variances in national implementations. Consequently, their goal was not the establishment of a complete or even partial VAT ontology for representing VAT-specific concepts. Instead, their contribution was oriented towards laying the groundwork with key conceptual ideas that could inform the development of a specialized VAT ontology.

The scarcity of research in developing VAT-specific ontologies can be attributed to a multitude of factors. Primarily, the complexity of VAT legislation poses significant challenges for both legal experts and computer scientists in accurately reconstructing this intricate legal and conceptual domain. VAT, governed at the European level by Directive 2006/112/CE, operates under a unique legislative framework. European Directives set objectives for EU countries, granting them the autonomy to formulate their laws to achieve these goals. This results in Member States incorporating the Directive into their national legal systems through domestic laws that adapt and interpret the Directive's content, often drawing on national terminologies and concepts. This variation in implementation is particularly evident in older member states, where VAT legislation predates deeper harmonization efforts at the European level, leading to reliance on national terminologies. In contrast, states that have more recently legislated in this domain tend to adhere more closely to the Directive's wording. Despite overarching harmonization efforts, numerous VAT concepts remain defined solely at the national level, adding complexity to ontology development.

Additionally, VAT regulation intersects with other legal domains like civil, commercial, and criminal law. It also incorporates 'common language' terms that acquire specific meanings within the VAT context (e.g., terms related to goods shipment or delivery). Therefore, creating a VAT ontology requires not only a comprehensive understanding of VAT law but also connectivity to other legal areas.

A notable challenge in VAT ontology development arises from the undefined nature of many VAT concepts in both the Directive and national legislation. These concepts are often clarified over time through the case law of the Court of Justice of the European Union (CJEU), which standardizes the interpretation and application of European law across member states. Consequently, modeling VAT concepts necessitates a multi-layered analysis, encompassing European and national legislations and CJEU case law. This process demands legal expertise across multiple jurisdictions and languages, coupled with a thorough understanding of European jurisprudence. The requirement to traverse multiple legal fields and common language terms further complicates the task, making it a time-intensive and highly specialized endeavor.

As far as OntoVAT is concerned, we decided to build an ontology at an intermediate-low layer of abstraction while committing it to already existing upper ontologies. In this regard, there are already many other upper ontologies designed to represent higher levels of abstraction, including the Legal Knowledge Interchange Format (LKIF), an upper ontology designed for legal knowledge [7]).

Another important aspect behind the design of OntoVAT is that it has an applicative intended use. As partly anticipated, we built an ontology of the main concepts especially focusing on VAT taxable/exempt transactions with the twofold aim of testing the possibility of automatically linking the judgements of a dataset to the most relevant concepts in the domain and organising legal knowledge. So, the objective was to capture the concepts which might be crucial in the legal reasoning of VAT-related judgments and especially with decisions concerning taxable/exempt VAT transactions. Hence, we had to focus both on relatively abstract concepts such as "exemption" or "territoriality", which were frequently mentioned in the above-mentioned decisions, as well as on more specific concepts belonging to the domain of VAT (such as the concepts of "medical service" or "country"), or to specific areas of knowledge (for example "investment fund" or "human blood"). The above-mentioned challenges are related to the difficulty of building an ontology capable of being expressive and representing such a large number of layers of abstractions belonging to different conceptual areas. A further challenge was to ensure the consistency of the resulting model from a formal point of view. For this reason, we decided to create this ontology in OWL format, so as to provide the scientific community with a first formal ontology, on which to explore automated reasoning experiments. Here, we describe the first version of OntoVAT as a multilingual ontology implemented in English, Italian, and Bulgarian (which has been also implemented as a graphical tool: https:// adele-tool.eu). After having described OntoVAT, we will also present the design of an application use based on the combination between OntoVAT and Large Language Models (LLMs), showing some preliminary insights.

3   Methodology

For the creation of OntoVAT, we were inspired by [12], which adopted a methodology to minimise the difficulties for legal operators to define a legal ontology.

We followed a top-down approach applied on legal sources (Directive 2006/ 112/CE and national implementations such as d.p.r. 633/1972 in Italy) and made more robust by the partial reuse of pre-existing ontology patterns [6]. Our results are evaluated by using foundational ontologies (in particular LKIF [7], DOLCE [4] and DUL [1]), and we followed the principles in the OntoClean [5] method, according to which each ontological concept can be evaluated based on three meta-properties: "identity" (making sure that a class uniquely identifiable), "unity" (making sure that instances of a class form cohesive and meaningful wholes) and "rigidity" (whether a property is essential to the instances of a class or if it can change over time).

Our validation involved a strongly interdisciplinary group, mostly composed of computer scientists, lawyers, and philosophers, which allowed an integrated expertise coming from different disciplines.

We can summarise our approach in the following steps:

(i)   tax lawyers from Italy and Bulgaria selected approximately 500 judgements decided by Italian and Bulgarian courts related to the domain of VAT;

(ii) the judgements were analyzed and the portions of text related with the judges' motivations were annotated (structure and argumentative patterns);

(iii) Italian and Bulgarian legal experts analysed the most important concepts mentioned in the judgements, checking these concepts against their respective national regulations;

(iv) the selected concepts were sent to a technical team composed by computer scientists and legal experts for building the ontology;

(v) for each element of the ontology our legal experts provided a range of linguistic variations/synonyms, a definition, the most common examples instantiating that concept, the most common related terms, and any relevant normative references related to the concept (both national and European rules);

(vi) the gathered results were validated by the legal team that returned them to the technical team who implemented the new information in the ontology;

(vii) the steps from (iii) to (vi) were iterated several times to refine the ontology;

The implementation of an algorithm which uses the OntoVAT to determine whether an ontological concept is relevant in judgements related to VAT, i.e. if a specific decision deals with one or more of the ontological concepts, is currently under development, but we will give some insights at the end of the paper. This process can be summarised as follows:

1. legal experts were asked to select from OntoVAT the ontological concepts which are considered more relevant in the decisions of judges;
2. considering the concepts selected in the previous step, legal experts were asked to manually annotate nearly 70% of the judgements by including the information of whether each selected concept is relevant in each judgement by associating a binary value, where 0 means "non relevant" and 1 means "relevant" (the concept is considered relevant if the court's decision concerns that concept from the substantial point of view);
3. an algorithm designed by the technical team encodes the information contained in the ontology to predict whether or not a concept is relevant (comparing the results with the gold standard defined in the previous step);

We are currently in the process of completing step 2 and implementing step 3. Our preliminary results shows that by using OntoVAT we can catch the most important concepts in the judicial decisions. While to develop an ontology to be used in a database by lawyers the ontology must cover all the most important aspects of the tax, to test the feasibility of automatically linking the concepts of an ontology to a group of judgements, it is necessary to focus on the aspects of the tax that are dealt with in the decisions. This requires a time-consuming activity to be performed by lawyers in reading the decisions and selecting the most notions mentioned within them. As a consequence, the analysis of the legislation is necessary but must be complemented by the analysis of the case law. Moreover, since the ontology intervened in a harmonised field but was intended for the national courts it is necessary to address all the difficulties related to the implementation of the European concepts in the national legal system through notions and definitions that are not identical. This is why the above-mentioned list of synonyms and reference to national legislation were crucial.

This methodology can be generalized and applied to different domains and it can be easily extended to other languages. For example, we employed the same approach for the development of another ontology, PaTrOnto, related to the domain of patents and trademarks [9]. The main difference between PaTrOnto and OntoVAT is related to the above-mentioned step (iii), since the legislation for the field patents and trademarks is completely different, also in terms of harmonisation at the European level.

4 OntoVAT

4.1 Core Concepts

It is worth mentioning that the ongoing effort behind this work is the result of the cooperation between computer scientists and legal experts in the VAT domain. Regarding the design of OntoVAT, we proceeded by taking into account different sources of information. First of all, we considered the European VAT Directive, which is the main legal source at the European level. The Directive provides a harmonized and coherent perspective on the ontological concepts of the VAT domain and it is compatible with our target of creating a multilingual VAT ontology, as it is available in all the official languages of the European Union. Moreover, we also considered another source of information, namely the case law of the CJEU, which we found particular useful to find key concepts which were not defined by the Directive. In fact, in the field of VAT the case law of the CJEU has a peculiar and crucial role. According to the European treaties, the CJEU shall have jurisdiction to give preliminary rulings concerning the interpretation of the Treaties (art. 267 TFEU). Through preliminary rulings the Court grants the uniform interpretation and application of Europeal law within the states. In the field of VAT the European case law is fundamental. First of all, there is a huge number of judgments in this field. Secondly, many fundamental principles in the VAT area and especially many concepts not defined in the original legislation have been defined by case law over time. Hence, the building of OntoVAT required a careful analysis of the case law.

Finally, we tried to model the key ontological concepts with an even more concrete source of information, namely the (above-mentioned) dataset of VAT-related judgments adopted by national courts. More specifically, we analyzed which concepts were particularly important in the legal reasoning of national judges, and how these concepts were employed by them. Thus, while the Directive was the fundamental starting point of the work, this was complemented by further research aimed at identifying the concepts that were actually relevant in real cases decided by national courts or relying on the definitions of concepts provided by the European case law. Therefore, one of the first challenges was to reconcile these two aspects (i.e., the more abstract normative dimension and the more concrete dimension of judicial cases).

Inspired by the first articles of our first source (i.e., the EU VAT Directive), we decided to put at the center of our ontology the concept of "Transaction", around which we added all the other concepts. The core ontological concepts are shown in Fig. 1.

According to Directive 2006/112/EC VAT is a general tax on consumption which applies to the supplies of goods and services performed by taxable persons

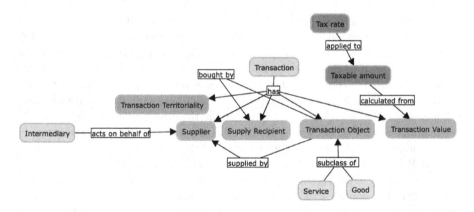

Fig. 1. The core elements of OntoVAT.

and which is exactly proportional the price of such goods and services. Thus, the idea is that any transaction which may be subject to VAT will have some persons involved (a supplier, a recipient, and sometimes intermediaries), an exchanged object (a service or a good), and a consideration from which the taxable amount is calculated. This transaction can be qualified as a supply of good or supply of service. VAT regulation includes a common list of exemptions for public purposes or other technical reasons. Hence, transactions can be taxed or exempted, depending on several conditions. As different rules apply depending on the place of the transaction concepts related to territoriality were included in the ontology. Starting from these core ontological concepts, we then further developed the ontology by extending their modeling. For example, a challenging step during the design of the ontology was related to the modeling of the *objective profiles* and the *subjective profiles* of the transaction, i.e., to which people (taxable persons) and to which transactions (e.g., types of goods and services) VAT applies. In fact, especially in the case of Italy, it implemented the VAT Directive rules concerning the taxable person and taxable transaction relying on national concepts identified though a terminology which was different from the European one (e.g., the VAT Directive defines the taxable persons referring to "any person who, independently, carries out in any place any economic activity", while Italian legislation provides a definition of taxable person which includes specific national concepts, such as "entrepreneurs" and "professionals"). Furthermore, we included the concept of "Exemption" and "Right to deduction", modeling also the relation with the concept of "VAT Chargeable Event", since we realized that these concepts were very relevant in our dataset of national decisions.

4.2 Design and Lexicalisation

The ontology is currently composed of 129 concepts (i.e., OWL classes) and 36 properties (relationships between classes), 578 disjoint class pairs and 101 subclass relations.

OntoVAT is a multilingual OWL ontology enriched with a SKOS lexicalisation and implemented in English, Italian and Bulgarian. This OWL+SKOS multilingual implementation has been implemented using VocBench 3 and is a powerful approach to mitigate the issue of semantic non-uniformity in multilingualism, which has been pointed out in previous research [8]. Thanks to the use of SKOS, each ontological concept (i.e. each OWL class) is enriched with some specific properties which are incorporated in the SKOS data model, namely: skos:definition, skos:scopeNote, skos:altLabel, skos:hiddenLabel, skos:example.

The addition of these properties to each ontological concept (in English, Italian and Bulgarian) facilitates the integration of crucial information within the ontology, making OntoVAT particularly expressive and powerful. In particular, **skos:definition** contains the definition of each single OWL class (i.e., the definition of each single concept). In **skos:scopeNote**, we added relevant specifications about the skos:definition field (whenever was necessary to further specify the interpretative angle of the chosen definition). Furthermore, scopeNotes also contain all relevant normative references (if any) describing the concept. We also added any relevant synonyms in the three different languages as **skos:altLabel** properties. In **skos:example**, we added some examples of the concept (which might look like further potential subclasses of the concept). Finally, the property **skos:hiddenLabel** is used to store terms in natural language which might signal the presence of the concept in the text (this can be useful for any application layers built on top of OntoVAT).

As mentioned before, we built OntoVAT using concepts taken from the European VAT Directive to grant a coherent and harmonic conceptual framework. Therefore all concepts are already designed to be appropriate for both Italy and Bulgaria. In fact, Italy and Bulgaria must grant the uniform application of European law.

In most cases, the semantic meaning of concepts is therefore harmonic between Italy and Bulgaria. In these cases, for each OWL class, a skos:definition is just provided in English and translated into Italian and Bulgarian with no adjustments. However, in few cases, definitions of concepts (i.e., their semantic meaning) vary at national level. In these situations, priority was given to national definitions, therefore the skos:definition in Bulgarian/Italian will not be just a translation from English, instead it will be a different definition (coherent with the national legislation). Moreover, whenever further specifications are needed to explain the scope of the concepts' meaning (at Bulgarian, Italian, and European level), we employed a skos:scopeNote property in Bulgarian/Italian/English.

Lastly, since national legislation may have alternative terms for referring to the Directive's concepts, we handled alternative terms as synonyms (skos:altLabel) in Italian/Bulgarian. For the time being we did not introduce any country-specific class, as our goal was to develop a common ontology which could be used by both Italian and Bulgarian judges. Moreover, the creation of a common ontology may be useful in developing a common conceptual framework that promotes the uniform application of EU law in a harmonised field. In the future, we will consider extending our ontology by adding specific classes based on concepts which are used by the legislator in national implementation. This might be useful for national judges, who might be more familiar with different country-specific concepts.

Hence, we handle the issue of multilinguality by specialising the skos properties skos:definitions, skos:scopeNotes and skos:altLabels whenever needed, without affecting the coherence of the ontological concepts or their relations (Fig. 2 shows an example of how multilinguality is handled for a specific concept/class).

We carefully assigned a definition to each concept by giving priority to definitions coming from the domain-specific legislative sources, whenever the concept exists in that domain. If the concept is not mentioned neither in the national nor in the European legislative sources, we searched for a definition in the case law of the Court of Justice of the European Union (CJEU). If the concept is not defined neither in the legislation nor in the case law of the CJEU, as it frequently happens for "factual concepts", it is defined following a simple description based on legal encyclopedias or dictionaries. In this way, we made sure that the every concept definitions was linked to the legals sources.

Fig. 2. An example of multilingual lexicalisation, related to the OWL class (i.e. the concept) "Taxable Importation of Goods".

4.3   Commitment and Scope

Figure 3 shows a simplified conceptual map that gives a clearer understanding of the formal structure of the ontology, showing most ontological classes and properties which can be found in the OWL ontology (relations such as "has" connecting to a target concept are represented in OWL as "hasTargetConcept",

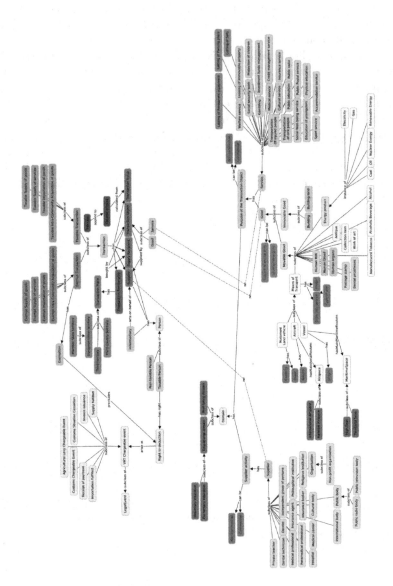

Fig. 3. Simplified map of the main concepts and relations in OntoVAT.

while relations such as "can be" are translated in OWL as datatype properties with a Boolean value). In this map, one can see the previously mentioned core elements having the class "Transaction" as central concept, as we previously described in Fig. 1. To make the picture more readable, the classes "Supplier", "Good" and "Service" have been duplicated and expanded at the bottom of the map and some classes have been omitted. Please see Fig. 4 for the complete hierarchies of classes and properties in OntoVAT.

Fig. 4. All hierarchies of classes and properties.

To grant ontological robustness across the conceptual framework, most classes in OntoVAT are designed to be disjointed. The only class we decided not to disjoin are **VAT Chargeable Event**, **Domain**, and **Supplier**.

As can be seen in Fig. 5, we did not disjoin the subclasses of "VAT Chargeable Event" to allow an instance of VAT chargeable event to belong to multiple types of chargeable event. Regarding the "Domain" concept, we preferred to allow an instance of domain to belong to multiple classes because the supplier's activity might sometimes involve an overlap of multiple domains, and because a domain might sometimes be defined as an intersection of multiple sub-domains. For the same reason, we also wanted to allow potential overlaps in the subclasses of the concept "Supplier".

These choices of allowing the overlap in the above mentioned cases (i.e., VAT chargeable events, domains and suppliers) might be made clearer with an example: an individual of the class "Dentist" could also be, in principle, an individual of the class "Private Teacher". Similarly, we decided that it was safer to leave potential overlapping among the sub-classes of "VAT chargeable event" as well as among the sub-classes of "Domain".

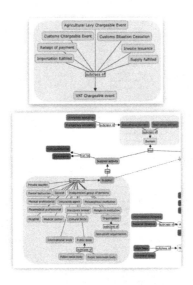

Fig. 5. The portions of OntoVAT which allow internal overlaps (i.e. where individuals can belong to multiple classes) are the subclasses of "VAT Chargeable Event" (image in top), "Domain" and "Supplier" (both depicted in the image at the bottom).

4.4   Alignment with Upper Ontologies

To make OntoVAT more robust and interoperable, we are exploring alignments to other well-known legal upper ontologies, in particular LKIF (Legal Knowledge Interchange Format) [7]. We also align to the Descriptive Ontology for Linguistic and Cognitive Engineering (DOLCE) and to the DOLCE+DnS Ultralite (DUL) ontology [1].

We list the alignment of our classes in Table 1, while Fig. 6 shows the alignments and commitment to the upper ontologies as described in Table 1.

5   Application

In this section, we elucidate a practical application of OntoVAT through an automated pipeline that detects the relevance of ontological concepts from a dataset

Table 1. Alignment and interoperability with upper ontologies.

OntoVAT class	Aligned with class	In	Comment
Airspace	place:Place	LKIF	
Domain	expression:Qualification	LKIF	
Exemption	norm:Norm	LKIF	An "exemption" is the result of interactions between norms, which are meant to assess if an exemption occurs.
Legal Event	top:Spatio Temporal Occurrence	LKIF	
Maritime Space	place:Place	LKIF	
Measurement	dul:Unit Of Measure	DUL	
Purpose Of The Transaction Object	expression:Qualification	LKIF	
Person	legal-action:Legal Person	LKIF	
Right To Deduction	norm:Right	LKIF	
Supplier	legal-role:Legal Role	LKIF	
Supplier Activity	expression:Qualification	LKIF	
Supply Recipient	legal-role:Legal Role	LKIF	
Taxable Amount	dul:Amount	DUL	
Tax Rate	dul:Amount	DUL	
Transaction	action:Trade	LKIF	action:Trade seems more appropriate than action:Transaction
Transaction Intermediary	legal-role:Legal Role	LKIF	
Transaction Object	dolce:Substantial	DOLCE	Regarding its subclasses, "Good" aligns to "dolce:Agentive physical Object"; "Service" aligns to "dolce:SocialObject"
Transaction Place	place:Place	LKIF	
Transaction Territoriality	norm:Norm	LKIF	The concept of "territoriality" is the result of interactions between norms, which are meant to assess a given geographical space (i.e. the "Transaction Place").
Transaction Value	dul:Amount	DUL	
TypeOfUse	expression:Qualification	LKIF	

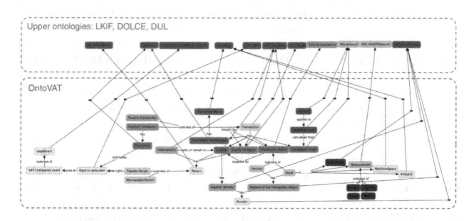

Fig. 6. OntoVAT alignments with upper ontologies.

of judicial decisions. This application exemplifies the ontology's utility in providing machine-readable and reusable legal knowledge, particularly within the realm of Value Added Tax (VAT) jurisprudence. **Semantic Encoding and Similarity Assessment:** The judicial decisions are firstly preprocessed to extract only the motivations of the judgment. This is possible because our corpus is encoded in XML and has a special tag for identifying the motivation part. We wanted to focus on the motivation only because the motivation is where the main legal reasoning of the judge is expressed Each motivation, parsed using the spaCy library, is then segmented into sentences. These sentences, in turn, undergo a transformation into numerical embeddings via the SentenceTransformer library. This is conducted using 13 Large Language Models (LLMs) - as shown in Table 2 - selected among the most powerful legal and non-legal (i.e. general-purpose) LLMs, among those available to the Open Source community. We also employed a suite of 4 similarity measures, namely cosine, euclidean, angular, and spearmanr. With 13 LLMs and 4 similarity measures, we tested a total of 52 experimental scenarios. More specifically, we evaluated the similarity between the judgements' segmented sentences within their motivations and 99 "targeted" concepts of our ontology (i.e. those ontological classes that our domain experts considered particularly important to be detected) out of 129. We therefore tried to assess whether these 99 targeted ontological concepts where relevant in a given judgement's motivation by calculating the above mentioned similarity measures between the embeddings of the judgement' sentences and the embeddings of five ontological components which are available in our ontological classes: skos:prefLabel, skos:altLabel, skos:example, skos:definition, and skos:scopeNote. Therefore, the similarity is actually calculated between text and the strings within these SKOS components. A threshold-based mechanism is employed to identify "relevant" ontological concepts. A concept is tagged as relevant if its similarity score surpasses a specific threshold (e.g. 0.90 for the cosine similarity, 80 for angular and spearmanr). Since the similarity is between each sentence in the motivation and the 5 SKOS components of each single concept, then a single concept can overcome the threshold multiple times. The process iterates across our dataset of judgement, calculating the similarity between sentence embeddings and the SKOS ontological components' embeddings for each one of the 99 targeted classes. Only classes surpassing the stipulated similarity threshold are selected as relevant. Moreover, to assess whether the similarities are capable of identifying relevant ontological concepts in our judgments, this iteration is actually performed over a subset of the dataset consisting of nearly 115 judgements. In fact, for this 115 judgments, our legal experts annotated whether or not the 99 targeted ontological concepts are relevant. In this way, we were able to consider a *ground truth* against which we could compare our pipeline, enabling us to compute the evaluation metrics. **Preliminary Insights and Limitations:** Our preliminary findings, shown in Table 1 are reported in terms of False Positive Rate (which measures the model's tendency to incorrectly identify negative cases as positive ones, and therefore the lower the score the better). These results provide some first interesting insights into the performances of different LLMs in terms of the expressiveness of their embeddings. We employed 3 among the most powerful (and arguably the most powerful) open source generative model: Zephyr-7B, Mistral-7B and LLAMA-2 [16]. We also used 8 non-generative LLMs recently proposed in the community and specifically created for the legal domain [11]. Finally, we use 2 general-purpose LLMs: BERT [2], DistilBERT [13]. In particular, so far, we noticed that (a) models like Zephyr-7B and Mistral-7B (which have been recently proposed as the most performative generative open source LLMs) seem to be more performative when using the euclidean similarity (with a huge difference wrt to other LLMs) and the spearmanr similarity; (b) the other generative model we used (i.e. LLAMA-2 by Meta) seem more performative with the spearmanr similarity (but not so much more than the previous two generative models); (c) the first 2 generative LLMs and the last 3 legal LLMs in the table seem the best models overall (confirming the importance of having *legal* LLMs).

Table 2. False Positive Rate (FPR) for Different Models and Similarities

Model	Cosine Similarity	Euclidean	Angular	Spearmanr	Type
zephyr-7B	0.1287	**0.0098**	0.5821	**0.0032**	Generative
mistral-7B	0.1857	**0.0074**	0.6135	**0.0043**	Generative
llama2converted	0.3932	0.6568	0.6474	**0.0012**	Generative
bert-large-uncased	0.6069	0.6576	0.6493	0.6478	Non-Generative
distilbert-base-uncased	0.6411	0.6576	0.6509	0.6497	Non-Generative
legal-roberta-base	0.6473	0.6576	0.6552	0.6313	Legal Non-Gen.
legal-roberta-large	0.5964	0.6576	0.6376	0.5558	Legal Non-Gen.
legal-longformer-base	0.6476	0.6576	0.6553	0.6328	Legal Non-Gen.
legal-longformer-large	0.5951	0.6576	0.6273	0.5560	Legal Non-Gen.
casehold-legalbert	0.6119	0.6576	0.6501	0.6156	Legal Non-Gen.
legal-xlm-longformer-base	**0.0019**	0.6576	**0.3075**	0.0009	Legal Non-Gen.
legal-xlm-roberta-base	**0.0602**	0.6576	0.4470	**0.0097**	Legal Non-Gen.
legal-xlm-roberta-large	0.3309	0.6576	0.5728	**0.0093**	Legal Non-Gen.

6 Conclusion

In this paper, we have described OntoVAT, a formal ontology tailored to the VAT legal domain. This ontology is the result of a collaborative effort between domain experts and computer scientists and is meticulously structured to encapsulate critical elements pertaining to VAT within judicial rulings. Crafted in OWL and enhanced with multilingual SKOS lexicalization, it spans three languages-English, Italian, and Bulgarian-demonstrating its versatility and broad applicability. Moreover, this research explores a preliminary application scenario by assessing the capabilities of 13 open-source LLMs. Our system employs a range of 4 mathematical measures to calculate the similarities between vector representations (embeddings) derived using LLMs, to pinpointing relevant VAT-related concepts in judicial decisions. The use of similarity measures to combine our ontological framework with the power of LLMs represents just one aspect of OntoVAT's potential utility, and we believe that OntoVAT can have many other useful applicative uses. For the future, we plan to test system on the whole judgments (instead of the motivation only), and explore more insightful metrics beside FPR, as well as other similarity measures.

References

1. Borgo, S., Masolo, C.: Foundational choices in DOLCE. In: Staab, S., Studer, R. (eds.) Handbook on Ontologies. IHIS, pp. 361–381. Springer, Heidelberg (2009). https://doi.org/10.1007/978-3-540-92673-3_16
2. Devlin, J., Chang, M.W., Lee, K., Toutanova, K.: Bert: pre-training of deep bidirectional transformers for language understanding. arXiv preprint arXiv:1810.04805 (2018)
3. Dimou, A., et al.: Airo: an ontology for representing AI risks based on the proposed EU AI act and ISO risk management standards. In: Towards a Knowledge-Aware AI: SEMANTiCS 2022-Proceedings of the 18th International Conference on Semantic Systems, 13-15 September 2022, Vienna, Austria, vol. 55, p. 51. IOS Press (2022)
4. Gangemi, A., Guarino, N., Masolo, C., Oltramari, A., Schneider, L.: Sweetening ontologies with DOLCE. In: Gómez-Pérez, A., Benjamins, V.R. (eds.) EKAW 2002. LNCS (LNAI), vol. 2473, pp. 166–181. Springer, Heidelberg (2002). https://doi.org/10.1007/3-540-45810-7_18
5. Guarino, N., Welty, C.A.: An overview of OntoClean. In: Staab, S., Studer, R. (eds.) Handbook on Ontologies. IHIS, pp. 201–220. Springer, Heidelberg (2009). https://doi.org/10.1007/978-3-540-92673-3_9
6. Hitzler, P., Gangemi, A., Janowicz, K.: Ontology engineering with ontology design patterns: foundations and applications, vol. 25. IOS Press (2016)
7. Hoekstra, R., Breuker, J., Di Bello, M., Boer, A., et al.: The LKIF core ontology of basic legal concepts. LOAIT **321**, 43–63 (2007)
8. Kerremans, K., Temmerman, R., Tummers, J.: Representing multilingual and culture-specific knowledge in a VAT regulatory ontology: support from the termontography method. In: Meersman, R., Tari, Z. (eds.) OTM 2003. LNCS, vol. 2889, pp. 662–674. Springer, Heidelberg (2003). https://doi.org/10.1007/978-3-540-39962-9_68
9. Liga, D., Amitrano, D., Markovich, R.: Patronto, an ontology for patents and trademarks. In: New Frontiers in Artificial Intelligence: JSAI-isAI 2023 Workshops, AI-Biz, EmSemi, SCIDOCA, JURISIN 2023 Workshops, Hybrid Event, June 5–6, 2023, Revised Selected Papers. Springer (2024)
10. Liga, D., Fidelangeli, A., Markovich, R.: Ontovat, an ontology for knowledge extraction in vat-related judgments. In: New Frontiers in Artificial Intelligence: JSAI-isAI 2023 Workshops, AI-Biz, EmSemi, SCIDOCA, JURISIN 2023 Workshops, Hybrid Event, June 5–6, 2023, Revised Selected Papers. Springer (2024)
11. Niklaus, J., Matoshi, V., Stürmer, M., Chalkidis, I., Ho, D.E.: Multilegalpile: a 689gb multilingual legal corpus. arXiv preprint arXiv:2306.02069 (2023)
12. Palmirani, M., Martoni, M., Rossi, A., Bartolini, C., Robaldo, L.: Pronto: privacy ontology for legal compliance. In: Proceedings of 18th European Conference Digital Government (ECDG), pp. 142–151 (2018)

13. Sanh, V., Debut, L., Chaumond, J., Wolf, T.: Distilbert, a distilled version of bert: smaller, faster, cheaper and lighter. arXiv preprint arXiv:1910.01108 (2019)
14. Sartor, G., Casanovas, P., Biasiotti, M., Fernández-Barrera, M.: Approaches to Legal Ontologies: Theories, Domains Methodologies. Law. Governance and Technology Series. Springer, Dordrecht (2011)
15. Temmerman, R., Kerremans, K.: Termontography: ontology building and the sociocognitive approach to terminology description. In: Proceedings of CIL17, vol. 7, p. 1 (2003)
16. Touvron, H., et al.: Llama 2: open foundation and fine-tuned chat models. arXiv preprint arXiv:2307.09288 (2023)

An Example of Argumentation Scheme from Liability: The Case of Vicarious Liability

Davide Liga[(✉)][iD]

University of Luxembourg, Esch-sur-Alzette, Luxembourg
davide.liga@uni.lu

Abstract. In this work, we explore a new argumentation pattern in legal discourse, referred to as the 'Argument from Vicarious Liability.' Central to our discussion is the 'Respondeat Superior' principle, commonly applied in Tort Law, which associates the accountability for an act with a supervisory figure, rather than the direct perpetrator. Our investigation highlights the need for more in-depth analysis of how liability functions within legal argumentation schemes. We introduce what we believe to be the first argumentation scheme focused explicitly on liability and its indirect ties with causality. While showing how this scheme is already used in some important judicial cases, we will also discuss how this specific argumentative pattern might be related to, or build upon, existing schemes in argumentation.

Keywords: Argumentation Schemes · Liability · Legal Knowledge Representation

1 Introduction

The landscape of structured argumentation has garnered heightened attention in contemporary research, notably in the arena of argumentation schemes. These schemes, unlike the monolithic atomic constructs observed in abstract argumentation, boast a multi-faceted internal composition. This structure is inherently influenced by the chosen *model of argument*, such as Toulmin's framework, which encompasses elements like claim, ground, and warrant [12], or Walton's model, characterized by a premise-conclusion relationship [16].

In the intersection of Argumentation and Artificial Intelligence (AI), Walton's model has emerged as particularly influential, underscoring its applicability in

This work was supported by the Fonds National de la Recherche Luxembourg through the project Deontic Logic for Epistemic Rights (OPEN O20/14776480) and through the project INDIGO which is financially supported by the NORFACE Joint Research Programme on Democratic Governance in a Turbulent Age and co-funded by AEI, AKA, DFG and FNR, and the European Commission through H2020 (agreement No 822166).

M. Bono et al. (Eds.): JSAI-isAI 2023 Workshops, LNAI 14644, pp. 132–147, 2024.
https://doi.org/10.1007/978-3-031-60511-6_9

AI dynamics, especially in argumentative contexts [2,4,6,9]. These schemes, recognized as typical inferential patterns [10], are articulated in natural language, encapsulating the inferential steps commonly utilized in persuasive and argumentative discourse. Take, for instance, the well-known 'argument from negative consequences' scheme (see Table 1), a ubiquitous inferential pattern in everyday dialogue.

Table 1. Structure of the argument from negative consequences, which is composed of one single premise and a conclusion.

Premise	If A is brought about, bad consequences will plausibly occur
Conclusion	Therefore, A should not be brought about.

These argumentation schemes serve as pivotal tools for dissecting and evaluating arguments across diverse disciplines, including philosophy, law, and AI. They act as argumentative templates [7] that can be adapted to the unique nuances of language use and contextual specifics. Moreover, these templates are instrumental in discerning the robustness of an argument, aided by critical questions designed to rigorously test the argument's validity.

While Walton's work has provided a comprehensive overview of prevalent argumentation schemes [16], there's a growing interest in legal argumentation schemes [15]. In our study, we aim to contribute to this developing field by tentatively shedding some light on a relatively unexplored aspect: the connection between liability and legal argumentation. Our focus is primarily on beginning to understand how causal and legal responsibility intertwine within the argumentative dimension of legal reasoning, a critical area that, until now, has not been extensively examined. Given that so far only little account has been given to the role of liability in legal argumentation schemes, including the interplay between causal responsibility and legal responsibility, we wanted to explore an argumentative dimension where the interplay between liability and causality is quite idiosyncratic, in the sense the idea of 'Respondeat Superior' is an example of situation where the liability is somehow *going beyond* the dimension of the causality, creating a very peculiar relation between the dimensions of causality and legal responsibility. In this sense, the kind of interconnections between liability an causality and how these kind of interconnections are intertwined with the argumentative dimension are open research areas.

In our investigation, we spotlight a specific legal argumentation scheme that centers on liability following this concept of 'Respondeat Superior': the argument from vicarious liability. This scheme not only serves as the primary focus of our study but also marks the starting point for a broader research trajectory, underscoring the need to understand better argumentative patterns grounded in legal and causal responsibilities.

Referencing the comprehensive compendium by Walton, Macagno, and Sartor [15], which delves into legal statutory interpretation through schemes like the argument from precedent or rule application, we propose a potential integration within this framework. Our proposition revolves around incorporating the dynamics of *causality* and *liability* within these legal argumentation schemes. Despite the pivotal role of causal and legal responsibilities in legal reasoning, their representation in existing literature on argumentation schemes, with a few exceptions (e.g., [1]), remains relatively scant. This observation motivates us to advocate for the development of legal argumentation schemes that specifically address causality and liability, which appear to be relatively underrepresented in current academic discourse.

To stimulate these research directions and to show that some important argumentation schemes could fall under these two umbrellas (i.e. causality and liability), we describe and formalise a quite relevant argumentative pattern which directly take into account liability (and, indirectly, also causality). Our objective is twofold: firstly, to encourage further exploration into legal argumentation schemes rooted in causality and liability, with a particular emphasis on the latter; and secondly, to underscore the intricate yet often overlapping nature of liability and causality in legal discourse, advocating for their inclusion in the formalization of legal argumentation schemes. Our exploration begins with a first case study which explicitly focuses on a legal argumentation scheme *from liability* (and which simultaneously account for elements of causality). Specifically, we focus on the principle of *vicarious liability*, a concept frequently invoked by judges to support or challenge argumentative positions in legal proceedings. To illustrate the significance of this scheme, we reference two landmark judgments where it played a crucial role: *Mohamud v WM Morrison Supermarkets plc [2016] UKSC 11, 2 March 2016]* and *Cox v Ministry of Justice [2016] UKSC 10, 2 March 2016*. Through these cases, we aim to offer a formalized framework for this argumentation scheme, complete with critical questions, showcasing its application by judges in legal reasoning.

In our analysis of the argument from vicarious liability, we aim to explore potential argumentative and ontological connections between our proposed scheme and the established Waltonian schemes. This exploration is crucial as it seeks to bridge the gap between Walton's original compendium and the *legal compendium* in [15]. Our goal is to elucidate how legal argumentation schemes not only align with, but also diverge from, non-legal ones, and how they interact within the broader Waltonian framework, particularly in terms of support and attack mechanisms.

Furthermore, it is worth mentioning that our scheme from vicarious liability is a perfect example to show that the relation between causality and liability deserves more attention from the argumentative point of view. In this regard, while showing that causal responsibility and legal responsibility does not necessarily coincide, we would also like to suggest that there might be complex (but stereotypical and thus frequent) interactions between these two spheres, which might have corresponding argumentation schemes.

To our knowledge, this study represents the first exploration of a legal argumentation scheme specifically addressing liability. By exploring this area, we hope to pave the way for subsequent research that will further shed some light on how liability and causality are intricately woven into the fabric of legal argumentation. In Sect. 2, the concept of vicarious liability is elucidated, encompassing an overview of its fundamental principles and doctrinal underpinnings. Afterwards, the relative scheme from vicarious liability is formalised. This section not only presents the formal structure of the scheme but also explores its interconnections with other established schemes, particularly focusing on the interplay between causality and liability in the context of vicarious liability.

Following this, Sect. 3 delves into an in-depth analysis of the landmark legal case *Mohamud v WM Morrisons Supermarkets*, while Sect. 4 similarly examines the case of *Cox v Ministry of Justice*. These sections aim to apply the previously discussed vicarious liability scheme to real-world judicial scenarios.

The penultimate section, Sect. 5, engages in a critical discussion of various facets of the vicarious liability scheme, considering also its applicability and implications in legal reasoning, as well as the connection between liability and causality. Finally, Sect. 6 concludes the paper.

2   Argumentation Scheme from Vicarious Liability

2.1   Vicarious Liability

Vicarious Liability, a fundamental concept in legal theory, is intrinsically linked to the 'Respondeat Superior' doctrine. This Latin term translates to 'let the master answer', encapsulating the idea that one party may bear responsibility for actions undertaken by another. A typical example is the potential liability of employers for actions executed by their employees, provided these actions occur within the employment scope. This principle, often termed the 'master-servant rule', is a staple in both civil and common law systems.

At its core, Vicarious Liability is a blend of strict and secondary liability. 'Strict liability' refers to legal accountability for certain actions irrespective of fault or intent (*mens rea*). On the other hand, 'secondary liability' is implicated when a party significantly aids or induces actions that lead to direct infringement by others. Thus, these forms of liability create legal responsibility even without a direct causal link between the wrongdoing and the person who is target of the liability. In the case of Vicarious Liability specifically, the transfer of liability from the perpetrator to another party hinges on the nature of their relationship (e.g., employer-employee) and the context of the wrongful act, which should have transpired within the boundaries of this relationship.

Delving deeper, the doctrine of vicarious liability stipulates that employers can be deemed liable for their employees' civil wrongs if there's a demonstrable link between the employer and the employee (who is the primary wrongdoer), and if the wrongful act is *closely related* to the employment. In essence, confirming vicarious liability involves a two-step process: firstly, establishing the relationship between the wrongdoer and the party being held vicariously liable; and secondly, determining whether the misconduct occurred in the context of this relationship. This dual-test framework was notably established in the landmark case of *Lister v Helsey Hall [2001] UKHL 22* and has been instrumental in numerous legal rulings.

The interpretation of this two-stage test is inherently subjective, hinging on the specific circumstances of each case, thereby opening avenues for legal reasoning and argumentation. For example, certain cases may emphasize the first part of the test, assessing the nature of the relationship, such as in *Cox v Ministry of Justice*. Conversely, others might focus on the second part, the 'close connection' test, as seen in *Mohamud v WM Morrison Supermarkets plc*. Before diving into these notable cases, our next section will introduce a model for the argument from vicarious liability.

2.2 The Scheme

This scheme is quite frequent in tort law and is based on the above-mentioned idea of vicarious liability, according to which a the legal responsibility (i.e., the liability) of a wrongdoing is channeled from the wrongdoer (who has the direct or causal responsibility of the wrongdoing) to a second agent who has a relevant hierarchical relationship with the wrongdoer (e.g., a relationship employer-employee). This transfer of liability is traditionally evaluated through a binary inquiry: firstly, does a significant relationship (like employment) exist between the perpetrator and the third party? Secondly, is there a sufficient link between this relationship and the misconduct?

From an argumentation standpoint, these queries can be viewed as *critical questions* employed by judges to determine the likelihood of vicarious liability. Shifting to an argumentative lens, the two-stage test essentially aims to validate the argument that the vicarious liability doctrine is applicable in a given scenario. Even though switching to this argumentative perspective makes it easier to see the critical questions behind the two-stage test, we still do not have a formal structure for the scheme from vicarious liability to which these critical questions are referred. In other words, what is the argumentative structure that this two-stage test tries to stress-test? First of all, an argument from vicarious liability must consider that a wrongdoer is responsible for a wrongdoing (first premise). Secondly, one need to consider not just the wrongdoer, but a second person who has a specific (i.e., relevant) relationship with the wrongdoer (second premise). Furthermore, the wrongdoing must be located in the context of such relationship (third premise). Finally, the conclusion must be that the second person is vicariously liable for the wrongdoing. Hence, we propose to design the argumentation scheme from vicarious liability as follows:

(P1) Agent A is causally responsible for wrongdoing W through Action D **[Causal Responsibility Premise]**

(P2) Agent L has a relevant vicarious relationship R with Agent A **[Vicarious Relationship Premise]**

(P3) Action D occurred in the scope of relationship R **[Vicarious Wrongdoing Premise]**

(C) Therefore, Agent L is vicariously responsible for wrongdoing W **[Conclusion]**

(CQ1) Is it really the case that there is a relevant relationship between Agent A and L? **[Vicarious Relationship Critical Question]**

(CQ2) Is the connection between relationship R and wrongdoing W sufficiently close? **[Sufficient Connection Critical Question]**

(CQ3) Is Agent A causally responsible for wrongdoing W? **[Causal Responsibility Critical Question]**

As can be seen above, the critical questions reflect the two-stage test, while adding a further critical question to stress test the very first premise. In fact, other studies have shown that each premise can be attacked on the bases of the content it provides, and premises generally provide the argument structure with their own piece of semantic information (the semantic link by which each premise give support the underlying inferential process towards the conclusion), which can have different natures (e.g., causal, factual, definitional) [8].

In general, we can consider arguments as structures which may be attacked (or supported) at specific critical points of their structure. In this regard, we can say that the hold of an argumentation scheme has a minimum amount of critical positions which corresponds to the number of premises (because each premises can be questioned) plus *at least* one critical point for the inferential step connecting the premises to the conclusion, plus at least one rebuttal stating the negation of the conclusion. Applying this framework to the argument from vicarious liability, we can identify five primary critical points in its structure. These are delineated in the corresponding figure illustrating the scheme (refer to Fig. 1).

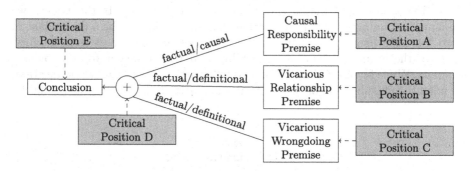

Fig. 1. Structure of the Argument from Vicarious Liability, showing the semantic link connecting the premises to the conclusion. Dashed connections are potential attacks or supports heading towards the critical positions of the scheme.

Critical Questions are positioned at critical position A, B and C. At these positions, other arguments might give an attack (or a support), which will directly attack (or support) the semantic link provided by the corresponding premise.

The first premise, for example, can be attacked or supported by a causal argumentation scheme. Instead, at position B and C the support or attack to the hold of the argumentative structure can come from a verbal classification scheme, since the premises' semantic information is mostly dedicated to factual/definitional elements (namely the nature of the relationship between wrongdoer and the potentially liable agent, as well as the nature of the scope under which the wrongdoing occurred). At position D, attacks/supports are meant to target the inferential steps from premises to conclusion. This also includes the attack to the structure as a whole. In other words, attacks at critical position A, B and C are referred to the so-called *undermining* attack, while an attack at position D refers to the *undercut* attack. Finally, we also mentions critical position E, the position for the *rebuttal* attacks, which occur when the conclusion is directly attacked by another argument.

Relationships with Other Schemes. As mentioned before, the first critical position can be "stress-tested" when the first premise is attacked (or supported). Having a causal semantic link, this critical position is physiologically prone to be attacked (or supported) by causal schemes [3, 16] such as the argument from cause to effect, the argument from correlation to cause. Regarding the other two premises, they can be stressed (or supported) by the use of a verbal classification schemes [13], which are meant to further specify, semantically, the nature of the involved relationship or the scope under which the wrongdoing occurred (since these two premises can be attacked/supported mostly with respect to the definition of the two key concepts they convey, namely the words "relevant" and "scope").

Another important aspect which is worth mentioning is that we see this scheme from vicarious liability as a part of a more general family of schemes from liability, which are not yet available in literature, and whose internal relationship should be explored on the basis of the existing legal theory. In this regard, we assume that an argument from vicarious liability is likely to be a descendant of two "parent schemes" belonging to the family of the arguments from liability, namely the argument from strict liability and the argument from secondary liability. While further research is needed to explore this ontological classification, a potential classification of these schemes might look like the scheme in Fig. 2.

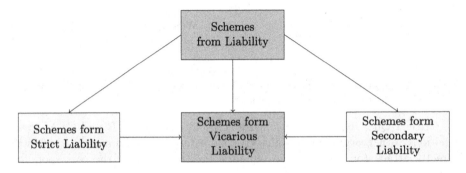

Fig. 2. Classification of some of the envisaged schemes from liability.

Interactions Between Liability and Causality in Legal Argumentation
Although this paper does not aim at describing the complex interplay between liability and causation [11,17], we argue that more efforts are required to clarify some of the main interactions between these two spheres from the argumentative point of view, providing an account of how this interplay is represented in different schemes from liability.

From this point of view, the scheme from vicarious liability offers a privileged perspective, because it is located in the context of strict liability, where liability arises even if the person who is targeted by liability is not aware of the wrongdoing for which he is considered liable. This kind of liabilities may be considered, from an argumentative point of view, as belonging to what we call *argumentation schemes from strict liability* (as depicted in Fig. 2). From a more abstract theoretical point of view, they dramatically remind us the necessity to keep in mind the difference between causal and legal responsibilities when evaluating wrongdoings.

In the case of our scheme from vicarious liability, it seems that liability can be generated from a fact even if there is no causal link between the person considered vicariously liable and the wrongdoing. This has the effect of extend somehow the scope of the liability for that wrongdoing, creating a "transfer" of liability from the wrongdoer (whose liability coincide with the actual causation) to the agent who is hierarchically responsible for the wrongdoer's actions if these actions occur in the context of the relationship between the two agents (and this "extended" liability thus goes beyond actual causation). It would be interesting to see what kind of potential interactions exist from the argumentative point considering different types of schemes from liability. In other words, it would be interesting to explore argumentation schemes as tools for understanding the interactions between liability and causality in legal reasoning. We leave this to future research.

3   Mohamud v. WM Morrison Supermarkets

The case *Mohamud v VM Morrison Supermarkets* is a very famous example of vicarious liability. The case was focused on the interpretation of the second limb of the above-mentioned two-stage test, which is sometimes referred to as "close connection" or "sufficient connection" test.

Facts. A man named Mr. Mohamud, who is of Somali descent, pulled over at a Morrison petrol station. The station's employee, Mr. Khan, was working at the kiosk and had the responsibility of serving customers and ensuring the proper functioning of the petrol pumps and the kiosk. Mr. Mohamud went inside the shop to inquire about printing some documents, to which Mr. Khan responded with swear words. Upon objecting to being sworn at, Mr. Khan ordered Mr. Mohamud to leave and used foul and racist language. Mr. Mohamud left the shop, got back in his car, and was about to drive away when Mr. Khan approached him, opened the passenger door, and told him never to return to the petrol station. When Mr. Mohamud asked Mr. Khan to step out of the car, he punched him in the head. Mr. Mohamud got out of the car to close the passenger door, but Mr. Khan continued to attack him, striking him and kicking him until he fell to the ground. Despite the efforts of his supervisor to stop him, Mr. Khan carried out the attack. As a result of the assault, Mr. Mohamud filed a personal injury claim against Morrison, raising the question of whether the company was vicariously liable for Mr. Khan's violent actions.

County Court Decision. The Court ruled that vicarious liability could not be established as the "close connection" test was not satisfied. The trial judge was unable to determine that the company was vicariously responsible for Mr. Khan's actions. In evaluating the second aspect of the vicarious liability test and applying the "close connection test" from the Lister case, the judge was unable to establish a sufficient connection between Mr. Khan's employment and the unprovoked assault. While it was acknowledged that Mr. Khan's job entailed some customer interaction, serving and assisting them, this was not deemed "sufficiently closely connected" to warrant holding the company vicariously liable for the attack. Another key factor in the trial judge's decision was that Mr. Khan had taken a deliberate action by leaving the kiosk and pursuing Mr. Mohamud onto the forecourt, going against his employer's instructions.

Court of Appeal Decision. Mr Mohamud appealed the first instance decision but the Court of Appeal upheld the decision. The reasoning was similar to the first instance decision but went further by stating that, since Mr. Khan's responsibilities did not involve a high likelihood of conflict, merely having interaction with customers in his role was not enough to make his employer vicariously liable for his violent behavior.

Supreme Court Decision. Mr. Mohamud took his case to the Supreme Court and asked for the "sufficient connection" test to be replaced with a "representative capacity" test. This proposed test was broader and asked whether a reasonable observer would consider the employee to be acting in a representative capacity for the employer at the time the tort was committed. This focus would not be on the closeness of the connection between the employee's work and the tortious conduct, but would relate to the setting the employer created. Mr. Mohamud argued that the "representative capacity" test was met as Mr. Khan, an employee responsible for serving customers at the petrol station, was the human representative of the employer and the employer created the setting by placing Mr. Khan in close physical contact with him. However, the Supreme Court rejected the "representative capacity" test, considering it unnecessary as it did not differ substantially from the Lister test. The judges preferred the broad application of the "close connection" test, which considered Mr. Khan's violent act to be sufficiently closely connected to his employment for Morrison to be vicariously liable. One of the judges argued that Mr. Khan leaving the kiosk to follow Mr. Mohamud to his car did not break the connection, stating that it would not be fair to say that Mr. Khan had "taken off his uniform metaphorically" when he stepped out from behind the counter. Therefore, the Supreme Court upheld Mr. Mohamud's claim and determined that Morrison was vicariously liable for Mr. Khan's actions.

Argumentative Analysis. The first judge refuted the argument of the appellant according to which Morrison Supermarkets were vicariously liable because the second question (related to the "close connection") was answered negatively. The trial judge reached this conclusion by using the critical question of the sufficient connection (i.e., the "close connection test" from the case of Lister v Hesley Hall), to which he answered negatively: according to the trial judge the connection between the wrongdoing and the relationship is not sufficient, i.e., the wrongdoing did not happen in the sufficiently within the employer-employee relationship. The judge supported this conclusion that the sufficient connection was not met by adding that Mr Khan went out of the shop against the instructions of his employer. Once the judge undermined the third premise by answering negatively to the sufficient connection critical question, the inferential step from the premises to the conclusion was not acceptable.

The second judge presented a similar reasoning, using the critical question of the sufficient connection to affirm that the wrongdoing did not happen within the scope of the employer-employee relationship. This time the judge used an even stronger argument by stating that Mr Khan responsibilities did not include the likelihood of a conflict and the mere confrontation with a customer does not justify the vicarious liability of the defendant. Again, this meant that the inferential passage from the premises to the conclusion of the argument from vicarious liability was rejected, because the third premise was undermined.

The last judge, instead, answered positively to the sufficient connection critical question. Therefore granting the inferential passage from the three premises to the conclusion. It is interesting to note that the appellant, coming from two negative decisions on the sufficient connection critical question, proposed to replace such critical question with a new one, in order to facilitate the inferential passage to the conclusion of the argument from vicarious liability.

Figure 3 summarises the inferential steps that judges undertook with respect to the argument from vicarious liability.

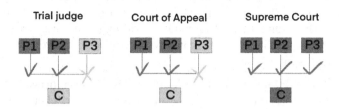

Fig. 3. Inferential processes of the three judicial level of judgment for the case Mohamud v WM Morrison supermarkets with respect to the argument from vicarious liability.

4   Cox v. Ministry of Justice

If in *Mohamud v WM Morrison Supermarkets* the Supreme Court decided about the second limb of the vicarious liability two-stage test, i.e., about the connection between the vicarious relationship and the tortious act, in *Cox v Ministry of Justice*, the Court decided instead about the first limb of the two-stage test, which is related to the relationship between the defendant (the potential vicariously liable person) and the wrongdoer.

Facts. Mrs Cox was the catering manager at HMA Swansea and had responsibility for the kitchen operation. She supervised 4 employees and 20 prisoners. During a kitchen supplies delivery, a prisoner dropped a sack on her back while trying to carry two past her, causing injury. The incident was deemed negligent. Mrs Cox claimed that the Ministry of Justice was vicariously liable for the actions of the prisoner orderly and sought compensation for her injuries. The problem here was to assess whether a relevant relationship existed between the defendant (Ministry of Justice) and the wrongdoer. Prison rules state that convicted prisoners in state or private prisons must do useful work for up to 10 h a day. The defendant's policy is that work instills a hard-working ethos and teaches vocational skills. Prisoners can apply to work in prison kitchens and are selected after assessments. They may be paid £11.55 per week by the Secretary of State to encourage participation. Without prisoner work, the prison service would need to incur additional costs for staff or contractors. Judges reasoned about these elements to assess whether the vicarious relationship critical question was positive. Is the relationship between the Ministry of Justice and the prisoner relevant to accept vicarious liability?

County Court Decision. The trial judge ruled that the prison service was not vicariously responsible for the prisoner's negligence. He evaluated if the connection between the prison service and the prisoner was similar to that of an employer and employee and found it was not. He acknowledged that there were similarities, but noted a crucial difference. Employment is a mutual agreement where each party benefits. With prisoners, the situation is different. The prison is legally obliged to provide work and pay for it, not as a choice but as part of their penal policy. The work is meant for the prisoner's discipline, rehabilitation, and fulfillment of their duty to the community. Although the prisoner's work may improve the prison's efficiency and economy, it's not seen as furthering the prison service's business interests.

Court of Appeal Decision. The Court of Appeal overturned the previous ruling. It argued that the work done by prisoners in the kitchen was crucial to the prison's operation, and if not performed by prisoners, it would have to be done by someone else. Therefore, the work was performed on behalf of the prison service and for its benefit, as part of its operations and running of the prison. In essence, the prison service gained from this work, so it should also bear its responsibilities. Although the relationship between the prisoners and the prison service was not a typical employment one, as the prisoners were connected to the prison service not by agreement but by their sentences and their wages were nominal, these differences actually made the relationship even closer to an employment one. It was based on obligation rather than mutuality.

Supreme Court Decision. The Supreme Court held in favour of the claimant. They found that the defendant, the Ministry of Justice, was vicariously liable for the prisoner's negligence. This was because the prisoners worked for the defendant's benefit, which created the risk of negligence.

Argumentative Analysis

The trial judge held that the Ministry of Justice was not vicariously liable because the relationship between the defendant (Ministry of Justice) and the wrongdoer was not sufficiently relevant. In other words, the judge undermined the second premise of the scheme by answering negatively to the critical question related to vicarious relationship, thus preventing the inferential step from premises to the conclusion.

However, the Court of Appeal and the Supreme Court found that the relationship between the Ministry of Justice and the prisoner was sufficiently close and that the Ministry of Justice gained advantages from prisoner works, and therefore should also bear its responsibilities. In this way the judges allowed the inferential passage from the three premises to the conclusion.

5   Discussion and Limitations

There are two points which are worth discussing regarding the argumentation scheme proposed in this paper. The first point is related to the nature of this scheme and the possibility that this scheme is a more specific implementation of the argument from rule. The second point is related to whether this schema is applicable universally or not.

Regarding the first point, in the analysed case study, the burden of proof is clearly related to whether or not the vicarious liability should be applied. We showed the most frequent ways in which this schema is supported or attacked (at least in Common Law). When judges argue w.r.t. the applicability of vicarious liability, their arguments mostly focus on Critical Question 1 and Critical Question 2 (related to relationship R and to its "sufficient connection" with wrongdoing W) which can be used to support or undermine (perhaps even undercut) the schema. We also showed where this happens (see critical positions in Fig. 1) with specific examples of how different judges undermined the schema (Fig. 3). In other words, judges build their arguments in support or attack of such applicability by checking whether some tests is passed (e.g., the "sufficient connection" test). For this reason, we believe that there is a relation with the most general argument from rule. While a simple argument from rule would be too general, this schema can better express the argumentative strategies of judges in the context of vicarious liability. The argument from vicarious liability could therefore be considered a descendant of the argument from rule, but instantiated in the context of liability (see Fig. 4).

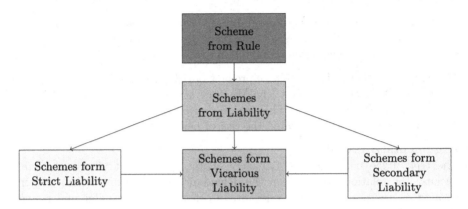

Fig. 4. Classification of some of the envisaged schemes from liability and the potential relation with the argument from rule.

Regarding the second point, although this schema shows a very common argumentative pattern and can be used as it is in the context of Common Law, we believe that the situation might be slightly different in countries which are not under the umbrella of Common Law. In particular, after some first analysis, it seems that we might need more Critical Questions and premises do deal with the legal systems of some countries in Civil Law. For this reason, we think that the schema proposed in this paper can be considered as a "basic" schema, similarly to how the "basic slippery slope" has been proposed by Walton as the basic pattern underlying more specialised "slippery slope" schemes [14].

Finally, we would like to remark again that this schema should be considered as a first attempt to tackle a huger long-term research goal, namely the analysis of what we call schemes from liability. By shedding some light in this direction, we believe that some interesting discussions can be undertaken. For example, we might understand the way in which argumentative patterns are developed in the context of different kind of liability (secondary liability, strict liability, shared liability, and so on).

5.1   The Relation Between Liability and Causality

The interplay between liability and causality in legal argumentation presents a complex landscape, often characterized by their varying degrees of interconnectedness and precedence. Understanding this dynamic is crucial in legal reasoning, especially in contexts where liability is not directly tied to the causation of harm. One prominent example of liability taking precedence over causation is seen in the above-mentioned concept of vicarious liability. In such cases, the focus shifts from who directly caused the harm to who is ultimately responsible for the actions leading to that harm. This *liability shift* often occurs in employer-employee relationships, where employers can be held liable for the actions of their employees, provided these actions were within the scope of employment.

Here, the causal link, while still relevant, becomes secondary to the established relationship between the employer and the employee. Another striking example is found in strict liability cases. Strict liability implies responsibility for damages irrespective of intent or negligence. In these scenarios, the emphasis is not on establishing a causal chain leading to harm but rather on the mere occurrence of a particular action or event. This approach significantly alters the traditional causality-driven narrative, as the defendant's liability is determined without considering the direct causal role in the damage caused.

Apart from this idea of "priority", other kinds of interconnections between liability and causality exist. For instance, in cases of *contributory negligence*, both causality and liability are intricately linked and *distributed* among various parties. Here, the causal contribution of each party to the harm is evaluated, and liability is apportioned accordingly.

Moreover, in certain legal doctrines like *proximate cause*, causality plays a pivotal role in determining liability. This doctrine assesses the directness of the causal link between an act and its consequences. The legal system uses this concept to establish the extent to which the act in question can be deemed responsible for the resultant damages.

The relationship between liability and causality also extends into areas like *product liability*. In such cases, manufacturers may be held liable for damages caused by their products, even when there is no direct fault on their part. The causal link here is established based on the product's nature and the expected duty of care, rather than on a specific negligent act.

In conclusion, the relationship between liability and causality in legal contexts is diverse and context-dependent. It ranges from scenarios where liability overrides direct causation, as seen in vicarious and strict liability, to situations where both aspects are intricately woven, like in contributory negligence and proximate cause doctrines. Understanding these varied interconnections is essential for a comprehensive grasp of legal argumentation and reasoning.

An interesting research direction would be that of assessing (a) what are the main existing scenarios of interaction between liability and causality and (b) what are their constitutive elements, i.e. those elements (possibly contextual/non-causal) that might determine an argumentative shift towards/against the application of liability.

6   Conclusion

In our study, we proposed an unexplored yet fundamental direction for legal argumentation schemes, focusing on the importance of defining liability patterns in legal reasoning. Our foundational premise was the observation of a gap in existing literature regarding liability within argumentation schemes, notwithstanding the crucial efforts detailed in [15]. We recognized the frequent yet complex interplay of liability and causality (or legal and causal responsibilities) in legal discourse, noting an absence of a detailed argumentative analysis of their relationship. Motivated by these insights, our research first established the necessity to further explore what we term "schemes from liability". We introduced a specific scheme fitting this category, illustrating the distinct divergence between causal and legal responsibilities, a scenario often encountered in instances of strict liability. We called this argumentative pattern "Argumentation Scheme from Vicarious Liability".

Our analysis underscored the significance of this scheme in legal contexts, demonstrated through two key case studies. These cases were pivotal in showcasing how judges navigate the applicability of vicarious liability through this argumentative framework.

We acknowledged that our proposed scheme, while foundational, may require adaptations for broader applicability beyond the realm of Common Law. Moreover, we posited that this scheme could be a derivative of the argument from rule, specifically tailored to the vicarious liability context.

Our current endeavors are directed towards creating a computational model for this scheme. Future research should aim to comprehensively map out the entire spectrum of liability-centered argumentation schemes, examining their relations from an ontological and logical point of view. Additionally, the intricate dynamics between causality and liability in legal argumentation deserves further investigation. It would also be beneficial to probe deeper into how these liability-based schemes interact with other argumentation schemes, particularly in light of the new legal compendium proposed in [15]. Exploring these schemes' connections with case-based reasoning [18] and recent studies on the legal presumption of causality in argumentation [5] will also provide valuable insights.

References

1. Contissa, G., Laukyte, M., Sartor, G., Schebesta, H.: Assessing liability with argumentation maps: an application in aviation law. In: JURIX, pp. 73–76 (2013)
2. Feng, V.W., Hirst, G.: Classifying arguments by scheme. In: Proceedings of the 49th Annual Meeting of the Association for Computational Linguistics: Human Language Technologies, pp. 987–996 (2011)
3. Hahn, U., Bluhm, R., Zenker, F.: Causal Argument. Oxford University Press, Oxford (2017)
4. Lawrence, J., Reed, C.: Argument mining using argumentation scheme structures. In: COMMA, pp. 379–390 (2016)
5. Liepiņa, R., Wyner, A., Sartor, G., Lagioia, F.: Argumentation schemes for legal presumption of causality. In: Proceedings of the Nineteenth International Conference on Artificial Intelligence and Law, pp. 157–166 (2023)
6. Liga, D.: Argumentative evidences classification and argument scheme detection using tree kernels. In: Proceedings of the 6th Workshop on Argument Mining, pp. 92–97 (2019)
7. Liga, D., Palmirani, M.: Argumentation schemes as templates? Combining bottom-up and top-down knowledge representation. In: CMNA@ COMMA, pp. 51–56 (2020)
8. Liga, D., Palmirani, M.: Uncertainty in argumentation schemes: negative consequences and basic slippery slope. In: Dastani, M., Dong, H., van der Torre, L. (eds.) CLAR 2020. LNCS (LNAI), vol. 12061, pp. 259–278. Springer, Cham (2020). https://doi.org/10.1007/978-3-030-44638-3_16

9. Macagno, F.: Argumentation schemes in AI. Argument Comput. **12**(3), 287–302 (2021)
10. Macagno, F., Walton, D., Reed, C.: Argumentation schemes. history, classifications, and computational applications. In: History, Classifications, and Computational Applications, pp. 2493–2556 (2017)
11. Moore, M.S.: Causation and Responsibility: An Essay in Law, Morals, and Metaphysics. Oxford University Press on Demand (2009)
12. Toulmin, S.E.: The uses of argument (1958)
13. Walton, D.: Argument from definition to verbal classification: the case of redefining 'planet' to exclude Pluto. Inf. Logic **28**, 129–154 (2008)
14. Walton, D.: The basic slippery slope argument. Inf. Logic **35**(3), 273–311 (2015)
15. Walton, D., Macagno, F., Sartor, G.: Statutory Interpretation: Pragmatics and Argumentation. Cambridge University Press, Cambridge (2021). https://doi.org/10.1017/9781108554572
16. Walton, D., Reed, C., Macagno, F.: Argumentation Schemes (2008)
17. Wright, R.W.: Causation in tort law. Calif. L. Rev. **73**, 1735 (1985)
18. Wyner, A., Bench-Capon, T.: Argument schemes for legal case-based reasoning. In: JURIX, pp. 139–149 (2007)

SCIDOCA 2023

Seventh International Workshop on Scientific Document Analysis (SCIDOCA 2023)

SCIDOCA is an annual international workshop focusing on various aspects and perspectives of scientific document analysis for their efficient use and exploration. The recent proliferation of scientific papers and technical documents has become an obstacle to efficient information acquisition of new information in various fields. It is almost impossible for individual researchers to check and read all related documents. Even retrieving relevant documents is becoming harder and harder. This workshop gathers all the researchers and experts who are aiming at scientific document analysis from various perspectives and invites technical paper presentations and system demonstrations that cover any aspects of scientific document analysis. The Eighth International Workshop on Scientific Document Analysis (SCIDOCA 2023) is associated with the JSAI International Symposia on AI 2023 (IsAI-2023).

Relevant topics include, but are not limited to, the following:

- Text analysis
- Document structure analysis
- Logical structure analysis
- Figure and table analysis
- Citation analysis of scientific and technical documents
- Scientific information assimilation
- Summarization and visualization
- Knowledge discovery/mining from scientific papers and data
- Similar document retrieval
- Entity and relation linking between documents and knowledge base
- Survey generation
- Resources for scientific documents analysis
- Document understanding in general
- NLP systems aiming for scientific documents, including tagging, parsing, coreference, etc.

Among all submitted papers reviewed by experts in the field, we discussed intensively nominating the best of them with sufficiently high quality for inclusion in the LNAI proceedings.

We thank all the Steering Committee, Advisory Committee, and Program Committee of SCIDOCA 2023, all authors who submitted papers, and all the members of the Organizing Committee of JSAI-isAI.

Minh Le Nguyen

Directional Generative Networks; Comparison to Evolutionary Algorithms, Using Measurements for Molecules

Yasuaki Ito$^{(\boxtimes)}$ and Le-Minh Nguyen

Japan Advanced Institute of Science and Technology, 1-1 Asahidai, Nomi, Ishikawa 923-1292, Japan
{yasuaki_ito,nguyenml}@jaist.ac.jp

Abstract. Various methods have been proposed to search for molecules with desired properties. However, it is still a challenging task due to the vastness of the search space. In recent years, machine learning methods such as deep learning have achieved remarkable results in various fields. Although machine learning methods depend on data sets, it is sometimes difficult to prepare good-quality data for some tasks, and unsupervised learning methods have also been studied.

A method called Directional Generative Networks (DGN) uses Deep Learning models as regression models. DGNs can generate molecules with desirable features by using the values of an evaluation function, even in the absence of a dataset of molecules. Given the lack of applications of this method, this study attempts to extend the evaluation function for molecular search applications using DGN. While previous studies have used three different functions to evaluate molecules, this study adds three more, resulting in six evaluation functions compared to the Evolutionary Algorithm (EA).

Furthermore, DGN incorporates random numbers as input, and we discuss the impact of the degree of freedom of the input during the training phase. A large degree of freedom in the input increases the number of variations of molecules generated, and it causes the training models to become more challenging to converge. Conversely, when the degree of freedom of the input is small, the training convergence becomes more manageable, but the variation of the generated molecules decreases.

Keywords: Generative Model · Unsupervised Learning · Evolutionary Algorithm · Generative Adversarial Networks

1 Introduction

Drug discovery, which contributes to people's health, is one of the most critical fields of research and development. Huge budgets and time tend to be consumed in the process of drug discovery. Discovering new molecules, e.g., candidates for new drugs, is still a challenging task due to the vastness of the search space [1]. In

M. Bono et al. (Eds.): JSAI-isAI 2023 Workshops, LNAI 14644, pp. 151–166, 2024.
https://doi.org/10.1007/978-3-031-60511-6_10

addition to physical discovery using high-throughput screening (HTS) and other methods, recent advances in computational power have led to the experimentation of various virtual discovery methods. Computational methods for obtaining new molecules with desirable characteristics can be roughly classified.

(1) Virtual Screening (VS) [2].
(2) Randomized algorithms such as Evolutionary Algorithms(EA) [3].
(3) Generative models based on Deep Learning [5].

(1) VS methods include Substructure search, Similarity, Docking, and QSAR [6]. The substructure search method searches for molecules that contain the desired substructure in a given database of molecules. The similarity method searches a database of molecules for molecules similar to the molecule with the desired property. Docking methods search the database for molecules that fit the target enzyme or receptor. QSAR stands for Quantitative Structure-Activity Relationship. The QSAR method searches for molecules with predicted activity from the database based on the activity data of the compound.

(2) EA is well known as a typical randomized algorithm. The advantage of EA is that it can be applied even if the differentiability of the evaluation function is not certain. Genetic Algorithm(GA) is one of the EAs proposed by Holand. J. [3]. A unique aspect of GA is its emphasis on crossovers. Within the research area of the method of finding new molecules with desirable features, Lee et al. proposed a method of stacking two GA models [7]. This is intended to focus on a desired region of the search space. The method uses the similarity to a specific molecule prepared from the data set and the desired features as a score for individual selection.

(3) Generative Models: Variational Autoencoder(VAE) [8] is known as a likelihood-based generative model. Samanta et al. applied VAE to the graph structure of molecules [24]. Generative Adversarial Networks(GAN) [9] is well-known as a likelihood-free generative model. The advantage of likelihood-free models is their applicability to complex data structures. The disadvantage is low explanatory power and difficulty in model training.

Most of the methods rely on the datasets of molecules. Conversely, DGN [25] does not necessarily need datasets for training. It uses the results of evaluation functions as ground truth for training. This study attempts to extend the DGN method and compare it with EA.

2   Related Works

Most molecular search methods using EA require heuristical techniques to reduce search space for real problems. The method of stacking two GA models [7] previously mentioned has the same purpose. If the search space is small enough, EA methods work well.

In applications of GAN, ORGAN [11] and MolGAN [10] can generate desirable molecules. This model uses multiple discriminators to learn the correctness of molecules and generates a group of molecules with desirable properties as a GAN. This makes it possible to generate molecules with favorable scores for Drug-likeness [21], logP [22], and Synthesizability [23]. However, depending on the dataset used for learning, the variation of molecules generated may be limited. If the number of data used to train a GAN is insufficient, the output may be identical to those in the data set used for training. In MolGAN, molecules with specific characteristics are selected and used as training data. Therefore, it is likely that the same molecules as those used for training are generated, resulting in a smaller Uniqueness score.

DGN can avoid drawbacks derived from datasets by combining evaluation functions and not using training data. Since neural networks are known to be able to approximate arbitrary functions [5], This allowed the incorporation of the evaluation function into the model without rewriting it in a back-propagatable method.

3   Directional Generative Networks (DGN)

Model Structure. The model structure of DGN is shown in Fig. 1. G: Generator, is neural network-based model that generates SMILES [18] with one-hot encoding. The input of G has two parts: a few initial atoms that are randomly generated and a mask based on the atom number of the molecule. F_0 is a function that takes x, the generated SMILES as input, and returns the SMILES with the grammatically incorrect parentheses and ring numbers corrected as output. F_1 is a function that include the RDKit [14] module, an open source toolkit for chemical informatics. F_1 takes the generated SMILES as input and returns the QES, SAS, and logP measurements. These measurements are described in Sect. 4. Two methods based on domain knowledge were used in DGN: masking the positions of sequences that exceed the required number of atoms by a factor of 0 and using the function F_0 to convert them into a form suitable for the SMILES grammar.

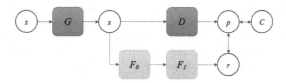

Fig. 1. DGN Structure. G, D: Estimator of Calculation model D receives x, the generated SMILES as input. D learns with the output of $F_1(F_0(x))$ as ground truth. Thus, the output of D gradually close the output of $F_1(F_0(x))$. When learning G, the weights of D are fixed when updating the weights of G. c is constant for the target measured values as ground truth.

GANs or GANs-lile models are known to be challenging to train. Without careful tuning of hyperparameters, they can easily cause mode collapse [15]. This study did not use graph convolutional networks (GCNs) [12,13] to use data representation by strings in SMILES notation. To make easier tuning of hyperparameters, U-net [17] and self-attention [16] were commonly used for the central part of the DGN's generator G, and estimator D as shown in Fig. 2. D receive x, the generated SMILES. D is trained with the output of r, $F_1(F_0(x))$ as ground truth. Thus, p, the output of D gradually approaches the output of $F_1(F_0(x))$. In other words, if D had trained enough, it acts as an approximate function of $F_1(F_0(x))$. The weights of D are fixed when updating the weights of G. c is constant target values and desired molecular features. For example, if you want 0.6 for the QED value of the molecule to be generated, set 0.6 at the corresponding position in C (Fig. 2).

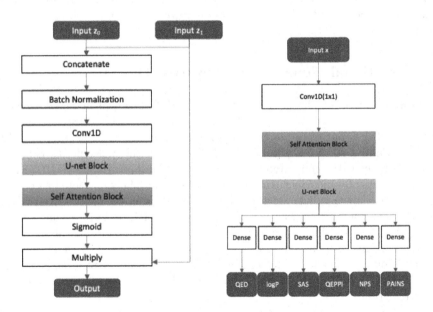

Fig. 2. Models in DGN; The lefthand is the Generator, and the righthand is the Estimator. They both contain a U-net block and a Self-Attention block. The degree of freedom of the generator's input is tuned as a hyperparameter. The generator's output is a molecule represented with a one-hot encoding array as SMILES. The output becomes input of the estimater. The estimator is a regression model. Therefore, the last layers do not have activation functions.

Data Representation. In DGN, the following list of SMILES [18] elements has been used.

```
['C', 'N', 'O', 'C=', 'N=', 'O=', 'C1', 'C2', 'C3',
'N1', 'N2', 'N3', 'C(', 'N(', 'C1(', 'C2(', 'C3(',
'N1(', 'N2(', 'N3(' ]
```

Table 1. Data representation examples; the lefthand is the input example, and the lefthand is the output one. Each row represents the index of the token list; each column represents the order of atoms in the generated molecule. The degree of freedom explained in Sect. 4 is 38 (=2by19) in the input example. The number of atoms in a generated molecule is randomly generated in the input. In this example, the number of atoms is eight. The first two atoms are randomly generated, and the rest are not yet determined as input. The output is multiplied by the input at the last layer in the generator.

token index		0	1	2	3	4	5	6	7	8	...	62	63		0	1	2	3	4	5	6	7	8	...	62	63
C	0	0	0	1	1	1	1	1	1	0	...	0	0		0	0	1	0.2	0.9	0.8	0.3	0.3	0	...	0	0
N	1	0	0	1	1	1	1	1	1	0	...	0	0		0	0	0.1	0.3	0.7	0.7	0.4	0.6	0	...	0	0
O	2	1	0	1	1	1	1	1	1	0	...	0	0		0.4	0	0.2	0.1	0	0	0.2	0.2	0	...	0	0
C=	3	0	0	1	1	1	1	1	1	0	...	0	0		0	0	0.2	0.3	0.1	0.1	0.3	0.3	0	...	0	0
N=	4	0	0	1	1	1	1	1	1	0	...	0	0		0	0	0.2	0.9	0.4	0.4	0.1	0.1	0	...	0	0
O=	5	0	0	1	1	1	1	1	1	0	...	0	0		0	0	0.6	0.3	0.3	0.4	0.4	0		...	0	0
C1	6	0	1	1	1	1	1	1	1	0	...	0	0		0	0.7	0.4	0.2	0.5	0.5	0.9	0.1	0	...	0	0
C2	7	0	0	1	1	1	1	1	1	0	...	0	0		0	0	0.4	0.2	0.3	0.3	0.4	0.4	0	...	0	0
⋮		⋮	⋮	⋮	⋮	⋮	⋮	⋮	⋮	⋮		⋮	⋮		⋮	⋮	⋮	⋮	⋮	⋮	⋮	⋮	⋮		⋮	⋮
C3(	16	0	0	1	1	1	1	1	1	0	...	0	0		0	0	0.5	0.6	0.5	0.5	0.4	0.4	0	...	0	0
N1(	17	0	0	1	1	1	1	1	1	0	...	0	0		0	0	0.4	0.6	0.5	0.5	0.2	0.2	0	...	0	0
N2(	18	0	0	1	1	1	1	1	1	0	...	0	0		0	0	0.4	0.6	0.1	0.1	0.1	0.1	0	...	0	0
N3(	19	0	0	1	1	1	1	1	1	0	...	0	0		0	0	0.2	0.2	0.4	0.4	0.1	0.1	0	...	0	0

SMILES: O C1 C N= C C C1 N

SMILES stands for Simplified molecular-input line-entry system. C, N, O, and F stand for carbon, nitrogen, oxygen, and fluorine, respectively. The character "=" means a double bond between atoms. Hydrogen is included in the generated molecules but is not explicitly indicated. Parentheses denote branches, and numbers indicate the starting and ending points of the ring. Parentheses are used in pairs, and the ring number's occurrences must be even. However, unclosed parentheses can occur, and the number of occurrences of the ring number can be odd. Therefore, a method to easily obtain a grammatically correct sequence of SMILES tokens has been proposed by O'Boyle N et al. [20].

A one-hot encoding representation that draws the index of the above list was used. An example of input data for DGN is shown in Table 1 lefthand. The righthand in Table 1 is an example of generator output, one-hot encoding SMILES.

Evaluation Functions. In the training phase of DGN, evaluation functions, F_0 and F_1, are used to prepare minibatch. The procedure of f_0 is shown in Algorithm 1. During the preparation of minibatch, F_0 converts generated x to string s. In s, the parentheses in even-numbers are replaced with the righthand parenthesis to be paired. If the last parentheses are odd-numbered, the last one is omitted. The aim is to increase the probability of SMILES grammar correctness. Then, s is tried to convert the Mol object of RdKit, m. If s is successfully converted, F_0 returns m. Otherwise, F_0 returns $error$, and the x is discarded.

The procedure of f_1 is shown in Algorithm 2. F_1 calculates six measurements described later, with input m. The measurements are normalized QED qed, normalized logP $logP$, normalized SAS sas, normalized QEPPI $qeppi$, normalized NPS nps, and normalized PAINS $pains$. This function f_1 returns them.

f_0 and f_1 are also used in Random Generation and Evolutionary Algorithms at experiments in this study.

Algorithm 1. Function F_0 Procedure

1: Input array x
2: Convert x to String s
3: Replace even-numbered "("with")" in String s
4: **if** the last parentheses is odd-numbered **then**
5:    the last parentheses is omitted
6: **end if**
7: Try to convert s to Mol object m
8: **if** s is converted to m **then**
9:    Return m
10: **else**
11:    Return *error*
12: **end if**

Algorithm 2. Function F_1 Procedure

1: Input Mol object m
2: Calculate normalized QED *qed* with input m
3: Calculate normalized logP *logP* with input m
4: Calculate normalized SAS *sas* with input m
5: Calculate normalized QEPPI *qeppi* with input m
6: Calculate normalized NPS *nps* with input m
7: Calculate normalized PAINS *pains* with input m
8: Return list $[qed, logP, sas, qeppi, nps, pains]$

Training. The following pseudo-code 3 shows the training procedure of DGN. The hyperparameters on the training batch size are 8, the number of training iterations is 8192, and using Adam [19] optimizer with a learning rate of 10^{-5}

Algorithm 3. Training Procedure D, G

1: **for** number of iteration **do**
2:    **while** mini-batch is not filled **do**
3:       z_0, z_1: Randomly generate initial atoms and number-of-atom mask
4:       **if** $F_0(G(z_0, z_1))$ is grammatically correct in SMILES **then,**
5:          $z_0 c = z_0, z_1 c = z_1$
6:          Add the data to the mini-batch.
7:       **end if**
8:    **end while**
9:    Gathering mini-batch with size m:
10:   $\left\{ z \,|z_{0c}^{(0)}, \cdots, z_{0c}^{(m)}, z_{1c}^{(0)}, \cdots, z_{1c}^{(m)} \right\}, \left\{ x \,|G(z_{0c}^{(0)}, z_{1c}^{(0)}), \cdots, G(z_c^{(m)} z_{1c}^{(m)}) \right\}$
11:   Updating D and G with the mini-batch
12:   $\nabla_{\theta D} \left[\frac{1}{m} \sum_{k=0}^{m} [logcosh(F_1(F_0(x)), D(x))] \right.$
13:   $\nabla_{\theta G} \left[\frac{1}{m} \sum_{k=0}^{m} [logcosh(C, D(G(z)))] \right.$
14: **end for**

for G Generator, 10^{-4} for D Estimator of Calculation model. F_0 is a function that takes x, a generated SMILES, as an argument and returns the Mol object of RDKit as output. Here, x, a one-hot encoding, is converted to a SMILES string as an index of the SMILES elements list. The last parenthesis is eliminated if the number of parentheses in the SMILES string is odd. If the number of ring numbers in the SMILES string is odd, the last number is also eliminated. Also, the even-numbered left parenthesis is converted to a right parenthesis.

F_1 is a function that returns the values of QED, SAS, $logP$, $QEPPI$, NPS and $PAINS$ described in Sect. 4 with Mol object of RDKit output by F_0 as an argument. Three measurements, QED, SAS, and $logP$, are normalized using code provided by the authors of MolGAN [10].

The function $logcosh$ at operation 12 and 13 in the Algorithm 3 is defined in Eq. (1).

$$logcosh(p, y) = \log\left(\frac{e^{p-y} + e^{-p+y}}{2}\right) \tag{1}$$

As the two models cooperate, they gradually approach the desired solution. As the prediction accuracy of the computational results around the search area improves, more favorable molecules will be generated.

Even if the function F_0 or F_1 were not differentiable, $D(x)$ could approximate $F_1(F_0(x))$ as a differentiable function. The generator, G, is trained with the error between the constant values c and the output r of $F_1(F_0)$. After a sufficient number of iterations, The generator G outputs $G(z_c)$ such that the output r of $F_1(F_0)$ is sufficiently close to c. In other words, the outputs to be generated can be directionally learned by giving constants as their targets.

4   Experimental Details

Random generation, EA, and DGN were compared as unsupervised learning. As a reference, ORGAN and MolGAN were compared as supervised learning methods.

We also confirmed the degree of freedom (DOF) affection. The DOF means the variety of input arrays of the generator model in DGN.

Measurements. The measurements of this experiment are as follows:

- **Validity** indicates the percentage of the generated SMILES that returned 0 in the function F_0. In other words, for molecules converted to Rdkit [14] Mol objects, we consider them to be grammatically correct SMILES and show the percentage of them.
- **Diversity** indicates the ratio of the number of molecules remaining after eliminating duplicates to the number of molecules generated.
- **QED** stands for Quantitative Estimate of Druglikeliness [21]. QED uses the following eight descriptors to quantify "drug-likeness". Molecular Weight (MW), logP, number of hydrogen bond donors (HBDs), number of hydrogen bond acceptors (HBAs), polar surface area (PSA), rotatable bonds (ROTBs),

number of aromatic rings (AROMs), and number of structural alerts to avoid as a drug (ALERTS).

- **SAS** stands for synthetic accessibility score [23]. SAS rates ease of synthesis on a scale of 1 to 10 based on frequency of occurrence and complexity. We used normalized values from 0 to 1.
- **logP** is the predicted octanol/water partition coefficient and is used for estimating fat solubility [22].
- **Sum_3** is a sum of normalized QED, SAS, and logP.
- **QEPPI** is stands for Quantitative Estimate of Protein-Protein Interaction [26]. It is targeting Drug-likeness.
- **NPS** is stands for Natural Product-likeliness Score [27].
- **PAINS** is derived from New substructure filters for removal of pan assay interference compounds [28].
- **Sum_6** is a sum of normalized QED, SAS, logP, QEPPI, NPS, and PAINS.

For QED, SAS, logP, QEPPI, NPS, and PAINS, these values are normalized to values between 0 and 1. To standardize QED, SAS, and logP, we used the module provided by the authors of MolGAN [10].

4.1   Comparison

Random generation and EA are compared with DGN. The number of atoms ranges from 8 to 32 in the experiment. Hydrogen is not included in the number of atoms.

Random Generation. For a random generation, random numbers are used to generate indices for the list of atoms listed in the data representation above. In each experiment, 10000 molecules are generated in SMILES format for each number of atoms. The number of molecules generated is 250000. The procedure is shown in Algorithm 4. F_0 and F_1 are the same as DGN and are used to obtain the measurements. Molecules that cannot be converted to Rdkit's Mol objects are considered invalid.

Algorithm 4. Random Generation Procedure

1: **for** Number of atoms range **do**
2:     **for** number of iteration **do**
3:         z: Generate random array with uniform distribution
4:         Calculate $F_1(F_0(z))$
5:     **end for**
6: **end for**

Evolutionary Algorithm. In this comparison, we used the simplest Evolutionary Algorithm(EA) presented by Bäck. T. [4]. The algorithm is shown in Algorithm 5. In EA, if the SMILES grammar of the generated molecule is correct, the score of the generated molecule is computed with the function $F_1(F_0(x))$;

if the grammar is incorrect, $F_1(F_0(x))$ returns 0, and the difference between that value and the desired score c is calculated as fitness. As the configuration of EA, the number of generations is from 10 to 40. The best molecules were obtained in smiles format for each atomic number ranging from 8 to 32. The number of molecules obtained is 750 for the experiment. The number of individuals in the population is 64. The crossover probability is 0.9. And the probability of an individual mutating is 0.1. As normalized targets, QED is 0.8, SAS is 0.9, logP is 1.0, QEPPI is 0.6, NPS is 0.9, and PAIN is 1. The measurements of the molecules generated in each step and the mean squared error (MSE) of the target were calculated. Based on the MSE, the individual with the best fit was allowed to survive as the next generation.

The function *mse* at operation 10 in the Algorithm 5 stands for mean squared error.

Algorithm 5. Evolutionary Algorithm Procedure

1: **for** Number of atoms range **do**
2:    **for** number of population **do**
3:        Generate x as individuals with uniform distribution for initial *population*
4:    **end for**
5:    evaluate *population*
6:    $fitness = mse(F_1(F_0(x)), c)$
7:    **for** number of generation **do**
8:        Apply crossover and mutation on the *population*
9:        evaluate *population*
10:        $fitness = mse(F_1(F_0(x)), c)$
11:        Select individuals from *population* based on the *fitness* as next generation
12:    **end for**
13:    Get individual with the best result x_{best}
14:    Calculate $F_1(F_0(x_{best}))$
15: **end for**

DGN. As a verification phase of the DGN, a randomly generated input is given to the Generator, G. The number of initial atoms in the generator's input is two as DOF. In each experiment, 100 molecules were generated in SMILES format for each number of atoms. The number of molecules obtained is 2500. As in the training phase, the list shown in data representation in Sect. 3 generated the molecules. If the generated molecule was parsable, QED, SAS, LogP, QEPPI, NPS, and PAINS were calculated with $F_1(F_0(G(z_0, z_1)))$ as shown in Algorithm 6 The target of measurements is the same as the target of EA.

Algorithm 6. DGN Validation Procedure

1: **for** Number of atoms range **do**
2:     **for** number of iteration **do**
3:         z_0, z_1: Randomly generate initial atoms and number-of-atom mask
4:         **if** $F_0(G(z_0, z_1))$ is parsable **then**
5:             Calculate $F_1(F_0(G(z_0, z_1)))$
6:         **end if**
7:     **end for**
8: **end for**

Result. A comparison of the molecules generated by unsupervised learning (Random, EA, DGN) and supervised learning (MolGAN, ORGAN) is shown in Table 2. The QED, SAS, logP, QEPPI, NPS, and PAINS in the table are the mean of the generated molecule values. ORGAN, MolGAN, and MolGAN(QM9) results were obtained from the Objective ALL row of Table 2 from the original paper [10]. QED corresponds to Druglikeliness, SAS to Synthesizability, logP to Solubility, QEPPI to Quantitative Estimate of Protein-Protein Interaction, NPS to Natural Product-likeliness Score, and PAINS to pan assay interference compounds. Sum3 in the table is the sum of the QED mean, SAS mean, and logP mean. Sum6 is the sum of QED mean, SAS mean, logP mean, QEPPI mean, NPS mean, and PAINS mean.

Table 2. In the results table, QED corresponds to Druglikeliness, SAS to Synthesizability, logP to Solubility, QEPPI to Quantitative Estimate of Protein-Protein Interaction, NPS to Natural Product-likeliness Score, and PAINS to pan assay interference compounds. *1: Div; diversity is the remaining ratio after eliminating duplicates and is uniqueness that is not included in training data at ORGAN and MolGAN. *2: based on MolGAN paper [10]. *3: Sum3 is the sum of QED, SAS, and logP. *4: Sum6 is the sum of QED, SAS, logP, QEPPI, NPS, and PAINS. *5: The original QM9 dataset contains 133885 molecules. Easily convertible to RdKit mol objects were 133247.

Algorithm	Sample	Validity	Div*1	QED	SAS	logP	QEPPI	NPS	PAINS	sum3*3	sum6*4
Random	250000	0.10	1.00	0.35	0.02	0.09	0.14	0.53	0.93	0.47	2.08
GA	750	1.00	0.99	0.64	0.39	0.67	0.23	0.59	1.00	1.70	3.51
DGN	2500	0.97	0.18	0.43	0.65	0.91	0.12	0.55	1.00	1.99	**3.66**
DGNr	2500	0.09	1.00	0.39	0.04	0.14	0.16	0.54	0.92	0.56	2.18
ORGAN*2	6400	96.1	0.89*1	0.52	0.71	0.53	–	–	–	1.76*3	–
MolGAN*2	6400	97.4	0.02*1	0.47	0.84	0.65	–	–	–	1.96*3	–
MolGAN (QM9)*2	6400	98.0	0.02*1	0.51	0.82	0.69	–	–	–	2.02*3	–
QM9	133247*5	1.00	1.00	0.46	0.22	0.28	0.14	0.60	0.99	0.96	2.69

For each unsupervised learning method, the distribution of the score, the sum of QED, SAS, logP, QEPPI, NPS, and PAINS at each number of atoms is shown in Fig. 3 as a kernel density estimate. The EA and DGN scores are higher than the randomly generated ones for all atomic numbers. The scores of EA and DGN are close. However, for EA, the scores tend to decrease as the number of atoms increases, as shown in Fig. 3 and Fig. 4. The increase in the number of atoms means an increase in the number of combinatorial patterns and the complexity of the problem. The increased complexity makes it difficult for a random choice algorithm such as EA to obtain good scores for individuals with mutation and crossover in the next generation. DGN, on the other hand, can obtain relatively high scores even as the number of atoms increases.

This is due to the difference in search strategies between EA and DGN. EA is always hopping in the search space. DGN is trained by gradient descent. Perhaps DGN tends not to escape local minimum in narrow search space with steep parts. DGN can consistently gradually decent to a favorable area in vast search space, although GA tends not to obtain a desirable solution due to combinatorial explosion.

Images of generated molecules are show in Figs. 5, 6, and 7. Randomly generated molecules have a higher complexity than the others. For EA, molecules become more complex as the number of atoms increases. For DGN, many are relatively simple even as the number of atoms increases (Fig. 4).

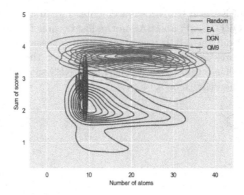

Fig. 3. The kernel density estimation of the score distribution according to the number of molecules. The x-axis is the number of atoms in the generated molecules. The y-axis is the sum of QED, SAS, logP, QEPPI, NPS, and PAINS. Blue is random generation, orange is EA, and green is DGN. Red is not generated but is a direct calculation of the original QM9 dataset for reference. Random scores were lower than the others. As the number of atoms increases, the score decreases. EA scores generally well, but performance declines as the number of atoms increases. DGN performs well, and performance does not decrease as the number of atoms increases. (Color figure online)

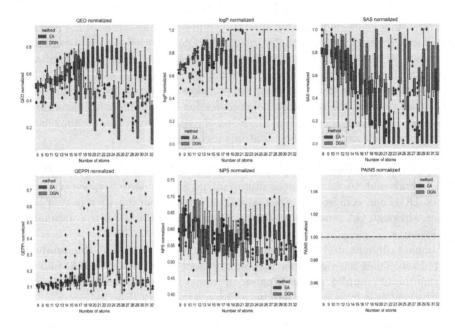

Fig. 4. Comparison of EA and DGN measurements. The first row, from the left to the right column, shows QED, LogP, and SAS normalized scores for each number of atoms. On the second row, from the left to the right column, these show QEPPI, NPS, and PAINS normalized scores for each number of atoms. For the molecules with a large number of atoms, EA has better QED, QEPPI, and NPS scores than DGN, but DGN is superior to EA in the other scores.

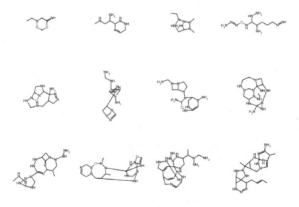

Fig. 5. Molecular examples that ramdomly generated. (number of atoms excluding hydrogen, 8–32). Many molecules have complex shapes.

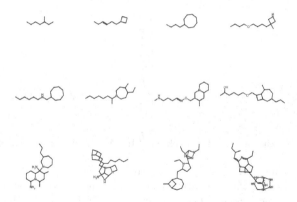

Fig. 6. Generated molecular examples with EA, duplicates are eliminated. (number of atoms excluding hydrogen, 8–32). Molecules with a small number of atoms are often simple. Molecules with more than 20 atoms have more complex shapes.

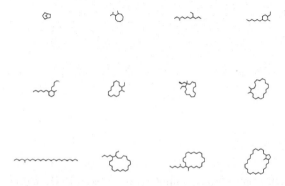

Fig. 7. Generated molecular examples with DGN, duplicates are eliminated. (number of atoms excluding hydrogen, 8–32). Molecules are often simple. Even when the number of atoms exceeds 20, they maintain their simple shapes.

4.2   Degree of Freedom (DOF) of DGN Input

The DOF means the variety of input arrays of the generator model in DGN.

DGN(DOF=38(=2by19)) and DGNr(DOF=1216(=64by19)) are compared. As a result, in table 2 and score distribution in Fig. 9, the scores of DGNr are much lower than DGN. It is almost the same as random generation. However, Div: diversity of DGNr is greater than DGN. During training, loss values of DGNr are greater than DGN in Fig. 8. It clearly shows that DGNr needs to be better trained.

According to these results, DOF affects the convergence ability of training and the diversity of products. It is a trade-off. You might have to determine DOF depending on the complexity of the problem to solve.

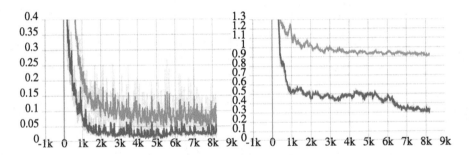

Fig. 8. Comparison of time-history of loss values during training; The lefthand is the loss value transition of the estimation model. The righthand is the loss value transition of the combined model. The blue line is DGN(DOF=38), the orange one is DGNr(DOF=1216(=64by19)). DGNr is difficult to converge. (Color figure online)

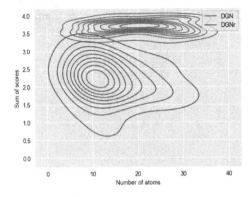

Fig. 9. Comparison to Sum6 score between DGN and DGNr

5   Conclusion

The results of this study suggest that DGN without datasets can generate molecules with features comparable to models from supervised learning, even with a problem for six measurements. In general, the dataset used for training is smaller than the search space, and the features obtained by the dataset do not necessarily encompass the desired solution. Suppose the function that evaluates the generated object, in this study, the evaluation of the molecule by F_0 and F_1, satisfies the necessary and sufficient conditions. In that case, the DGN can function as an excellent generator. A similar method is EA, but EA's performance degrades as the complexity of the problem increases due to combinatorial explosion. On the other hand, DGN can asymptotically approach the solution by gradient descent even when the problem is complex and thus is more likely to produce a good solution than EA. Since preparing datasets for training is still expensive, DGNs can effectively complement conventional supervised learning.

As a disadvantage of DGN, the evaluation function, e.g., $F_1(F_0(x))$ in this study, is often simpler than in reality. If the evaluation function satisfies the

necessary conditions but not the sufficient conditions, the output of the DGN
may be biased. Therefore, when using DGNs, applying appropriate constraints
based on domain knowledge to the input data or model is desirable.

For future research, it is necessary to devise a data representation less prone
to stagnation near the local optimum. Increasing the input degrees of freedom is
necessary to obtain various solutions in GAN-like models. However, high input
degrees of freedom have the side effect of making learning convergence more difficult. By considering data representations that can maintain appropriate outputs, such as grammatical correctness, we expect to achieve diverse outputs and
learning convergence, even with various inputs.

References

1. Polishchuk, P.G., Madzhidov, T.I., Varnek, A.: Estimation of the size of drug-
   like chemical space based on GDB-17 data. J. Comput.-Aided Mol. Design **27**(8),
   675–679 (2013). https://doi.org/10.1007/s10822-013-9672-4
2. Rester, U.: From virtuality to reality - virtual screening in lead discovery and lead
   optimization: a medicinal chemistry perspective. Curr. Opin. Drug Discov. Dev.
   11(4), 559–568 (2008)
3. Holland, J.H.: Adaptation in Natural and Artificial Systems: An Introductory
   Analysis with Applications to Biology, Control and Artificial Intelligence. The University of Michigan Press (1975). ISBN-10-0472084607
4. Bäck, T., Fogel, D., Michalewicz, Z. (eds.): Evolutionary Computation 1: Basic
   Algorithms and Operators. Institute of Physics Publishing, Bristol (2000)
5. Goodfellow, I., Bengio, Y., Courville, A.: Deep Learning. MIT Press (2016). http://
   www.deeplearningbook.org/ Accessed 19 Sept 2021
6. Sheridan, R.P., Kearsley, S.K.: Why do we need so many chemical similarity search
   methods? Drug Discov. Today **7**(17), 903–911 (2002). https://doi.org/10.1016/
   s1359-6446(02)02411-x
7. Lee, Y., Choi, G., Yoon, M., Kim, C.: Genetic algorithm for constrained molecular
   inverse design (2021)
8. Kingma, D., Welling, M.: Auto-encoding variational bayes (2013)
9. Goodfellow, I., et al.: Generative adversarial networks (2014)
10. De Cao, N., Kipf, T.: MolGAN: an implicit generative model for small molecular
    graphs. In: ICML 2018 Workshop on Theoretical Foundations and Applications
    of Deep Generative Models (2018). https://github.com/nicola-decao/MolGAN.
    Accessed 1 Jan 2023
11. Guimaraes, G., Sanchez-Lengeling, B., Outeiral, C., Farias, P., Aspuru-Guzik, A.:
    Objective-reinforced generative adversarial networks (ORGAN) for sequence gen-
    eration models (2017)
12. Kipf, T., Welling, M.: Semi-supervised classification with graph convolutional net-
    works (2016)
13. Simonovsky, M., Komodakis, N.: Dynamic edge-conditioned filters in convolutional
    neural networks on graphs (2017)
14. Landrum, G.: Rdkit Open source toolkit for cheminformatics (2006). https://www.
    rdkit.org. Accessed 15 Oct 2022
15. Arjovsky, M., Bottou, L.: Towards principled methods for training generative
    adversarial networks (2017)

16. Mnih, V., Heess, N., Graves, A., Kavukcuoglu, K.: Recurrent models of visual attention (2014)
17. Ronneberger, O., Fischer, P., Brox, T.: U-net: convolutional networks for biomedical image segmentation. In: Navab, N., Hornegger, J., Wells, W.M., Frangi, A.F. (eds.) MICCAI 2015. LNCS, vol. 9351, pp. 234–241. Springer, Cham (2015). https://doi.org/10.1007/978-3-319-24574-4_28
18. Weininger, D.: SMILES, a chemical language and information system. 1. Introduction to methodology and encoding rules. J. Chem. Inf. Comput. Sci. **28**(1), 31–36 (1988)
19. Kingma, D., Ba, J.: Adam: a method for stochastic optimization (2014)
20. O'Boyle, N., Dalke, A.: DeepSMILES: an adaptation of SMILES for use in machine-learning of chemical structures. ChemRxiv. Cambridge Open Engage, Cambridge (2018). https://chemrxiv.org/engage/chemrxiv/article-details/60c73ed6567dfe7e5fec388d. This content is a preprint and has not been peer-reviewed
21. Bickerton, G.R., Paolini, G.V., Besnard, J., Muresan, S., Hopkins, A.L.: Quantifying the chemical beauty of drugs. Nat. Chem. **4**, 90–98 (2012)
22. Wildman, S., Crippen, G.: Prediction of physicochemical parameters by atomic contributions. J. Chem. Inf. Comput. Sci. **39**(5), 868–873 (1999)
23. Ertl, P., Schuffenhauer, A.: Estimation of synthetic accessibility score of drug-like molecules based on molecular complexity and fragment contributions. J. Cheminform. **1**(1), 8 (2009)
24. Samanta, B., De, A., Jana, G., Chattaraj, P., Ganguly, N., Gomez-Rodriguez, M.: NeVAE: a deep generative model for molecular graphs (2018)
25. Ito, Y., Nguyen, M.L.: Directional generative networks (2023). https://ssrn.com/abstract=4474512, http://dx.doi.org/10.2139/ssrn.4474512
26. Kosugi, T., Ohue, M.: Quantitative estimate of protein-protein interaction targeting drug-likeness. In: 2021 IEEE Conference on Computational Intelligence in Bioinformatics and Computational Biology (CIBCB), pp. 1–8. IEEE (2021)
27. Ertl, P., Roggo, S., Schuffenhauer, A.: Natural product-likeness score and its application for prioritization of compound libraries. J. Chem. Inf. Model. **48**(1), 68–74 (2008)
28. Baell, J.B., Holloway, G.A.: New substructure filters for removal of pan assay interference compounds (PAINS) from screening libraries and for their exclusion in bioassays. J. Med. Chem. **53**(7), 2719–2740 (2010)

Reference Classification Using BERT Models to Support Scientific-Document Writing

Ryoma Hosokawa[1]([✉])([iD]), Junji Yamato[1], Ryuichiro Higashinaka[2], Genichiro Kikui[1], and Hiroaki Sugiyama[2]

[1] Kogakuin University, Tokyo, Japan
em22020@g.kogakuin.jp
[2] NTT Corporation, Tokyo, Japan

Abstract. We are presently developing a document clustering method to group reference papers based on semantic similarity to support the writing of scientific papers by organizing the citations more appropriately. Currently, no dataset can be used for clustering experiments and evaluations for this purpose. In this study, we created two datasets of papers and corresponding references from PMC, an online medical paper archive. Then we performed clustering of the reference papers based on their abstracts using BERT, BioBERT, SciBERT and PubMedBERT. In this case, we input the number of clusters for clustering. Clustering by BERT-based models trained on the similarity of pairs of references was more accurate than clustering by embedding the abstracts of references in each BERT model. Moreover, the trained BERT-based models had a clustering accuracy better or comparable to human experts. In addition, we predicted the number of clusters that used information from the references. The prediction accuracy for the number of clusters was about 40%. Evaluation measures for the clustering results are also discussed.

Keywords: Classification · Clustering · Natural Language Processing (NLP) · Neural Networks · Text Classification · Transformer · Word Embedding

1 Introduction

The number of scientific papers continues to increase rapidly. As the number of authors increases, so does the number of people seeking support with paper writing. As a result, research to support the writing of scientific papers has become increasingly important [1]. Paper summarization [2], citation recommendation [3], and generation of citation text tasks [4] have been reported.

Narimatsu et al. [5] were the first to present the big picture of scientific writing support and summarize the necessary tasks for each research stage.

This paper addresses the "citation categorization task" defined by Narimatsu et al. [5]. According to Narimatsu et al., tasks to support scientific paper writing include citation extraction tasks, citation worthiness tasks, citation allocation

M. Bono et al. (Eds.): JSAI-isAI 2023 Workshops, LNAI 14644, pp. 167–183, 2024.
https://doi.org/10.1007/978-3-031-60511-6_11

tasks, citation recommendation for sentence tasks, and citation categorization tasks. Of these tasks, the citation categorization task has the highest priority in terms of being researched because it is related to other tasks and has not yet been reported. This task facilitates writing-related work sections by categorizing each reference into an appropriate cluster when a set of reference papers is given so that the citations can be more appropriately organized.

This task will be combined with the two subtasks that follow. There are citation sentence generation tasks and citation text generation tasks. This group of tasks aims to generate related work sections automatically. The citation categorization task assumes a situation in which a group of citations is given, and support is needed for beginners writing scientific papers.

To accomplish the citation categorization task, we need a dataset showing the correspondence between a paper and which references papers are cited in the paper's related work section. However, no dataset shows these correspondences. Therefore, we created two separate datasets for this study and evaluated two methods with three BERT models. We also compared the clustering results with those of human experts.

In this paper, we adopted four BERT-based models for the citation categorization task: BERT and three fine-tuned models for scientific vocabulary called BioBERT [12], SciBERT [13] and PubMedBERT [21]. We utilized them to vectorize the abstracts of reference papers and used their vector similarity for clustering. In addition, we also fine-tuned the BERT models to calculate the similarity between a pair of papers by learning whether each pair of reference papers appears in the same paragraph of the citing papers in a related work section. We then clustered the references based on their similarity by k-means or hierarchical clustering.

We collected the papers from Pub Med Central (PMC) and listed the reference papers cited as related work in the "background" sections of the citing papers. We utilized references cited in one paragraph as one cluster. Specifically, the clustering problem is defined as performing clustering on all the papers cited in the background section of one paper based on a similarity measure of the cited papers. We then evaluated the correctness of the clustering by comparing it with the actual groups corresponding to paragraphs of the background section. Note that to perform BERT-based clustering, we use only the abstracts of the reference papers as the max length of the tokens of the BERT models is restricted. In this study, the number of clusters was given when clustering the reference papers. As an additional experiment, we predicted the number of clusters from the information in reference papers.

Our research questions are as follows.

– RQ1: Does fine-tuning BERT-based models contribute to the clustering performance?
– RQ2: Do BERT models achieve better clustering than humans with abstract information?

To answer these, we constructed two datasets from the PubMed archive (Sect. 3) and conducted two experiments to evaluate the clustering performances (Sect. 4).

2   Related Work

Much has already been done to support writing for scientific documentation. Citation sentence generation, citation context classification, cited text identification, citation recommendation, and multi-label classification of scientific documentation have already been researched [16–19]. Arita's study proposed citation sentence generation based on sentences in the citing paper and the cited papers [16]. These studies have been particularly advanced in recent years.

For the citation categorization task, TF-IDF-based methods have been standard [6] for years, but Transformer-based models such as BERT [7] and XLNet [8] have recently delivered outstanding accuracy in a variety of NLP tasks. BERT models have demonstrated excellent performance with document clustering tasks as well [9–11]. However, these prior studies have not targeted scientific documents. Therefore, we conducted a clustering of scientific papers. In the clustering of conventional methods for scientific papers, the clustering was performed based on citation networks [20]. The aim of this study is to perform clustering based on the semantic similarity of abstracts in papers. Since datasets for the clustering of scientific papers have not been constructed, we built datasets composed of scientific papers. Moreover, we evaluated the clustering performance for references.

We made the BERT models vectorize the abstracts of the references. We also let the BERT models learn the abstracts of the references that appeared in pairs for each cluster. Then, based on the learning, we calculated the similarity of the pairs of references in papers used for testing. Using that information, we used k-means or hierarchical clustering to cluster the references. We then predicted the number of clusters and envisioned what actual scientific documentation support would look like. Comparisons were also made with the result of reference clustering done by human experts to demonstrate validity. We also discuss an evaluation measure for the clustering results. In future work, we will work with other tasks to support scientific documentation writing.

3   Creation of Datasets

We obtained paper data from PMC, an online medical article archive, to build datasets with different search queries for the clustering experiments. PMC has data from many papers. Moreover, we can get that data in XML format. Accordingly, we can quickly analyze the data. Also, in this archive, there are many past papers. Thus, we considered it likely that we could obtain all the references as well.

For this purpose, PMC was selected as the paper archive. First, we collected 194,787 papers retrieved using the query words "artificial intelligence," "deep learning," or "image recognition." The papers thus collected were set as Dataset 1.

Second, we collected 137,998 papers retrieved using the query word "echocardiography." The papers thus collected were set as Dataset 2. The reason for the multiple queries for the first set of collected papers was to ensure that the number of papers was sufficient. We chose echocardiography because we will use our laboratory as a model case. In this study, it was necessary to target papers in the medical field to serve as a model case for the research areas of related topics being pursued by the authors.

Among these obtained papers, we eliminated papers whose type was "case report" to extract research articles. Case reports are common among medical papers. Case reports and other documents were eliminated from the datasets because they were deemed to have a different structure than the scientific papers intended for this study. In addition, we extracted those that begin with the background section (which is supposed to include related work information). For this reason, papers beginning with an introduction section instead of a background one were eliminated. For medical papers, the related work section is often described in the background section. In addition, we then selected only papers written in English. This process resulted in 12,178 papers for Dataset 1 and 7,599 for Dataset 2.

Figure 1 shows an example of a background section. We extracted each paragraph from the reference papers. Table 1 shows an example entry from Dataset 1, which includes three paragraphs in a background section citing 14 papers.

We obtained an abstract from PubMed for each reference in the papers we obtained. Unfortunately, not all of these papers could be used for our clustering experiments because some of the reference papers were missing in PubMed, and we could not obtain the abstracts. If we eliminated papers with at most one reference paper missing, the dataset would be too small; therefore, we decided to allow for two missing references as a compromise. We also eliminated papers with only one paragraph in the background section because the number of clusters has to be more than one to perform the clustering properly.

As a result, the final number of papers for Datasets 1 and 2 was 2,752 and 3,890, respectively. This selection process is summarized in Table 2. We generated 768-dimension vectors from the reference abstracts of these papers using the

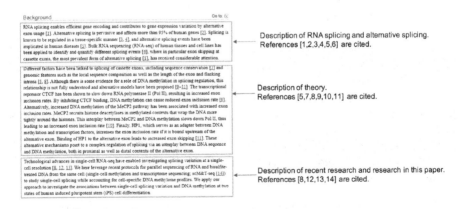

Fig. 1. Example of paragraph content and reference groups.

Table 1. Example of entry in the Dataset 1.

Paper ID	PMC6371455
Paragraph 1	[1,2,3,4,5,6]
Paragraph 2	[5,7,8,9,10,11]
Paragraph 3	[8,12,13,14]
Reference #1–#14	12626338, 23258890, 22909801, 20573213, 25525159, 18688268, 27717327, 28655331, 21964334, 23938295, 25704815, 28673540, 26740580, 26752769

The number in reference represents the PMID.

Table 2. Number of data per condition in the dataset.

	Dataset 1	Dataset 2
Query	Artificial intelligence OR Deep learning OR Image recognition	Echocardiography
Number of retrieved papers	194,787	137,998
Articles that are [research-article] AND Include a [background] section	12,178	7,998
Cluster number ≥ 2 AND Missing references <2	2,752	3,890

BERT, BioBERT, SciBERT, and PubMedBERT models. The tokenizer used during the pre-trained of each model was used to convert the abstract sentences into tokens. The BERT models have an upper limit on the length that can be converted into tokens. Therefore, we entered the longest possible abstract text into the BERT models. We vectorized the abstract for clustering references.

4 Methods

We conducted three experiments in this study. The first and second experiments used a given number of clusters. The first experiment regarded a clustering method that utilizes vectors of the abstracts of the references. The second experiment used the similarity learned from whether each pair of reference papers appears in the same paragraph of the citing paper. The similarity was defined as the reciprocal of the distance between references. The third experiment predicted the number of clusters.

4.1 Clustering Method

Four clustering methods were used: k-means, hierarchical clustering, x-means, and VBGMM (Variational Bayesian Gaussian Mixture Model). In this study, the k-means method and hierarchical clustering were given a number of clusters.

- *k-means method:*
  The k-means method is a basic clustering algorithm. First, the center of gravity of each cluster is set randomly. Then, for each dataset, the distance from the center of gravity of each cluster is calculated and assigned to the cluster with the closest distance. The above process is performed until the clusters to be assigned no longer change.
- *Hierarchical clustering:*
  Hierarchical clustering is a basic clustering algorithm. We used bottom-up hierarchical clustering. First, each piece of data is assigned to a cluster. Then, data that are close in distance to each other are merged into a single cluster. The above process is performed until the data are combined into a single cluster. Then, based on the generated dendrogram, we assign the data to an appropriate number of clusters.
- *X-means method:*
  The x-means method is an extension of the k-means method proposed by Dau [15]. This method allows for the prediction of clusters without giving the number of clusters. This is a significant difference from the k-means method. First, the k-means method is run with a small number of clusters to predict the number of clusters. Then, it is performed within the created clusters with k set to 2, and the clusters are divided. If the Bayesian Information Criterion (BIC) value increases, the clusters are split, and the number of clusters increases. The above process involves predicting the number of clusters by increasing the number of clusters from a small value.
- *VBGMM:*
  The VBGMM (Variational Bayesian Gaussian Mixture) is a clustering method for cases where the number of clusters is unknown. This method is an application of Variational Bayes to the Gaussian Mixture Model. This method assumes multiple Gaussian distributions, and clustering is performed by determining which Gaussian distribution each element belongs to. The Gaussian distribution is updated until convergence based on the input data.

4.2   Evaluation Measures

We used purity, pairwise F1, and pairwise accuracy to evaluate the clustering accuracy. Purity is known as a simple and transparent evaluation measure [14]. Equations (1) and (2) were used to calculate the purity, where N is the number of elements in a cluster, C_i is each generated cluster, and A_j is the cluster of correct answers.

In calculating pairwise F1 and pairwise accuracy, true positive is the number of correct reference pairs, not the number of elements, of reference pairs belonging to the same cluster.

$$\text{purity} = \sum_i \frac{|C_i|}{N} \max_j \text{Precision}(C_i, A_j) \tag{1}$$

$$\text{Precision}(C, A) = \frac{|C \cap A|}{|C|} \tag{2}$$

Purity is used in this study as the evaluation measure for clustering. This is a measure whose value varies depending on the correspondence between the clusters predicted and the clusters of correct answers. Therefore, when evaluating the clustering results in this study, all patterns of correspondence between the clusters created and the clusters of correct answers were calculated. The correspondence of the clusters with the best purity was then used as the clustering result.

4.3   Experiment 1: Vector-Based Clustering for Abstracts

In Experiment 1, we performed clustering on the dataset of papers created using the vectors of the abstracts of the references by the k-means method, with the number of clusters given. In this experiment, clustering was performed using three groups of vectors generated by BERT, BioBERT, and SciBERT, with each paper's abstract. The vectors of the abstracts of the references in this study came from the CLS token output of BERT.

BERT is a pre-training model with bidirectional transformers using large datasets [7]. SciBERT is a BERT model trained on 1.14 million scientific papers from Semantic Scholar [13]. BioBERT is a model trained using 4.5 billion words from paper abstracts in PubMed and 13.5 billion words from PMC papers. PubMedBERT is a model trained using abstracts from PubMed and full-text papers from PMC. PubMedBERT is distinct from other BERT models in that its vocabulary is exclusively based on PubMed. The model is trained using 3.1billion words from PubMed papers.

We utilized random clustering as a baseline for this experiment. Random clustering in this experiment refers to assigning each element such that each cluster has at least one element.

4.4   Experiment 2: Pairwise Learning Based Clustering

In Experiment 2, we used information on whether two references belong to the same cluster for training the four BERT-based models. We utilized the BERT-ForSequenceClassification[1] and prepared every combination of reference papers and a label, 1 or 0, meaning references belong to the same cluster (paragraph) or not the same cluster, respectively. BERTForSequenceClassification is a BERT model transformer with a sequence classification head on top. Figure 2 shows the sequence classification model. This allows the BERT model to classify sentences. We used the output of classification as a distance measure for clustering. In this experiment, we divided each dataset into training/validation/test sets at a ratio of 8:1:1.

For Dataset 1, 360,834 reference pairs generated from 2200 papers were used as training data, 45,754 references generated from 276 papers were used as validation data, and 276 papers were used as test data. For Dataset 2, we used 292,972 reference pairs from 3,112 papers for training data, 39,331 references

---

[1] https://huggingface.co/docs/transformers/model_doc/bert.

from 389 papers for validation data, and 389 papers for test data. Among the training data, 38% in the Dataset 1 and 42% in the Dataset 2 were labeled 1. Since there was a slight bias, we introduced class weights in the training process. The percentage of class labels determined the class weights. This improved the low amount of data for label 1. Based on validation loss, a model trained for one epoch was used to predict clusters for the test data.

The value of logit output normalized by a softmax function was used as the distance between a pair of references. The distance value ranges from 0 to 1, decreasing if the two references are similar. A distance matrix was created by finding the distance between all references. The distance matrix was used to cluster the references. The k-means method and hierarchical clustering were used with the number of clusters given. We evaluated the clustering accuracy using purity and pairwise F1.

Human Experts' Performance. We compared the accuracy of the clustering results to that of human experts. Collaborators with sufficient medical knowledge read the abstracts of the references and performed clustering, equivalent to the model in Experiment 2. We had them examine ten randomly selected sample papers and compare the average results of the BERT-based methods for the same ten papers. We recruited three human experts for each dataset using a crowdsourcing service[2] four under the condition of "licensed physicians or senior medical school students only."

The experimental collaborators were told the number of clusters for each paper. However, we did not give them the original reference numbers in the sample paper. This is because the referenced papers have a series of numbers, which we thought would give them a hint about clustering. Instead, we gave them a new number that we independently assigned to each referenced paper. They were asked to read the papers' abstracts and cluster them to reach a given number of clusters. In this experiment, the experts needed a long time to consider clustering. Therefore, we did not set a time limit for the clustering of each sample.

They were allowed to do it whenever they wanted, with no time or order restrictions. These reasons were to confirm the optimal clustering results by human experts. The clustering results obtained in this way were evaluated in terms of purity. These samples all contained references, and the number of clusters was given.

LLM Performance. ChatGPT 4 was used to cluster references for 10 papers. The papers used were identical to those used in the clustering experiment by human experts. We entered the abstract and number of clusters for each paper.

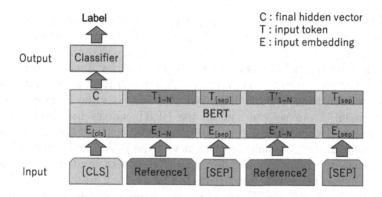

Fig. 2. Structure of BERT for sequence classification model.

4.5   Experiment 3: Predicting the Number of Clusters

In Experiment 3, we predicted the number of clusters. In the previous experiments of this study, clustering was performed with the number of clusters given. Here, the number of clusters was predicted using the following two methods. In this experiment, if the number of clusters predicted and the number of clusters of correct answers were different, we added empty sets until we had the same number of clusters.

X-Means Algorithm. For the first condition, the x-means algorithm was used. To predict the number of clusters in a paper, we used a vector of abstracts from the references used in Experiment 1, transformed by each BERT model.

The x-means method was used to determine how many clusters the vector was divided into. It was run with an initial number of clusters of 2. Hierarchical clustering was performed using the mode of the number of clusters obtained from ten runs of the x-means method and, as in Experiment 2, using the distance between references.

VBGMM Algorithm. For the second condition, we used the VBGMM algorithm to predict the number of clusters. Hierarchical clustering was then performed with the number of clusters obtained using the distance between reference papers.

5   Results

The results table shows each dataset's average value of the evaluation results. The bold type in the table indicates the maximum value of the evaluation for the dataset for each method. In Tables 9 and 10, bold type indicates the number of correct cluster predictions.

Tables 3, 4 and 5 show the clustering accuracy in the experiments. We can see that the clustering evaluation value of any of the BERT models was increased by learning pairs of references. From Table 3, we can see that the clustering result of DataSet1 by BioBERT was evaluated highly. On the other hand, we can see that the clustering result of Dataset2 by PubMedBERT was evaluated highly. As can be seen from Table 4, PubMedBERT also has the highest evaluation in Experiment 2. As we can see, all the BERT models had a higher purity and pairwise F1 than the random clustering result in Table 3 of Experiment 1. We can confirm that the pairwise accuracy of the BERT and SciBERT models is lower than the random clustering. In the results of random clustering, the number of elements in each cluster tends to take an average number. On the other hand, clustering by the BERT model results in some cases in a concentration of elements in one cluster. Pairwise evaluation tends to be lower when the cluster sizes are largely biased. As a result, the accuracy is considered to be lower than that of random clustering.

Table 6 shows the results of the cross-domain accuracy testing for each of the trained BERT models in different datasets. These results confirm that BERT, BioBERT, and PubMedBERT had higher purity when trained on Dataset 1 than when trained on Dataset 2. They also confirm that SciBERT had higher purity for the training datasets than for the different test datasets. Still, even for the different test datasets, all BERT-based models had better accuracy for purity than the random clustering of Experiment 1. The clustering accuracy was improved even when trained on a different domain than the test dataset.

Tables 7 and 8 show the clustering accuracy in Experiment 3. Table 7 confirms that the clustering results obtained with PubMedBERT had the highest purity and pairwise evaluation for Dataset 2. Table 8 confirms that the clustering results obtained with BioBERT had the highest pairwise evaluation. We can also confirm that both methods' clustering results obtained with PubMedBERT had the highest purity evaluation. Moreover, the results of Experiment 3 had better purity accuracy than the random clustering of Experiment 1.

Tables 9, and 10 show the number of correct papers and the percentage of proper papers for the number of clusters. In Tables 9 and 10, C indicates the number of correct clusters, and P indicates the number of predicted clusters. It can be seen that the number of predictions was often smaller than the number of correct answers. The results in Tables 9 and 10 also confirm that the VBGMM method was better at predicting the number of clusters. The results from the VBGMM method confirm that the prediction of the number of clusters correctly estimated by BioBERT was better. Still, the purity was lower than the other BERT models.

Table 11 shows a comparison with human clustering accuracy in terms of purity, where the human values show the average of the three human experts. The time required for one clustering task varied from person to person, ranging from 5 to 90 min. We found that there were individual differences in this task. As we can see, the results of the learned BERT models other than PubMedBERT were better than the human results for Dataset 1. In contrast, those of the humans were slightly better than SciBERT and BioBERT for Dataset 2.

In the result of Table 4, SciBERT and BioBERT also have a purity of 0.721 and 0.718, which is better than the human results. These results are based on a small number of samples, so it is difficult to say with certainty whether the performance of each domain is better or worse.

We didn't include the clustering results by ChatGPT in the table 11 as they are preliminary results. The purity of clustering results by ChatGPT was 0.627, while the average purity by humans was 0.699. This indicates that the ChatGPT clustering accuracy is lower than that of human experts. However, it is important to note that these are still preliminary results. Making definitive statements may be premature without more detailed and extensive experimental data. There is also room for improvement regarding prompts.

Table 3. Evaluation of clustering in Experiment 1.

Evaluation Measure	DS	BERT	SciBERT	BioBERT	PubMedBERT	Random
Purity	1	0.573	0.581	**0.652**	0.590	0.543
	2	0.605	0.618	0.600	**0.628**	0.578
Pairwise(F1)	1	0.367	0.364	**0.458**	0.387	0.319
	2	0.358	0.382	0.390	**0.400**	0.354
Pairwise(Accuracy)	1	0.504	0.506	**0.628**	0.583	0.516
	2	0.463	0.470	0.542	**0.555**	0.512

DS stands for dataset.

Table 4. Evaluation of clustering in Experiment 2 (purity).

Method	DS	BERT	SciBERT	BioBERT	PubMedBERT
k-means	1	0.693	0.699	**0.704**	0.692
	2	0.712	0.721	0.718	**0.722**
hierarchy	1	0.701	0.704	0.710	**0.712**
	2	0.714	0.721	0.723	**0.735**

6   Discussion

From the results of Experiment 1 in Table 3, we confirmed that the most accurate clustering for Dataset 1 was the one converted into a vector using PubMedBERT. This is presumably because PubMedBERT, a model specialized for medical vocabulary, could grasp the features of sentences better than the other three models since the paper data were medical papers from PMC. From the results of Experiment 2 in Table 4, we confirmed that the clustering accuracy was increased by learning pairs of references since the purity, accuracy, and F1 were higher than those of Experiment 1. From these results, we conclude that fine-tuning the vocabulary and domain knowledge contributed to the clustering performance to some extent (RQ1).

178   R. Hosokawa et al.

Table 5. Evaluation of clustering in Experiment 2 (pairwise).

Evaluation Measure	DS	BERT	SciBERT	BioBERT	PubMedBERT
F1	1	0.597	0.607	**0.615**	0.593
	2	**0.601**	0.596	0.600	0.592
Accuracy	1	0.701	0.711	**0.722**	0.708
	2	0.725	0.728	0.729	**0.733**

Table 6. Trained BERT model results per dataset (purity).

	BERT	Training		SciBERT	Training		BioBERT	Training		PubMedBERT	Training	
	DS	1	2	DS	1	2	DS	1	2	DS	1	2
Test 1	1	**0.693**	**0.675**	1	**0.699**	0.690	1	**0.704**	0.685	1	**0.712**	0.710
2	2	**0.726**	0.712	2	0.711	**0.721**	2	**0.726**	0.712	2	**0.736**	0.735

Table 7. Results of clustering by x-means in Experiment 3

Evaluation Measure	DS	BERT	SciBERT	BioBERT	PubMedBERT
Purity	1	0.666	0.685	0.673	**0.687**
	2	0.683	0.701	0.693	**0.710**
Pairwise(F1)	1	0.572	0.603	0.608	**0.610**
	2	0.558	0.599	0.583	**0.609**
Pairwise(Accuracy)	1	**0.664**	0.657	0.654	0.659
	2	0.693	0.696	0.693	**0.701**

Table 8. Results of clustering by VBGMM in Experiment 3

Evaluation Measure	DS	BERT	SciBERT	BioBERT	PubMedBERT
Purity	1	0.666	0.678	0.676	**0.681**
	2	0.703	0.703	0.692	**0.710**
Pairwise(F1)	1	0.605	0.617	**0.623**	0.598
	2	0.607	0.604	**0.613**	0.597
Pairwise(Accuracy)	1	0.670	0.683	**0.692**	0.675
	2	0.700	0.701	0.703	**0.711**

Table 9. Number of papers for which the number of clusters was correctly estimated (Dataset1, Experiment 3).

	Method	BERT	SciBERT	BioBERT	PubMedBERT
C < P	x-means	74	17	11	13
	VBGMM	45	42	39	50
C = P	x-means	74	85	83	84
	VBGMM	**93**	**93**	**103**	**89**
C > P	x-means	128	174	182	179
	VBGMM	138	141	134	137

C stands for number of correct clusters. P stands for a number of predicted clusters.

Table 10. Number of papers for which the number of clusters was correctly estimated (Dataset2, Experiment 3).

	Method	BERT	SciBERT	BioBERT	PubMedBERT
C < P	x-means	118	24	64	16
	VBGMM	60	68	44	59
C = P	x-means	148	152	141	156
	VBGMM	**160**	**154**	**169**	**159**
C > P	x-means	123	213	184	217
	VBGMM	169	167	176	171

C stands for number of correct clusters. P stands for a number of predicted clusters.

Table 11. Human clustering result (purity).

DS	BERT	SciBERT	BioBERT	PubMedBERT	Human
1	0.762	**0.765**	0.759	0.663	0.735
2	**0.739**	0.674	0.688	0.721	0.699

From the results in Table 6, we confirmed that the purity of the trained model for a dataset different from the training dataset was low. BERT had the lowest purity, indicating a difference in the dataset used for pre-training with the other BERT models. BERT, which had less pre-training for its area of expertise than the other BERT models, showed the most significant difference between the same training/test set result and the different training/test one. This might be because the pure BERT model without fine-tuning had the most significant margin to improve with domain knowledge.

From the results in Tables 4 and Table 11, the BERT-based models showed better or comparable accuracy in terms of purity to the human experts (RQ2). This demonstrates that using BERT-based models for categorizing references has a good potential to be used in the writing support task defined by Narimatsu et al. [5]. It also indicates that the information contained in an abstract may be sufficient for such a clustering task. It is also likely that the higher purity value of the BERT models than in Experiment 2 was due to the papers selected. Unlike the datasets for the other experiments, the papers selected for this experiment were those for which abstracts were obtained for all references. This allowed us to use data from each reference, and all relationships between references could be expressed. This is a merit that datasets with missing references do not have. There is merit in avoiding the need to take missing references into account when clustering. We believe this resulted in higher purity than the other data sets with missing references.

Regarding the prediction of the number of clusters by the x-means method, the results in Tables 9 and 10 confirm that even SciBERT, which is the most accurate, was correct only about 40% of the time. However, the results from SciBERT confirm that the most common case is that the number of clusters of correct answers was greater than the number of clusters of predictions. The errors in the number of predicted clusters and the number of correct clusters were generally 1. The number of clusters predicted by SciBERT was often two. The most common mistake was to predict the number of clusters to be 2 instead of 3. It is likely that the number of clusters predicted for papers with more than three clusters is wrong.

The results of BioBERT for Dataset 1 in Experiment 1 were superior to the other BERT models. However, BioBERT was also inaccurate in predicting the number of clusters with the x-means method in Experiment 3. This suggests that the method for predicting the number of clusters needs further improvement.

The VBGMM method was better at predicting the number of clusters, possibly because the features used differed from the x-means method. The x-means method used a vector of features from the abstracts of the references. However, VBGMM used the distance between references output by the trained model in Experiment 2. The output of the trained model showed better clustering results than the clustering using the output of the vectors by the BERT model. Therefore, the output was considered superior in predicting the number of clusters.

In this study, we used purity and pairwise evaluation to evaluate clustering. Pairwise evaluation can be performed regardless of the number of clusters. However, the evaluation decrease is significant if the wrong cluster belongs to a cluster with many elements. In contrast, the decrease is constant in purity evaluation no matter which element is mistaken. However, evaluation is difficult when the number of clusters is different. Therefore, we can evaluate the clustering method by checking the results of the two evaluation measures.

7   Conclusion and Future Work

In this paper, we investigated a citation categorization task in the context of support for scientific paper writing by creating two datasets for clustering references and proposed clustering methods. Our findings showed that the clustering accuracy is increased by having the BERT model learn labels that indicate whether two references belong to the same cluster. Moreover, the accuracy is better or comparable to human experts.

Future work will include clustering to allow common references for multiple clusters. In our experiments, a reference belongs to only one cluster because of the limitation of the clustering algorithm we used. However, a reference may sometimes belong to multiple clusters (paragraphs) in actual papers.

Future work will also include finding the adequate evaluation measure for clustering when the number of clusters is different from the correct number. In this study, we responded by adding an empty set when evaluating the basis of purity. The recall used in obtaining the F1 is characterized by a tendency to lead to a higher evaluation value when the number of clusters in the prediction is smaller than the number of clusters of correct answers. A problem with this property is that a lenient evaluation is obtained when the number of clusters is smaller than the true number.

The evaluation measure in this study should be able to correctly evaluate for common references and penalize an incorrect number of clusters in the prediction. Each of the clustering evaluation measures has its own merits. For this reason, we concluded to use multiple evaluation measures. In pairwise evaluation, it is possible to evaluate regardless of the number of clusters. On the other hand, purity evaluation is complex when the number of clusters differs. However, with purity evaluation, it is possible to evaluate even when multiple clusters do not have common references. In pairwise evaluation, clustering with no common references in the prediction results in a reduced evaluation. In addition, a disadvantage exists in that the range of decreases in the evaluation value is large when a cluster with a large number of elements mistakenly belongs to a cluster with a large number of elements.

The datasets for this experiment were created from the PMC archive. In the future, for non-medical papers, a dataset of papers and references in a particular field needs to be created. It will be important to construct datasets with a high acquisition rate of references.

In addition, clustering was performed by human experts with only ten samples out of the thousands contained in each dataset due to resource limitations. We plan to expand the sample size and the number of experts in the future.

In this study, clustering was performed using abstracts for the dataset, which is information that can be easily collected. For clustering, we used the abstract information from the references, so we need to consider other information that can be used for clustering. For example, we might use the amount of text per paragraph in the "background" section. Paragraphs with a large amount of text may have a large number of references. Thus, clustering accuracy may be improved by using information other than abstract information.

At the current stage, the results of clustering with LLMs may not yet match the achievements of human experts. However, they are approaching a level of accuracy that is comparable to human experts. Additionally, utilizing LLMs can make it easier to explain the clustering results. This is a unique advantage not found in other methods. In contrast, current methods using k-means or hierarchical clustering solely obtain clustering results based on features, and the clustering criteria are unclear. If we can determine the criteria used for clustering the references, it may potentially contribute a new method for supporting scientific paper writing

References

1. Bai, X., Wang, M., Lee, I., Yang, Z., Kong, X., Xia, F. : Scientific paper recommendation: a survey. IEEE Access **7**, 9324–9339 (2019)
2. Qazvinian, V., Radev, D.R.: Scientific paper summarization using citation summary networks. In: Proceedings of the 22nd International Conference on Computational Linguistics, vol. 1, pp. 689–696 (2008)
3. Huang, W., Wu, Z., Mitra, P., Giles, C.L.: Refseer: a citation recommendation system. in: IEEE/ACM Joint Conference on Digital Libraries, pp. 371–374 (2014)
4. Xing, X., Fan, X., Wan, X.: Automatic generation of citation texts in scholarly papers: a pilot study. In: Proceedings of the 58th Annual Meeting of the Association for Computational Linguistics, pp. 6181–6190 (2020)
5. Narimatsu, H., Koyama, K., Dohsaka, K., Higashinaka, R., Minami, Y., Taira, H.: Task definition and integration for scientific-document writing support. In: Proceedings of the Second Workshop on Scholarly Document Processing, pp. 18–26 (2021)
6. Bafna, P., Pramod, D., Vaidya, A.: Document clustering: TF-IDF approach. In: Proceedings of the 2016 International Conference on Electrical, Electronics, and Optimization Techniques (ICEEOT) (2016)
7. Devlin, J., Chang, M.W., Lee, K., Toutanova, K.: BERT: pre-training of deep bidirectional transformers for language understanding. In: Proceedings of the 2019 Conference of the North American Chapter of the Association for Computational Linguistics: Human Language Technologies, 2019, pp. 4171–4186 (2019)
8. Yang, Z., Dai, Z., Yang, Y., Carbonell, J., Salakhutdinov, R.R., Le, Q.V.: XLNet: generalized autoregressive pretraining for language understanding. In: Proceedings of the 33rd International Conference on Neural Information Processing Systems (2020)
9. Marcińczu, M., Gniewkowski, M., Walkowiak, T., BÇdkowski, M.: Text Document clustering: wordnet vs. TF-IDF vs. word embeddings. In: Proceedings of the 11th Global Wordnet Conference, pp. 207–214 (2021)
10. Li, Y., Cai, J., Wang, J.: A text document clustering method based on weighted BERT model. In: 2020 IEEE 4th Information Technology, Networking, Electronic and Automation Control Conference (ITNEC) (2020)
11. Shi, H., Wang, C.: Self-supervised Document Clustering Based on BERT with Data Augment, ArXiv, abs/2011.08523 (2020)
12. Lee, J., et al.: BioBERT: a pre-trained biomedical language representation model for biomedical text mining. Bioinformatics **36**(4), 1234–1240 (2020)
13. Beltagy, I., Lo, K., Cohan, A.: SciBERT: a pretrained language model for scientific text. In: Proceedings of the 2019 Conference on Empirical Methods in Natural Language Processing and the 9th International Joint Conference on Natural Language Processing (EMNLP-IJCNLP), pp. 3615–3620 (2019)
14. Schutze, H., Manning, C.D., Raghavan, P.: Introduction to Information Retrieval. Cambridge University Press, Cambridge (2008)
15. Pelleg, D., Moore, A.W.: X-means: extending K-means with efficient estimation of the number of clusters. In: Proceedings of the 17th International Conference on Machine Learning, pp. 727–734 (2000)

16. Arita, A., Sugiyama, H., Dohsaka, K., Tanaka, R., Taira, H.: Citation sentence generation leveraging the content of cited papers. In: Proceedings of the Third Workshop on Scholarly Document Processing, pp. 170–174 (2022)
17. Te, S., Barhoumi, A., Lentschat, M., Bordignon, F., Labbe, C., Portet, F.: Citation context classification: critical vs non-critical. In: Proceedings of the Third Workshop on Scholarly Document Processing, pp. 49–53 (2022)
18. Toney, A., Dunham, J.: Multi-label classification of scientific research documents across domains and languages. In: Proceedings of the Third Workshop on Scholarly Document Processing, pp. 105–114 (2022)
19. Medić, Z., Snajder, J.: Large-scale evaluation of transformer-based article encoders on the task of citation recommendation. In: Proceedings of the Third Workshop on Scholarly Document Processing, pp. 19–31 (2022)
20. Subelj, L., Van Eck, N.J., Waltman, L.: Clustering scientific publications based on citation relations: a systematic comparison of different methods. PLoS ONE 11(4) (2016)
21. Gu, Y., et al.: Domain-specific language model pretraining for biomedical natural language processing. In: Association for Computing Machinery (ACM), pp. 1–23 (2021)

Enhancing Legal Text Entailment with Prompt-Based ChatGPT: An Empirical Study

Chau Nguyen and Le-Minh Nguyen[✉]

Japan Advanced Institute of Science and Technology, Nomi, Ishikawa, Japan
{chau.nguyen,nguyenml}@jaist.ac.jp

Abstract. This research paper focuses on the task of legal text entailment, which involves determining whether a given statement logically follows from the facts stated in a legal text. In this paper, we perform experiments with ChatGPT, a large language model developed by OpenAI, for the task of legal text entailment. Among various prompt settings, we find that by using appropriate prompts while asking ChatGPT to output step-by-step reasoning, ChatGPT outperforms previous approaches by a large margin in the COLIEE 2022 dataset, achieving an improvement of up to 10.09% absolute. We also conduct an extensive analysis of how the model makes incorrect predictions, providing insights for potential improvements in future work. This research demonstrates the potential of using state-of-the-art natural language processing models, such as ChatGPT, to address complex legal tasks and advance the field of automated legal text entailment.

Keywords: Legal text entailment · ChatGPT · Large language model

1 Introduction

Legal text entailment is a task in natural language processing (NLP) that involves determining whether a given statement logically follows from the facts stated in a legal text. The development of automated systems for addressing the legal text entailment task is of critical significance, as it has the potential to provide substantial benefits to individuals with varying legal needs. First, it can help lawyers and legal professionals save time and effort analyzing large volumes of legal texts. Traditionally, lawyers have had to manually read and analyze legal documents to determine the relevant facts and legal arguments. With the help of automated legal text entailment systems, lawyers can quickly identify the most relevant information and arguments, which can help them make more informed decisions. Besides, it can help ensure consistency and fairness in legal decision-making. By using automated systems to analyze legal texts, legal professionals can reduce the risk of bias and errors when decisions are based on human interpretation alone. Furthermore, it is crucial for the development of advanced legal applications such as legal chatbots or legal question-answering

© The Author(s), under exclusive license to Springer Nature Switzerland AG 2024
M. Bono et al. (Eds.): JSAI-isAI 2023 Workshops, LNAI 14644, pp. 184–196, 2024.
https://doi.org/10.1007/978-3-031-60511-6_12

systems. These applications can help make legal services more accessible and affordable, particularly for people who cannot afford expensive legal advice.

The development of automated systems for addressing legal text entailment is an emerging area of research that has the potential to revolutionize legal services. However, this field is still in its infancy, and much work remains to be done to develop accurate and efficient systems. To this end, the Conference on Legal Information Extraction and Entailment (COLIEE [10]) has emerged as a prominent forum for advancing the development of automated legal text entailment systems. This annual international competition provides a platform for researchers and practitioners to showcase their latest advances in this field while promoting collaboration and knowledge sharing among participants. By spurring innovation and fostering collaboration, the COLIEE competition is playing a critical role in advancing the state-of-the-art in automated legal text entailment, with significant implications for the future of legal services.

ChatGPT[1] is a large language model developed by OpenAI[2] that is capable of understanding natural language text and generating human-like responses to prompts. Trained on a massive corpus of text data, ChatGPT has shown impressive performance across a wide range of natural language processing tasks, including language translation, summarization, and question-answering. We are interested in using ChatGPT to analyze legal texts, given its ability to understand the complex and nuanced language used in legal documents. Legal text entailment, which involves determining whether one text can logically entail another, is one such task where ChatGPT's natural language processing capabilities can be particularly useful.

In this paper, we perform experiments with ChatGPT in its prompt-based setting for the task of legal text entailment in COLIEE 2022 with various scenarios. Through these experiments, we find that if we ask ChatGPT to output step-by-step reasoning and with an appropriate prompt setting, ChatGPT outperforms previous approaches by a large margin in the COLIEE 2022 dataset, achieving an improvement of up to 10.09%, from 67.89% to 77.98%. We also extensively analyze how the model makes incorrect predictions, shedding light on potential improvements for future work.

2   Related Work

2.1   Introduction to ChatGPT

ChatGPT is trained with three stages. In the first stage of training ChatGPT, the transformer model is trained on diverse text data from the internet, such as websites, books, and articles, to generate text in various styles and contexts. The model is trained to perform various tasks like language modeling, summarization, translation, and sentiment analysis, but it is not trained for a specific task. Although the model is great at text completion and summarization, it is not

---

[1] https://chat.openai.com/.
[2] https://openai.com/.

built to chat about a particular topic, which leads to a misalignment in user expectations and the model's capabilities.

The second stage of training ChatGPT is Supervised Fine-Tuning (SFT), which involves training the model on specific tasks that are relevant to the user's expectations, such as conversational chat. In SFT, carefully crafted conversations are created by one human agent pretending to be a chatbot and another human agent providing ideal responses to each request. These conversations are then used to create the training data corpus, which is used to fine-tune the base GPT model using the Stochastic Gradient Descent Algorithm (SGD [8]). However, even after SFT, ChatGPT faces the issue of Distributional Shift, where the model's training is limited to the conversations it was trained on and may not be able to handle new or unexpected requests.

In Stage 3 of training the ChatGPT model, Reinforcement Learning through Human Feedback (RLHF [3,18]) is utilized to fine-tune the model's ability to generate responses. In RLHF, a reward function is created to evaluate the model's responses, which is established by having a real person chat with ChatGPT and rate alternate responses. Training pairs consisting of a request and response are used to help the reward model learn what responses are better. Proximal Policy Optimization (PPO [17]) is used to evaluate each action and decide what a good response is. To avoid over-optimization, the Kullback-Leibler divergence measure is added to the PPO model. Finally, the model is fine-tuned to generate better responses.

2.2   Approaches to Legal Text Entailment in COLIEE Competition

The Conference on Legal Information Extraction and Entailment (COLIEE) has facilitated the development of a diverse range of approaches for the task of legal textual entailment. In COLIEE 2020, participants employed a range of NLP techniques and models such as BERT [5], RoBERTa [13], GloVe [16], and LSTM [9]. The winning team, JNLP [15], fine-tuned BERT-based models with Japanese legal data and utilized TF-IDF to achieve superior performance. Rule-based ensembles, SVM [4], and attention mechanisms with word embeddings were also used to tackle the legal text classification task. In COLIEE 2021, the winning team HUKB [21] employed an ensemble of BERT models and utilized data augmentation, which outperformed the other approaches [6,11,14,20]. The 2022 competition saw further innovations, such as a method for selecting relevant parts from articles and employed an ensemble of BERT with data augmentation [22], an ensemble of rule-based and BERT-based methods with data augmentation and person name inference [7], used the longest uncommon subsequence similarity comparison model [12], or employed an ensemble of graph neural networks with textbook nodes and sentence embeddings [19]. These advances demonstrate the ongoing efforts to improve the performance of automated systems for legal text entailment, with significant implications for the future of legal services.

3 Methods

3.1 Using ChatGPT API

The ChatGPT API allows users to easily integrate the ChatGPT language model into their applications. When using the API, each message in the input list contains two properties: "role" and "content". The "role" property specifies the role of the message sender, which can be "system", "user", or "assistant" (i.e., ChatGPT). The "content" property contains the text of the message from the sender.

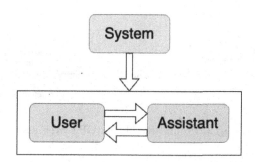

Fig. 1. Interaction of the "role" properties when prompting ChatGPT API

The "system" role can be used to provide high-level instructions for the conversation and can also be used to guide the behavior of the model throughout the conversation. Figure 1 demonstrates the interaction of the "role" properties. The messages in the list are processed in the order in which they appear, and the assistant responds accordingly. Suppose we want to ask ChatGPT to tell explain Artificial Intelligence as if it is a primary school teacher and the audience is a six-year-old child. We can send the following input to the ChatGPT API:

```
[
  {
    "role": "system",
    "content": "You are a primary school teacher and you exlain
    everything to a six-year-old child."
  },
  {
    "role": "user",
    "content": "Please explain Artificial Intelligence in one sentence."
  },
]
```

In response to a query regarding Artificial Intelligence, the ChatGPT API may return a message, such as "Artificial Intelligence is when machines are programmed to think and learn like humans.". However, if the role "system" and its corresponding content, which instructs ChatGPT to explain the concept to a six-year-old child, are not passed to the API, the returned message would be `"Artificial Intelligence is the simulation of human intelligence processes by machines, especially computer systems."`. The contrast between the two responses highlights the role of the "system" role in guiding ChatGPT to provide an explanation in language that is easy for a young child to comprehend.

3.2 Prompt-Based ChatGPT for Legal Textual Entailment

Fig. 2. Prompt-based ChatGPT overview

This study investigates the ability of ChatGPT to provide explanations for its predictions in the context of legal textual entailment, as explored in previous research [2,23] (Fig. 2). Three different prompt-based settings are employed to compare ChatGPT's performance when providing explanations versus when not prompted to do so. We design the prompts following the suggestions in [1]. The designed prompts are as follows:

1. Prompt 1: ChatGPT only outputs the answer.

```
{
  "role": "user",
  "content": "Given a query (which is delimited with triple
  backticks) and the related articles (which is also delimited
  with triple backticks). Is the query entailed by the related
  articles? Please provide a simple answer of either "Yes" or
  "No", without any explanation.

  Query: ```{query}```

  Related articles: ```{related_articles}```"
}
```

2. Prompt 2: ChatGPT outputs the answer and provides an explanation for its reasoning.

```
{
    "role": "user",
    "content": "Given a query (which is delimited with triple
    backticks) and the related articles (which is also delimited
    with triple backticks). Is the query entailed by the related
    articles? Please provide the answer of "Yes" or "No", then
    provide an explanation. Format your response as a JSON object
    with "Answer" and "Explanation" as the keys.

    Query: '''{query}'''

    Related articles: '''{related_articles}'''"
}
```

3. Prompt 3: ChatGPT provides a step-by-step reasoning process and concludes with an answer.

```
{
    "role": "user",
    "content": "Given a query (which is delimited with triple
    backticks) and the related articles (which is also delimited
    with triple backticks). Is the query entailed by the related
    articles? To answer, please use the following format:
        Step-by-step reasoning: <your step-by-step reasoning>
        Answer: <a clear "Yes" or "No" response>

    Query: '''{query}'''

    Related articles: '''{related_articles}'''"
}
```

In addition, the impact of providing the "system" role to ChatGPT on its performance is also examined, resulting in a total of six experimental settings. In particular, we add the "system" role to the messages that are sent to ChatGPT API. The "system" role is defined as follows:

```
{
    "role": "system",
    "content": "You are a legal AI assistant that is capable of
    accurately inferring whether a statement in a query is entailed
    by the related articles provided."
}
```

4 Experimental Results and Error Classification

4.1 Experimental Results

In the API, we need to set the `temperature` parameter, which determines the level of randomness in the generated output. For the purpose of ensuring reproducibility, we fix the `temperature` parameter to 0.

We experiment with the test data of COLIEE 2022 and compare them with the previous systems' highest performances. For each test sample, the task involves assessing whether a given statement in a query can be inferred from the related legal articles provided in a list. The obtained experimental results are presented in Table 1.

Table 1. Accuracy comparison of different methods

Method	Accuracy
Previous methods	
KIS	67.89%
HUKB	66.97%
LLNTU	60.55%
OvGU	57.80%
UA	54.13%
JNLP	53.21%
*Our methods: **no** "system" role*	
Prompt 1 (Only answer)	75.23%
Prompt 2 (Answer-then-Explain)	71.56%
Prompt 3 (Reason-then-Answer)	75.23%
*Our methods: **has** "system" role*	
Prompt 1 (Only answer)	73.40%
Prompt 2 (Answer-then-Explain)	67.89%
Prompt 3 (Reason-then-Answer)	**77.98%**

The experimental results demonstrate the effectiveness of our proposed methods for the legal textual entailment task. In particular, our approaches outperform previous methods, indicating the strength of ChatGPT for this task.

Moreover, we observed that the use of the "system" role may have a negative or positive effect on the performance, depending on the specific setting. For instance, when used with the setting of asking ChatGPT to answer before explaining, the "system" role may cause a negative effect (accuracy decreases from 75.23% to 73.40%). However, the performance can be further improved by asking ChatGPT to reason before providing an answer (accuracy increases from 75.23% to 77.98%). It may be because the "system" role is a better fit with the

Reason-then-Answer prompt than the others. It is also notable that prompt 1 (Only answer) performs better than prompt 2 (Answer-then-Explain) in both cases.

Overall, our proposed method achieved the highest results of 77.98%, which is more than 10% absolute improvement over the previous best-performing system. These results highlight the potential of ChatGPT for the legal textual entailment task and pave the way for further improvements in this area.

4.2 Error Analysis and Classification

To gain a better understanding of the errors made by ChatGPT for the Reason-then-Answer prompt, we conducted an analysis of 20 selected responses and classified the errors into four categories. These errors in ChatGPT's reasoning can be classified as follows:

- Category 1. Incorrect provision of facts by ChatGPT leading to incorrect conclusions (50% of the errors). For instance, in the given scenario, ChatGPT fabricates a fact during the reasoning process in step 6 (highlighted in yellow), consequently arriving at an incorrect conclusion:

Related articles:

Article 143:

(1) If a period is provided for in weeks, months, or years, the period is calculated in accordance to the calendar.

(2) If a period does not commence at the beginning of the week, month, or year, that period expires on the day immediately preceding the day which corresponds to the commencement day in the last week, month or year; provided, however, that if the period is provided for in months or years and the last month does not contain a corresponding day, the period expires on the last day of that month.

Query:

If an agreement is made at 11:00 a.m. on July 12 of a given year that the obligation will be fulfilled within one month, the period expires at 12:00 p.m. on August 13 of the same year, both of which do not fall on Sundays, holidays as provided in the Act on National Holidays, or any other holidays.

ChatGPT step-by-step reasoning:

1. The query states that if an agreement is made on July 12 of a given year that the obligation will be fulfilled within one month, the period expires at 12:00 p.m. on August 13 of the same year.

2. The query specifies that the period does not fall on Sundays, holidays as provided in the Act on National Holidays, or any other holidays.

3. Article 143(1) states that if a period is provided for in months, the period is calculated in accordance with the calendar.

---

4. Article 143(2) states that if a period does not commence at the beginning of the month, that period expires on the day immediately preceding the day which corresponds to the commencement day in the last month.

5. Since the agreement is made on July 12 and the period is for one month, the period will end on August 12.

6. Since August 13 is not a Sunday, holiday as provided in the Act on National Holidays, or any other holiday, the period can be extended to August 13.

7. Therefore, the query is entailed by the related articles.

ChatGPT answer: Yes

Gold answer: No

– Category 2. The inability of ChatGPT to draw correct conclusions from correct premises (25% of the errors). For instance, in the following scenario, ChatGPT can accurately identify the premises presented in both the query and the related article; however, it fails to draw an appropriate conclusion:

Related articles:

Article 548:

The right to cancel is extinguished if the holder of the right to cancel, intentionally or negligently, causes significant damage to, or makes it impossible to return the object of the contract, or converts the object into another kind of thing by processing or alteration; provided, however, that this does not apply if the holder of the right to cancel does not know of the holder's right to cancel.

Query:

If the holder of the right to cancel negligently makes it impossible to return the object of the contract, the right to cancel is extinguished even if the holder of the right to cancel does not know of the holder's right to cancel.

ChatGPT step-by-step reasoning:

1. The related article states that the right to cancel is extinguished if the holder of the right to cancel intentionally or negligently makes it impossible to return the object of the contract.

2. The related article also states that this provision does not apply if the holder of the right to cancel does not know of their right to cancel.

3. The query states that if the holder of the right to cancel negligently makes it impossible to return the object of the contract, the right to cancel is extinguished even if the holder of the right to cancel does not know of their right to cancel.

4. Therefore, the query is entailed by the related article.

ChatGPT answer: Yes

Gold answer: No

Enhancing Legal Text Entailment with Prompt-Based ChatGPT 193

– Category 3. Difficulties faced by ChatGPT while reasoning on "mutatis mutandis" articles (10% of the errors). In the following case, Article 558 pertains to contracts for sale, while Article 559 indicates that these provisions also apply to contracts for value other than contracts for sale with necessary modifications. However, ChatGPT fails to deduce the application of mutatis mutandis in this context:

Related articles:

Article 558:
The expenses associated with contracts for sale are borne equally by both parties.

Article 559:
The provisions of this Section apply mutatis mutandis to contracts for value other than contracts for sale; provided, however, that this does not apply when it is not permitted by the nature of the contract for value.

Query:
The expenses associated with conclusions of lease contracts are borne equally by both parties.

ChatGPT step-by-step reasoning:
1. The query is about the expenses associated with lease contracts.
2. Article 559 states that the provisions of the section apply to contracts for value other than contracts for sale.
3. However, it also states that this does not apply when it is not permitted by the nature of the contract for value.
4. Article 558 states that the expenses associated with contracts for sale are borne equally by both parties.
5. Since the query is specifically about lease contracts and there is no mention of lease contracts in the related articles, we cannot infer that the expenses associated with conclusions of lease contracts are borne equally by both parties. Therefore, the answer is No.

ChatGPT answer: No
Gold answer: Yes

– Category 4. Insufficiency of the related articles provided for ChatGPT to arrive at the gold answer (15% of the errors). In the following case, the lack of sufficient related articles led to confusion in ChatGPT, resulting in the model's inability to reach a conclusion. In this case, the articles 140, 141, 142 should be added to the list of related articles.

Related articles:
Article 143:
(1) If a period is provided for in weeks, months, or years, the period is calculated in accordance to the calendar.

(2) If a period does not commence at the beginning of the week, month, or year, that period expires on the day immediately preceding the day which corresponds to the commencement day in the last week, month or year; provided, however, that if the period is provided for in months or years and the last month does not contain a corresponding day, the period expires on the last day of that month.

Query:
If an agreement is made at 5:00 p.m. on January 30 of a non-leap year that the obligation would be fulfilled within one month, the period expires at 12:00 p.m. on February 28 of the same year, both of which do not fall on Sundays, holidays as provided in the Act on National Holidays, or any other holidays.

ChatGPT step-by-step reasoning:
1. The query states that if an agreement is made on January 30 of a non-leap year that the obligation would be fulfilled within one month, the period expires at 12:00 p.m. on February 28 of the same year.
2. Article 143(1) states that if a period is provided for in months, the period is calculated in accordance with the calendar.
3. Article 143(2) states that if a period does not commence at the beginning of the month, the period expires on the last day of that month.
4. Since the agreement in the query is made on January 30 and the period is for one month, the period would expire on February 28.
5. The query specifies that the period would expire at 12:00 p.m. on February 28, but neither Article 143(1) nor Article 143(2) mention anything about a specific time of day.
6. However, the query also specifies that the expiration date must not fall on Sundays, holidays as provided in the Act on National Holidays, or any other holidays, which is not addressed in the related articles.
7. Therefore, it cannot be definitively concluded whether the query is entailed by the related articles.

ChatGPT answer: No
Gold answer: Yes

5   Conclusion

In conclusion, the development of automated systems for addressing legal text entailment has the potential to revolutionize legal services, benefiting legal professionals and individuals with varying legal needs. Such systems can help lawyers save time and effort in analyzing large volumes of legal texts, ensure consistency and fairness in legal decision-making, and make legal services more accessible and affordable. The emerging area of research in automated legal text entailment still requires significant work to develop accurate and efficient systems. Our experiments with ChatGPT in its prompt-based setting for the task of legal text entailment in COLIEE 2022 with various scenarios demonstrate the potential of natural language processing capabilities in legal text analysis. Specifically, our findings show that by asking ChatGPT to output step-by-step reasoning with an appropriate prompt setting, the model can outperform previous approaches by a large margin in the COLIEE 2022 dataset. Our study also highlights potential improvements for future work by analyzing the model's incorrect predictions. These results suggest that the use of large language models such as ChatGPT can significantly enhance the accuracy and efficiency of automated legal text entailment systems.

Acknowledgements. This work is partly supported by AOARD grant FA23862214039.

References

1. ChatGPT prompt engineering for developers. https://learn.deeplearning.ai/chatgpt-prompt-eng
2. Chen, J., Chen, L., Huang, H., Zhou, T.: When do you need chain-of-thought prompting for ChatGPT? arXiv preprint arXiv:2304.03262 (2023)
3. Christiano, P.F., Leike, J., Brown, T., Martic, M., Legg, S., Amodei, D.: Deep reinforcement learning from human preferences. In: Advances in Neural Information Processing Systems, vol. 30 (2017)
4. Cortes, C., Vapnik, V.: Support-vector networks. Mach. Learn. **20**, 273–297 (1995)
5. Devlin, J., Chang, M., Lee, K., Toutanova, K.: BERT: pre-training of deep bidirectional transformers for language understanding. CoRR abs/1810.04805 (2018). http://arxiv.org/abs/1810.04805
6. Fujita, M., Kiyota, N., Kano, Y.: Predicate's argument resolver and entity abstraction for legal question answering: KIS teams at COLIEE 2021 shared task. In: Proceedings of the COLIEE Workshop in ICAIL (2021)
7. Fujita, M., Onaga, T., Ueyama, A., Kano, Y.: Legal textual entailment using ensemble of rule-based and BERT-based method with data augmentation by related article generation. In: Takama, Y., Yada, K., Satoh, K., Arai, S. (eds.) JSAI-isAI 2022. LNCS, vol. 13859, pp. 138–153. Springer, Cham (2023). https://doi.org/10.1007/978-3-031-29168-5_10
8. Harold, J., Kushner, G., Yin, G.: Stochastic approximation and recursive algorithm and applications. Appl. Math. **35** (1997)
9. Hochreiter, S., Schmidhuber, J.: Long short-term memory. Neural Comput. **9**(8), 1735–1780 (1997)
10. Kim, M.Y., Rabelo, J., Goebel, R., Yoshioka, M., Kano, Y., Satoh, K.: COLIEE 2022 summary: methods for legal document retrieval and entailment. In: Takama, Y., Yada, K., Satoh, K., Arai, S. (eds.) JSAI-isAI 2022. LNCS, vol. 13859, pp. 51–67. Springer, Cham (2023). https://doi.org/10.1007/978-3-031-29168-5_4
11. Kim, M., Rabelo, J., Goebel, R.: Bm25 and transformer-based legal information extraction and entailment. In: Proceedings of the COLIEE Workshop in ICAIL (2021)
12. Lin, M., Huang, S., Shao, H.: Rethinking attention: an attempting on revaluing attention weight with disjunctive union of longest uncommon subsequence for legal queries answering. In: Proceedings of the Sixteenth International Workshop on Juris-informatics (JURISIN 2022) (2022)

13. Liu, Y., et al.: RoBERTa: a robustly optimized bert pretraining approach. arXiv preprint arXiv:1907.11692 (2019)
14. Nguyen, H.T., et al.: ParaLaw nets–cross-lingual sentence-level pretraining for legal text processing. In: Proceedings of the COLIEE Workshop in ICAIL (2021) (2021)
15. Nguyen, H.T., et al.: JNLP team: deep learning for legal processing in COLIEE 2020. In: COLIEE 2020 (2020)
16. Pennington, J., Socher, R., Manning, C.D.: GloVe: global vectors for word representation. In: Proceedings of the 2014 Conference on Empirical Methods in Natural Language Processing (EMNLP), pp. 1532–1543 (2014)
17. Schulman, J., Wolski, F., Dhariwal, P., Radford, A., Klimov, O.: Proximal policy optimization algorithms. arXiv preprint arXiv:1707.06347 (2017)
18. Stiennon, N., et al.: Learning to summarize with human feedback. In: Advances in Neural Information Processing Systems, vol. 33, pp. 3008–3021 (2020)
19. Wehnert, S., Kutty, L., De Luca, E.W.: Using textbook knowledge for statute retrieval and entailment classification. In: Takama, Y., Yada, K., Satoh, K., Arai, S. (eds.) JSAI-isAI 2022. LNCS, vol. 13859, pp. 125–137. Springer, Cham (2023). https://doi.org/10.1007/978-3-031-29168-5_9
20. Wehnert, S., Sudhi, V., Dureja, S., Kutty, L., Shahania, S., De Luca, E.W.: Legal norm retrieval with variations of the BERT model combined with TF-IDF vectorization. In: Proceedings of the Eighteenth International Conference on Artificial Intelligence and Law, pp. 285–294 (2021)
21. Yoshioka, M., Suzuki, Y., Aoki, Y.: BERT-based ensemble methods for information retrieval and legal textual entailment in COLIEE statute law task. In: Proceedings of the Eigth International Competition on Legal Information Extraction/Entailment (COLIEE 2021) (2021)
22. Yoshioka, M., Suzuki, Y., Aoki, Y.: HUKB at the COLIEE 2022 statute law task. In: Takama, Y., Yada, K., Satoh, K., Arai, S. (eds.) JSAI-isAI 2022. LNCS, vol. 13859, pp. 109–124. Springer, Cham (2023). https://doi.org/10.1007/978-3-031-29168-5_8
23. Zhang, H., Liu, X., Zhang, J.: Extractive summarization via ChatGPT for faithful summary generation. arXiv preprint arXiv:2304.04193 (2023)

AI-Biz 2023

Artificial Intelligence of and for Business (AI-Biz 2023)

Takao Terano[1], Setsuya Kurahashi[2], and Hiroshi Takahashi[3]

[1]Chiba University of Commerce
[2]University of Tsukuba
[3]Keio University

1 The Workshop

In AI-Biz 2023, held on May 4, one excellent invited lecture and eight cutting-edge research papers were presented with a total of 15 participants. The workshop theme focused on various recent issues in business activities and the application technologies of Artificial Intelligence to them.

The invited lecture was "Teaching Artificial Intelligence in K-12 Education: The Policy Landscape and Research Directions" by Dr. Chathura Rajapakse of Department of Industrial Management, Faculty of Science, University of Kelaniya, Sri Lanka. In his presentation, he discussed some existing policy frameworks and challenges of teaching artificial intelligence in K-12 education into discussion. He focused on some ongoing initiatives in Sri Lanka to teach artificial intelligence at the pre-tertiary level.

The AI-Biz 2023 was the sixth workshop hosted by the SIG-BI (Business Informatics) of JSAI. We believe the workshop was held successfully because of the vast fields of business and AI technology. It includes Investment Strategy, Stock Market, Mergers and Acquisitions, Online Advertisement, Knowledge Extraction, Power Market, Collaborative Multi-agent, Visualization, COVID-19 Infections, Classification, Fake News, Wide and Deep Learning, and so on.

2 Synopsis of Presented Papers

Ten papers were submitted for the workshop, and eight of them were selected for oral presentation in the workshop (80% acceptance rate). After the workshop, they were reviewed by PC members again, and three papers were finally selected (30% acceptance rate). Followings are their synopses.

Takahiro Obata, Jun Sakazaki, and Setsuya Kurahashi introduced the concept of capital goods into a macroeconomic agent-based model developed for analyzing the propagation of economic shock effects. They implemented the model encompassing the major economic agents and incorporated improvements in interfirm supplier-customer relationships to bring firm behavior closer to reality.

Haruna Okazaki and Hiroshi Takahashi attempted to extract corporate trends from news data and employed BERTopic to group news containing various topics into several categories. Their study targeted news headlines of specific chemical companies listed on the Japanese stock market. The results of the analysis revealed the ability of

BERTopic to classify target news into multiple groups and the potential to efficiently obtain information about future corporate activities from the content of the news.

Akiko Ueno, Yuko Okiyama, Nozomi Masuda, Ken-ichi Yamaga, Aino Yamagata, Kazuto Yoshioka, Arata Abe, Koichi Kitanishi and Takashi Yamada investigated whether young people in regional cities of Japan have really shifted away from owning automobiles. They analyzed empirical data about driver's license statistics and consumer confidence surveys to clarify whether young people living in such places have really decided not to drive. They found that the ratio in regional cities is still much higher than the nationwide average, and views on having an automobile can be classified based on three factors.

3 Acknowledgment

As the organizing committee chair, I would like to thank the steering committee members. The members are leading researchers in various fields:

Chang-Won Ahn, VAIV Company, Korea
Ernesto Carella, University of Oxford, UK
Reiko Hishiyama, Waseda University, Japan
Manabu Ichikawa, Shibaura Institute of Technology, Japan
Yoko Ishino, Yamaguchi University, Japan
Hajime Kita, Kyoto University, Japan
Hajime Mizuyama, Aoyama Gakuin University, Japan
Matthias Raddant, Kiel University, Gemany
Chathura Rajapaksha, University of Kelaniya, Sri Lanka
Masakazu Takahashi, Yamaguchi University, Japan
Shingo Takahashi, Waseda University, Japan
Alfred Taudes, Vienna University, Austria
Takashi Yamada, Yamaguchi University, Japan
Chao Yang, Hunan University, China

The organizers would like to thank JSAI for its financial support. Finally, we wish to express our gratitude to all those who submitted papers, steering committee members, invited speakers, reviewers, discussants and the attentive audience. We are extremely grateful to all the reviewers. We would like to thank everybody involved in the sympodia organization that helped us in making this event successful.

Development of a Macroeconomic Simulator with an Elaborated Firm Sector

Takahiro Obata[1]([✉]), Jun Sakazaki[2], and Setsuya Kurahashi[1]

[1] University of Tsukuba, Tsukuba, Japan
obata_takahiro@hotmail.com
[2] Studio Flux, New York, USA

Abstract. We introduce the concept of capital goods into a macroeconomic agent-based model developed for analyzing the propagation of economic shock effects. This concept is based on a macroeconomic agent-based model encompassing the major economic agents and incorporates interfirm supplier-customer relationship improvements to bring firm behavior closer to reality. Based on a sensitivity analysis of the inventory ratio, if the intermediate goods inventory was estimated as larger than necessary, many of the products produced by firms would be sold to firms as intermediate input materials, while the quantity of products sold to households would decrease, reducing the household purchase volume. This would result in a negative cycle of reduced demand for the intermediate input material, further suppressing the production activity of firms.

Keywords: Agent-based simulator · Macroeconomic simulator · Supply chain network · Capital goods

1 Introduction

In this study, an agent-based model(ABM) suitable for analyzing the propagation of the effects of economic shocks is developed. With the COVID-19 pandemic as an impetus, extensive studies have been conducted on the propagation of the effects of economic and societal shocks using ABM.

The ABMs used in economic shock analysis can be classified into (1) a macroeconomics approach, in which a model is constructed covering all the major entities in the economy, (2) a sector-specific approach, in which a model is constructed focusing on a specific area of analysis, such as the corporate sector, and (3) an input-output approach that uses agents for each industry, unlike the aforementioned two approaches that use agents for a single firm or household. Each approach has its own advantages and disadvantages. Obata et al. (2023) constructed an ABM that incorporates the advantages of each aforementioned approach. In particular, based on a model structure that covers major economic entities such as households, firms, banks, governments, and central banks as in the macroeconomics approach, Obata et al. (2023) proposed a model that

M. Bono et al. (Eds.): JSAI-isAI 2023 Workshops, LNAI 14644, pp. 201–216, 2024.
https://doi.org/10.1007/978-3-031-60511-6_13

elaborates interfirm interactions by introducing an interfirm supplier-customer network [1].

In this study, we improve this model to bring it closer to real business activities by introducing the concept of capital equipment, which was found to be an issue in case of Obata' s model. The second half of this paper reports the results of a sensitivity analysis using the improved macroeconomic agent-based model (MABM).

The structure of this paper is as follows: Sect. 2 presents previous studies, while Sect. 3 presents a brief description of the model. Furthermore, Sect. 4 discusses the simulation analysis, while Sect. 5 presents a summary.

2   Related Works

As the germ of research using ABMs in macroeconomic analysis, some of the early studies (for example, [2] and [3]) were conducted around 1960; however, it was not until the mid-2000s that ABMs became widespread. In particular, when the financial crisis occurred in 2008, there was a movement to review economic analysis, partly because the crisis could not be predicted using conventional analysis. Thus, ABMs became recognized for their effectiveness, and their use expanded [4].

While various MABMs have been developed and proposed, a research paper that organized MABMs developed since the turn of the millennium [5] identifies seven major frameworks and summarizes the characteristics of each. One of these seven frameworks is the complex adaptive trivial system (CATS) and it is frequently used in studies focusing on emergent aspects of the macroeconomy. Caiani (2016) proposed a benchmark model as a basis for various analyses of the CATS framework [6]. Obata et al. (2023) listed macroeconomic, sector-specific, and input-output approaches for developing ABMs to analyze the impact of economic shock propagation. Obata' s MABM, while novel, was based on the benchmark model in [6], using the strengths of each approach, the characteristics of each of which are summarized now.

- The macroeconomics approach encompasses representative economic entities in the economy, such as firms, households, banks, governments, and central banks. The macroeconomic approach can analyze the interactions among economic agents. Conversely, the tendency to simplify the attributes and behavior of each entity is disadvantageous.
- The sector-specific approach is where the analytical target is narrowed down to a specific area, such as a business-to-business transaction network. Consequently, it is easy to construct an elaborate model of the domain. However, it is not able to capture interactions with domains outside the specific area. As an example, Hillman et al. (2021) analyzed by ABM the outbreak of the new Coronavirus and the subsequent economic stagnation. Therein the attributes of the corporate agents were adapted to the characteristics of various real corporate data [7]. Inoue & Todo (2019) analyzed the propagation of shocks from natural disasters by constructing a model of an inter-firm network of

approximately 890,000 corporate agents based on actual corporate attributes and supplier-customer relationship data [8]. Inoue & Todo extended their model a year later and analyzed the impact of a lockdown in Tokyo during the Coronavirus disaster [9].
- The input-output approach is a model that subdivides the entire firm sector into many subindustries and uses agents for each industry. The model is constructed on a macroscopic aggregate basis; therefore, it is assumed that a single firm is dominant in an industry and it is not possible to analyze interactions such as competition at the firm level. One of the pioneering studies in this field was that conducted by Hallegatte (2008), who proposed the framework of the adaptive regional input-output (ARIO) model [10]. Recent studies include [11], which analyzed the impact of supply shocks propagated through supply-chain networks in global markets, and [12], which analyzed the impact of lockdowns during the Coronavirus epidemic.

Obata et al.' s MABM was constructed by incorporating the advantages of these three approaches. In this study, Obata' s MABM is improved by introducing the concept of capital equipment.

3 Model

Our model proposed in this paper has many contributions from the benchmark model in [6] (hereinafter referred to as the benchmark model) and the model proposed in [13]. The similarities and differences between these models are described below.

The benchmark model has two types of firm agents: capital goods firms and final consumer goods firms. In the product flow, consumer goods firms purchase capital goods produced by capital goods firms. The consumer goods firms use the capital goods to produce final consumer goods and sell them to households. In other words, in the benchmark model, the product flow is unidirectional: capital goods firms → final consumer goods firms → households. The concept of intermediate input materials does not exist. Our model incorporates the capital equipment concept of the model in [13] having the similar modeling in this respect. The model in [13] and ours also have the similar properties for the concept of intermediate goods and the possibility of two-way business relationships between firms. The difference is whether the supplier–customer relationships between firms are maintained or not. In our model, the supplier–customer relationships established at the beginning of the simulation are maintained, while in the model in [13], the business relationships are established randomly at any point in time, so the transaction network structure is not maintained. The details of our model are explained in the following sections.

3.1 Overview of the Model

In our model, there are five types of economic agents: firms, banks, households, government, and the central bank. Each entity interacts through the five types of markets described below. The following is a detailed description of each agent.

- Firm agents: Firms develop a production strategy, secure the necessary la bor, capital goods, and intermediate input materials, and then manufacture products. Wages are paid to employees. Products are sold to households and firms through supplier-customer relationships. Firms also seek loans from banks to fund their operations and cover shortfalls. Furthermore, government taxes the profits earned from business activities. After-tax profit is distributed to households as dividends, and the remainder is held in bank deposits.
- Banking agents: Banks accept deposits from households and firms while lending to firms but not to households. When banks have excess funds, they invest them in government bonds. Furthermore, banks are subject to financial regulations, such as liquidity ratio regulations, and they must borrow short-term funds from the central bank when they have inadequate funds to meet these regulations. Banks do not employ workers.
- Household agents: Households provide labor to firms and the government in exchange for wages. Wages are accumulated in the form of bank deposits. Households spend their wages and some of their accumulated assets for consuming and purchasing goods from firms. Households do not borrow and are shareholders in firms and banks, depending on the size of their assets. They receive distributions from firm and bank profits. In addition, they earn interest on their bank deposits. Moreover, they receive unemployment benefits from the government while unemployed. They must pay income taxes to the government if they receive income from wages or dividends.
- Government agent: The government hires and compensates government employees. It also provides unemployment benefits to people who are unemployed. Revenue is generated by the amount of taxes collected from each entity, and if the fiscal balance is negative, the government issues government bonds.
- Central bank agent: The central bank is responsible for issuing legal tenders, maintaining central bank accounts for banks and the government, and holding central bank reserves. It also holds the portion of government bond issues that banks do not hold. The central bank lends short-term funds to banks to meet their funding needs. The government receives all interest income from government bond holdings and short-term lending. The central bank does not employ workers.

Each aforementioned agent interacts with one of the five model types. In the business-to-business (B2B) product trading market, products are ordered and delivered between firms through the supplier-customer relationship described as follows: In the business-to-household product trading market, households purchase unsold products and engage in consumption activities. Households, firms, and the government interact in the labor market. Firms and the government contract to pay the household's desired wage in exchange for the required labor from the latter. In the credit market, firms apply to banks for loans to cover capital shortages and banks review the applications and decide whether to accept or reject them. Furthermore, in the deposit market, households and firms interact with banks, which accept deposits from households and firms to secure funds for loans. Section 3.4 describes the details of the interactions in each market.

3.2 Flow of Events in a Step

In economic activities, for example, in a series of activities such as production planning, procurement of raw materials and labor, provision of necessary funds, product production, sales, profit determination, and return of profits to shareholders are repeated within a certain period for a company. In our model, a cycle of economic activity is represented as a single step, with events corresponding to the actions of economic agents occurring one after another within each step. Table 1 shows the sequence of events and their contents. Notably, one step in this model is assumed to be a quarter of year in reality.

3.3 Construction of Business-to-business Supplier-Customer Networks

In this model, each firm requires at least one product as an intermediate input material for production. Each firm's intermediate input material suppliers are predetermined, and the required quantities are purchased at each step via interfirm supplier–customer relationships. In constructing a supplier–customer network, we mainly referred to the method taken in the CAB model [7]. However, in the CAB model, the number of customers of a company is determined based on industry statistics, but in this study, the number of customers is assigned stochastically due to the lack of applicable data. The procedure for establishing a network of supplier–customer B2B relationships is as follows:

1. With the number of firm agents as ϕ_f, we generate a matrix $\phi_f \times \phi_f$ (called the SC matrix), where the rows of the SC matrix represent product sales destinations, and the columns represent intermediate input material suppliers. For example, the first row represents firm 1's product sales destination, and the first column represents the suppliers of intermediate input materials required by firm 1 to manufacture its product.
2. Determine the number of firms to which products are sold per firm according to the following probabilities
   $\{1 : 67\%, 2 : 22\%, 3 : 11\%\}$
   According to Fujiwara et al., the number of clients for Japanese firms follows a power distribution, $x^{-1.26}$ [14]. Such probabilities are based on Fujiwara et al. and have been adjusted to account for the number of firm agents.
3. For each firm, select a destination firm randomly from the remaining firms, excluding itself, based on the number of destination firms determined in the previous step. Accordingly, 1 is entered in the cell corresponding to the number of the destination firms in the row for the selling firm in the SC matrix. If a company does not have any intermediate input material suppliers, it is assigned a supplier.

Table 1. flow of events and their contents

No	Event	Outline
1	Production planning	Each firm updates its expected product sales and production volume
2	Firm labor demand	Each firm estimates the labor required
3	Price, interest rate, and wage setting	Each agent estimates the value of the goods that each entity can offer. (Firms, banks, and households determine product prices, deposit and lending rates, and desired wage levels, respectively)
4	Planning for ordering intermediate inputs and capital equipments	Each firm estimates the intermediate input materials and capital equipments required
5	Business-to-business product market (demand)	A customer firm places an order with the supplier firms for the number of intermediate inputs required. Note that the intermediate inputs ordered and received are used in production after the next step
6	Capital equipment order	Each firm place orders for capital equipments
7	Credit market (demand)	Each firm calculates its financing needs, selects a bank to apply for a loan, and applies for a loan
8	Credit market (supply)	Banks evaluate the loan applications received and provide loans to the successful applicants
9	Labor market	Firms and governments interact with households to secure labor
10	Production of products	Firms produce products based on capital equipments, intermediate inputs and labor inventories
11	Capital equipment supply	Each firm provides products based their market share
1211	Business-to-business product market (supply)	Supplier firms sell products to customer firms based on order quantity and production volume
13	Business-to-household product trading market	Households purchase products from firms and consume
14	Interest rates, government bonds, loan repayments	Arrangement of loan/loan relationships (firms repay part of the principal and pay interest on loans, the government repays the principal and pays interest on government bonds, and banks repay the principal and pay interest if they receive short-term funding from the central bank, along with interest payments on deposits)
15	Wages and unemployment benefits	The firms and government pay wages to households. The government pays unemployment benefits to the unemployed
16	Tax payments	Taxes on profits and income are paid to the government
17	Dividends	Firms and banks pay a portion of their after-tax profits as dividends to households
18	Bankruptcy	Bankruptcy resolution for any failed firms and banks
19	Depositor selection	Firms and households choose the bank where they deposit their cash holdings
20	Government bond purchases	The government issues new government bonds depending on fiscal balance, and the banks purchase them. The central bank holds any remaining amount
21	Short-term funds (liquidity) supply	The central bank provides short-term funds to banks upon the banks' request

4. The proportion of the value of intermediate input materials required for a firm to manufacture one product is distributed equally among the suppliers of intermediate input materials. The value ratio of intermediate input materials procured by firm i from intermediate input material supplier firm j is denoted by $inpv_{i,j}$. To determine the proportions of the values, we divide the value of each cell by the sum of the columns in the SC matrix.

Each column in the SC matrix created by the preceding procedure represents the value ratio of intermediate input materials required to manufacture products by the corresponding firm. Meanwhile, although firms with cell values greater than 0 in each row represent firms to which products are sold, the size of the cell value is not proportional to the number of sales. Each customer's sales amount varies depending on the number of orders received from the customer company. The quantity of intermediate input materials required for a firm to manufacture a product unit is calculated at the start of the simulation using the following formula.

$$inpq_{i,j} = 1 * costratio \ / \ \#of \ supplier_i \ (firm_j \in supplier_i) \qquad (1)$$
$$costratio = 1/\mu_I$$

$inpq_{i,j}$ denotes the quantity of intermediate input materials that firm i procures from intermediate input material supplier firm j to produce one unit of the product, $supplier_i$ is the set of supplier firms of firm i, $firm_j \in supplier_i$ denotes that firm j is a supplier of firm i. $\#of \ supplier_i$ is the total number of elements in the set of supplier firms of firm i, and μ_I is the raw material productivity, which in this study was 1.4.[1]

3.4   Demand Matching

Each market has a demand side that seeks the object of trade and a supply side that provides it. For example, in the labor market, labor is the object of exchange; households providing labor are on the supply side, and firms and governments seeking labor are on the demand side. Table 2 lists each market's demand and supply sides. The flow of transactions between the demand and supply sides in each market can be organized as shown in Algorithm 1, although some differences exist between markets. In the construction of this algorithm we mainly referred to [15].

The parameters varying from market to market in Algorithm 1 are listed in Table 3. When the matching quantity is set to "all demand", for example, if there is a demand for 10 items, all 10 demands will be met in a single matching. On the other hand, when "one at a time" is selected, only 1 of the 10 demands will

---

[1] According to the Basic Survey of Corporate Activities conducted by the Ministry of Economy, Trade and Industry (METI), the cost-to-income ratio of domestic firms has remained around 80% year after year. Note, 1.4 was chosen as the parameter that provides stable results when running the model because the reciprocal of 1.4 is close to this level at about 71%.

Table 2. Demand Side and Supply Side by Market

Market	Demand side	Supply side
Business-to-business product market	Firms	Firms
Business-to-household product market	Households	Firms
Labor market	Firms, government	Households
Credit market	Firms	Banks
Deposit market	Firms, households	Banks

be met, leaving 9 demands. In this case, the demand-supply matching process is executed again, starting from the first step of the demand-supply matching process. The matching quantity is set to "one at a time" only in the product trading market between firms and households because households are assumed to have demand for a variety of products rather than satisfying all of their demand with the products of a single supply agent. If the supply side' s capacity is less than that of the demand side, the matching volume is limited to the volume supplied by the supply side. In the business-to-business product trading market, supplier and customer relationships determined at the start of the simulation automatically determine the suppliers and quantities to be ordered. Introducing a mechanism that allows customers to change suppliers is an issue that must be addressed in the future. In the deposit market, whether depositors change from their current deposit location to another is probabilistically determined by the difference in interest rates. This was performed to avoid concentrating deposits in one bank.

Algorithm 1. Demand-supply matching process in the market

1: **while** Agents with demand exist, and agents with supply capacity exist and iterations < predetermined number **do**
2:    All agents with demand greater than zero on the demand side are extracted.
3:    The agents extracted in step 2 become randomly sorted.
4:    **for** The following steps are executed for the top of the sorted agents in order. **do**
5:       The predetermined number of agents with supply capacity on the supply side is extracted.
6:       The agents extracted in step 5 become sorted by the specified rule.
7:       **for** The following steps are executed in order for the top of the sorted agents on the supply side. **do**
8:          **if** Supply and demand match. **then**
9:             Transaction is executed.
10:          **end if**
11:       **end for**
12:    **end for**
13: **end while**

Table 3. Matching Parameters by Market

market	Repetitions	Extracts	Sort by	Matching quantity
B2B market	1	1	–	All demand
B2C market	5	5	Lowest price	One at a time
Labor market	20	10	Lowest asking wage	All demand
Credit market	3	3	Lowest loan interest rate	All demand
Deposit market	3	3	Highest interest rate	All demand

B2B market means business-to-business product market. B2C market means business-to-household product market.

3.5   Agent Behaviors

The behaviors of each agent are not described in this paper because of space limitations. For details, please refer to [1]. However, the concept of capital goods is unique to this model and will be explained in the following sections. For facilitating explanation, we will refer to the model in [1] as the reference model and to the model in this paper as the current model.

3.6   Major Differences Between Reference and Current Models

The concept of capital equipment, is introduced into the current model. All firms use capital equipment to produce their products. The productivity of capital equipment, μ_k, which represents the number of products that can be produced per piece of capital equipment, is set at 1.5 for all firms and all capital equipment. The labor capital equipment ratio, ι_k, which represents the maximum number of capital equipment that a worker can be equipped with, is 6.4. These two values were set referring to [6]. Thus, the maximum number of products that a worker can produce in one step is $1.5 * 6.4 = 9.6$. The durability period of capital equipment, η_k, is set to 20 steps (equivalent to 5 years in the real world). This is determined by referring to the table of useful lives of major depreciable assets published by the National Tax Administration Agency of Japan. Firms determine the desired number of capital facilities assumed for the current period using the following formula.

$$K_{fi,t}^{D} = (1 + g_{fi,t}^{D})K_{fi,t-1} \tag{2}$$

$$g_{fi,t}^{D} = \gamma_1 \frac{pcfr_{fi,t-1} - \bar{r}}{\bar{r}} + \gamma_2 \frac{u_{fi,t-1}^{D} - \bar{u}}{\bar{u}}, \tag{3}$$

where $K_{fi,t}^{D}$ denotes firm i's desired number of capital facilities in the period t, $g_{fi,t}^{D}$ denotes the desired capital facility growth rate, and $K_{fi,t-1}$ denotes the number of capital facilities owned in period $t - 1$, $u_{fi,t-1}^{D}$ represents the capital equipment utilization rate, which is calculated as the desired production volume of firm i in period t/(the number of capital facilities owned * The productivity of capital equipment). γ_1, γ_2, $\bar{r}$, and $\bar{u}$ denote constants and are set to 0.01, 0.02, 0.03, and 0.90, respectively. These values are taken from [6]. $pcfr_{fi,t-1}$ denotes the net asset cash flow multiplier for firm i in period $t-1$, where the total capital equipment held is added to the calculation of net assets, as defined in the reference model. The investment amount of capital equipment purchased in each period is not reflected in the operating cash flow calculation because it is a capital transaction. Therefore, the operating cash flows in the reference and current models are the same. The net asset cash flow multiples in the current model are as follows:

$$pcfr_{fi,t} = \frac{OCF_{fi,t}}{NW_{fi,t-1}} \qquad (4)$$

$$NW_{fi,t} = \text{reference models' } NW_{fi,t} + KV_{fi,t}, \qquad (5)$$

where $KV_{fi,t}$ denotes the total value of capital facilities owned by firm i in period t. The capital equipment owned by firm i is assumed to be depleted by $KV_{fi,t}/\eta_k$ in each period. Firm i orders the quantity of capital equipment it aims to own, i.e., $(1 + g_{fi,t}^D) * K_{fi,t}^D/\eta_k$, in each period. However, the ability to procure capital equipment based on the quantity ordered depends on the availability of sufficient products for capital equipment.

The mechanism for ordering and procuring capital equipment is based on [13], where the required quantity of capital equipment is aggregated on the basis of the industry attribute of the firms and the products produced by each firm are provided according to its share of product sales in the industry to which it belongs in the immediately preceding period, rather than directly between individual firms with supplier- customer relationships, as in case of product sales. Thus, a firm provides the products it produces in proportion to its share of product sales in its industry in the preceding period. Although the percentage of the products of each industry comprising a unit of capital equipment can be set differently for each industry, in the setting of the current model, the percentages of the products of each industry comprising a unit of capital equipment are assumed to be equal. The maximum quantity of products that a firm can provide for capital equipment in each period is limited to 3% of the quantity of products manufactured in the period.

The number of products a firm can produce is dependent on the number of workers and intermediate input materials it has in the reference model; however, in the current model, the number of products a firm can produce is also dependent on the number of capital facilities it has.

$$y_{fi,t}^{max} = min\{mat_{1,fi,t}/inpq_{fi,1}, mat_{2,fi,t}/inpq_{fi,2}, \cdots ,$$
$$mat_{n,fi,t}/inpq_{fi,n}, \mu_k \iota_k N_{fi,t}, \mu_k K_{fi,t}\},$$

where $mats_{,fi,t}$ denotes the quantity of intermediate input materials s in stock for firm i in period t. $inpq_{fi,s}$ denotes the quantity of intermediate input materials required by firm i to produce a unit of product, and $N_{fi,t}$ denotes the number of workers employed by firm i in period t.

Because of the introduction of the capital equipment concept in the current model, the method of updating product markups has changed from that in the reference model. The product markup is the percentage that firm i adds to the product manufacturing cost uc when setting the product price p in step t, and their relations can be expressed as $p_{fi,t} = uc_{fi,t} * (1 + mu_{fi,t})$. In the reference model, the only criterion for increasing or decreasing the product markup is whether the product inventory ratio exceeds the threshold value ν. However, in the current model, we introduced a capital equipment utilization criterion, $u_{threshold}$, and added another condition indicating whether $u_{threshold}$ is more than 95%. This was done to avoid raising the product markup when the product inventory ratio becomes low under the condition of low facility utilization. The current model differs from the reference model with respect to many other aspects because of the introduction of the capital equipment concept (e.g., the capital equipment sales volume is reflected in the calculation of the expected product sales volume). However, these are minor changes and will not be explained here.

4 Simulation Analysis

This section reports the simulation analysis results using the model described in the previous section.

4.1 Analysis Settings

Various hyperparameters must be determined before the simulation analysis can be performed. These hyperparameters were set referring to [1] and [6]. Table 4 summarizes the main hyperparameters of the model used in the study.

4.2 Simulation Results

This section reports the simulation results with the model parameters based on the reference model. Figure 1 plots the mean value and ±1 standard deviation of the results of each trial after running the 100-step simulation ten times. The price index is calculated by taking the weighted average of the average prices of firm and household products.

According to the transition in nominal GDP, the standard deviation is within a small range up to about 10 steps in the early stage of the simulation; subsequently, the standard deviation gradually increases. This trend is common for each index value. In the early stages of the simulation, the results of each simulation are similar, partly owing to the initial settings. Furthermore, for the real GDP growth rate and price growth rate, the standard deviation expands from approximately steps 10 to 20 and then shrinks in subsequent steps, staying within a narrow range. This can be attributed to the adjustments made in the model to the effects of the initial settings, etc.; the stability of the model increased with increasing number of steps.

Table 4. Hyperparameters setting

Category	Item	Symbol	Value
No. of agents	Firms	ϕ_f	110
	Households	ϕ_h	8000
	Banks	ϕ_b	10
	Gov	ϕ_g	1
	Central bank	ϕ_c	1
Product-related	Material productivity	μ_I	1.4
	Initial firm product markup	μ_{f0}	7%
	Initial household product markup	μ_{h0}	11%
	Estimated inventory ratio to product sales	ν	0.05
Finance-related	Initial interest rate on deposit	i_0^d	0.10%
	Initial interest rate on loan	i_0^l	0.75%
	Interest rate on government bond	i^g	0.25%
	Interest rate on short-term liquidity	$\bar{i}^{CB}$	0.50%
	Loan term	η	20 steps
Profit-related	Corporate tax rate, income tax rate	τ_π	18%
	Dividend payout ratio for firms and banks	ρ_g	90%
Capital-related	Capital equipment productivity	μ_k	1.5
	Labor capital equipment ratio	ι_k	6.4
	The components of the capital growth rate	$\bar{r}$	0.03
	The components of the capital growth rate	$\bar{u}$	0.9
	The components of the capital growth rate	$\gamma 1$	0.01
	The components of the capital growth rate	$\gamma 2$	0.02

Excluding the initial stage by the 35th step, where output fluctuations were significant, the average values per step (standard deviation in parentheses) were as follows: the nominal GDP growth rate was approximately 0.46% (0.26%), price inflation rate was 0.48% (0.06%), real GDP growth rate was -0.02% (0.25%) and unemployment rate of 23% (0.08%). These levels are close to the reference model's nominal GDP growth rate of 0.86% (0.9%), price inflation rate was 0.43% (0.08%), real GDP growth rate of 0.44% (0.9%), and unemployment rate of 19% (3.3%).

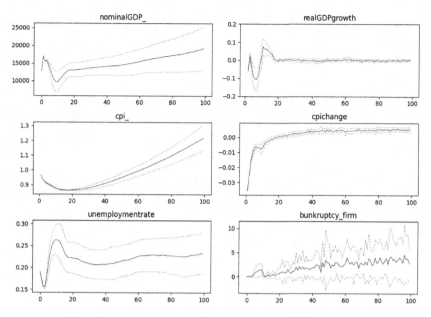

Fig. 1. Mean and standard deviation of each indicator value obtained from ten trials of simulation up to 100 steps

4.3   Sensitivity Analysis

For the sensitivity analysis, we compared the base scenario of holding two months' worth of intermediate input material inventories with that of 2.5, 1.5 and 1.0 month.

Figure 2 shows the transitions in the nominal GDP, unemployment rate, real production quantity, upper limit by labor, upper limit by input material, and upper limit by capital equipment. The upper limit by labor is the upper limit of the amount of product that can be produced based on the secured labor force, and the upper limit by input materials is the corresponding amount of product that can be produced based on the intermediate input material inventory. The values for each scenario are the average of ten simulations.

Figure 2 shows that the results of the base scenario (blue solid line) and the setting of 1.0 months worth of intermediate input material inventory (purple dashed line) are almost similar. The results of the 1.5 month inventory (green dotted line) show better performance than the others. Furthermore, the results of the 2.5 month inventory (orange dash-dot-dash line) show that the nominal GDP is suppressed as the simulation proceeds while the unemployment rate remains high throughout. The unemployment rate seems to have increased owing to a decrease in the number of workers required due to sluggish product production volume. One reason for the sluggish product production volume is that the upper limit by input material is lower than the required production quantity in later steps of the simulation, which is believed to restrain the production of products.

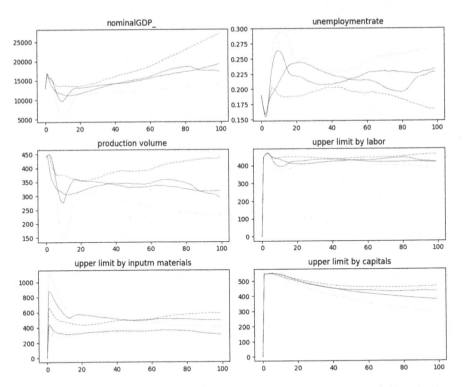

Fig. 2. Transitions in average of nominal GDP, unemployment rate, desired production quantities, real production quantities, upper limit by labor, and upper limit by input materials.

In a case where the inventory is 2.5 months worth of intermediate input materials, most of the products firms produce are sold to firms; further, firms are unable to prepare adequate quantities of products for households. The quantity of intermediate input materials needed for production declines with the decreasing quantity of household purchases. The aforementioned negative effects may have accumulated to suppress economic activity.

5 Summary

This study attempted to bring the behavior of firms in the model closer to real corporate behavior by introducing the concept of capital equipment into the model proposed by [1], which is a suitable MABM for analyzing the propagation of the impact of economic shocks. The transactions related to capital equipment were not conducted directly between firms, but rather a pool of capital goods was established, into which each firm provided products according to its market share, in reference to [13]. In the latter half of the study, we conducted a sensitivity analysis on the inventory quantity of intermediate input materials using the proposed model and found that if the inventory quantity to be secured in each period was estimated to be larger than necessary, most products will be sold to firms as intermediate input materials, while unable to produce adequate products to be sold to households, decreasing the household purchases. This would cause a negative spiral of reduced product production estimates by firms, further reducing production activity.

One issue that should be addressed in the future is how to perform an appropriate analysis and to set the scope of the analysis according to problem consciousness. The model in this paper can be analyzed from various perspectives due to the wide range of agent types and interdependent behaviors, but in contrast, there is a concern that the focus of the analysis may become ambiguous. Therefore, it is important to establish a clear agenda for the analysis. After resolving these issues, we believe the next challenge is adapting our analysis to real economic data. Specifically, we envision setting up model parameters compatible with real data using Japanese input-output tables and corporate statistics data and conducting analyses for various shocks.

References

1. Obata, T., Sakazaki, J., Kurahashi, S.: Building a macroeconomic simulator with multi-layered supplier-customer relationships. Risks **11**(7), 128 (2023). https://doi.org/10.3390/risks11070128
2. Cohen, K. J.: Simulation of the Firm. The American Economic Review, vol. 50, no. 2, Papers and Proceedings of the Seventy-Second Annual Meeting of the American Economic Association, pp. 534–540 (1960)
3. Shubik, M.: Simulation of the industry and the firm. Am. Econ. Rev. **50**(5), 908–919 (1960)
4. Fagiolo, G., Roventini, A.: Macroeconomic policy in DSGE and agent-based models. Rev. l'OFCE **124**(5), 67–116 (2012)
5. Dawid, H., Delli Gatti, D.: Agent-based macroeconomics. Handb. Comput. Econ. **4**, 63–156 (2018)
6. Caiani, A., Godin, A., Caverzasi, E., Gallegati, M., Kinsella, S., Stiglitz, J.E.: Agent based-stock flow consistent macroeconomics: towards a benchmark model. J. Econ. Dyn. Control **69**, 375–408 (2016)
7. Hillman, R., Barnes, S., Wharf, G., MacDonald, D.: A new firm-level model of corporate sector interactions and fragility: the corporate agent-based (CAB) model. OECD Economics Department Working Paper no. 1675 (2021)
8. Inoue, H., Todo, Y.: Firm-level propagation of shocks through supply-chain networks. Nat. Sustain. **2**, 841–847 (2019)
9. Inoue, H., Todo, Y.: The propagation of economic impacts through supply chains: the case of a mega-city lockdown to prevent the spread of COVID-19. PLoS One **15**, e0239251 (2020)
10. Hallegatte, S.: An adaptive regional input-output model and its application to the assessment of the economic cost of Katrina. Risk Anal. **28** (2008)
11. Otto, C., Willner, S., Leonie, W., Frieler, K., Levermann, A.: Modeling loss-propagation in the global supply network: the dynamic agent-based model acclimate. J. Econ. Dyn. Control **83**, 232–269 (2017)
12. Guan, D., et al.: Global supply-chain effects of COVID-19 control measures. Nat. Hum. Behav. **4**, 577–587 (2020)

13. Poledna, S., Miess, M., Hommes, C., Rabitsch, K.: Economic forecasting with an agent-based model. Eur. Econ. Rev. **151**, 104306 (2023)
14. Fujiwara, Y., Aoyama, H.: Large-scale structure of a nation-wide production network. Eur. Phys. J. B **77**, 565–580 (2010)
15. Riccetti, L., Russo, A., Gallegati, M.: An agent based decentralized matching macroeconomic model. J. Econ. Interac. Coord. **10**, 305–332 (2015)

Nowcasting Corporate Product Development Activities Through News Article by BERTopic: The Case of the Japanese Chemical Company

Haruna Okazaki$^{(\boxtimes)}$ (ID) and Hiroshi Takahashi$^{(\boxtimes)}$ (ID)

Graduate School of Business Administration, Keio University, 4-1-1 Hiyoshi, Kohoku-ku, Yokohama 223-8526, Japan
{okazaki.haruna,htaka}@keio.jp

Abstract. In this study, we attempt to extract corporate trends from news data. Specifically, in this analysis, we employed BERTopic to group news containing various topics into several categories. BERTopic is a tool for document clustering that utilizes BERT. The analysis focused on examining the relevance between topics related to products and corporate activities. The study targeted news headlines of specific chemical company listed on the Japanese stock market, covering a sample period of 24 years from 1996 to 2019. The results of the analysis revealed (1) the ability of BERTopic to classify target news into multiple groups and (2) the potential to efficiently obtain information about future corporate activities from the content of the news. These findings indicate the possibility of acquiring timely information about corporate trends through the analysis of news headlines using BERTopic.

Keywords: BERTopic · Nowcasting · Alternative Data · Asset Pricing

1 Background

Companies undergo constant changes such as growth or decline, and these changes are relevant to all stakeholders surrounding the company. For such stakeholders, the actions of a company that are relevant to them are captured by the term "corporate trends". Stakeholders include not only employees of the company but also various individuals and organizations, such as end users who use the products produced by the company and investors who provide funding for the company's growth.

For stakeholders, corporate trends can significantly impact their lives if the influence is substantial, or they may not need to be concerned if the impact is minor. Nonetheless, corporate trends, to varying degrees, have an influence. Precisely because they have an impact, it becomes necessary for stakeholders to follow corporate trends. In this study, we attempt to conduct an analysis focused on extracting valuable information about corporate trends from the perspective

M. Bono et al. (Eds.): JSAI-isAI 2023 Workshops, LNAI 14644, pp. 217–225, 2024.
https://doi.org/10.1007/978-3-031-60511-6_14

of investors, who play a notable role among stakeholders by providing funding for corporate activities [1].

To track corporate trends, various means are available. For instance, widely known methods include shareholder meetings that inform investors about the company's financial situation within the company and securities reports that compile information about the company's future strategies. Based on such information, investors make decisions on whether to invest in the company or not. However, shareholder meetings and securities reports are only published a few times a year, making it challenging to follow the company's detailed strategies and real-time focus on business. As a solution to such challenges, tracking news data can be highlighted as a means to capture nuanced corporate trends without missing out on the finer details.

In this study, we grouped news containing various topics into several categories using news data and analyzed the relevance between topics related to products and corporate activities. The analysis focused on the chemical industry, which is one of the industries known for its active research and development activities. In the midst of various news articles, efficient extraction of information related to research and development activities is crucial for investors. In the next section, we will discuss previous research, followed by the presentation of the analysis methods and results in Sect. 4, and finally, a summary in Sect. 5.

2   Previous Studies

An example of a prior study demonstrating the impact of news data on external factors is Chan's research [2]. In this study, Chan [2] shows that after the release of negative news, stock prices tend to decline, providing empirical evidence of the correlation between news and stock prices. Antweiler et al. [3] suggest the potential for changes in trading volume due to postings on platforms such as internet bulletin boards. Yamashita et al. [8] demonstrate, through an analysis using a sentiment dictionary, that there is a significant relationship between the stock index return changes and the negative (or positive) news classified by keywords.

Goshima et al. [4] utilizes deep learning to investigate the impact of news content on stock prices, demonstrating that news articles indeed influence stock prices. However, they mention the possibility of a lag in the impact on stock prices by news indicators. As a precedent study on how news content affects stock prices, Ryan et al. [5] sugguest that there is a consistent relationship between news content and stock market reactions. Nishi et al. [6,7] demonstrate that utilizing text generation techniques to create text for each polarity and incorporating it into model construction improves the accuracy of the model.

Zhang et al. [9] analyze the relationship between research and development activities and the stock market. In this study, they demonstrate that the research and development ratio has an impact on stock prices, suggesting the importance of appropriately disclosing information related to research and development activities. Matsumoto et al. [10] have analyzed the relationship between technological diversification and corporate value based on patent data for listed companies in Japan, demonstrating the occurrence of diversification discounts. Yonemura et al. [11] conducted visualization after acquiring vector representations of patent documents through natural language processing, comparing the temporal trends of patents held by different companies. Chen et al. [12] focused on patents from both Japan and the United States, estimating the temporal evolution of industrial compositions in each country through soft clustering of patent documents and highlighting differences between the two nations. In this study, the analysis is focused on research and development-oriented companies.

Among the diverse news delivered to the market, some contain information related to research and development. There is a study that suggests the possibility of using BERTopic to track the activities of different departments within a company from news articles [13]. Okazaki et al. [13] focused on Toshiba (Company Code: <6502.T>), a widely known company in the Japanese electronics industry, and applied BERTopic to classify topics in Toshiba's news. By focusing on news about specific products and tracking the temporal changes in news, they suggested the potential to analyze news and follow the trends of different departments within the company using BERTopic. Additionally, in a subsequent paper [14], Okazaki et al. [14] extended this method to track corporate trends more finely. Instead of summarizing data for several years and classifying topics with BERTopic, they classified topics annually and compared them with information announced by the company, such as annual reports. They reported that this approach allows for detailed tracking of corporate trends. While these previous studies suggest the effectiveness of information extraction using BERTopic in the electronics industry, they do not demonstrate its effectiveness in other industries. In this analysis, we focus on the chemical industry as a different sector, particularly on FujiFilm (Company Code: <4901.T>), a company known for its diversification.

3   Analytical Methods

In this study, to verify the possibility of understanding corporate trends in the chemical industry from news data, we follow the procedure outlined by Okazaki et al. [13,14]. The specific steps are as follows: 1. Extract news data from Thomson Reuters News, 2. Conduct topic classification on the extracted news data using BERTopic, and 3. Compare the results of topic classification with relevant company reports, such as financial statements and production numbers of products, and reveal the relationship between the compared results and the results of topic classification.

3.1   News Data

The news data used in this study will be sourced from the global multimedia organization Thomson Reuters. The analysis will focus on news from the fiscal years 1996 to 2015.

3.2 Extracting News Data

First, we will extract news data for the target company, FujiFilm (Company Code: <4901.T>), from the aforementioned news dataset. We will consider news related to the specified company by identifying articles where the stock code of FujiFilm (Company Code: <4901.T>) is present in both the headline and body of the news. Extraction will be performed based on these criteria from the entire dataset.

3.3 Topic Classification

For grouping news articles, we employ a topic model called BERTopic [15] in this study. Traditional topic models involve creating a sentiment dictionary, assigning scores to phrases, calculating scores for individual sentences, comparing sentences, and computing the similarity between sentences to classify topics. Other methods include classification based on the probability of word occurrence in sentences. BERTopic, on the other hand, enables more context-aware topic classification by utilizing BERT (Bidirectional Encoder Representations from Transformers) [16] to vectorize individual sentences, taking context into account during topic classification.

3.4 Comparison with Securities Report

From the results of topic classification, we will select topics that reveal the characteristics of the target company. In this study, topics that provide insights into the industry or products of the target company are considered as its characteristics. The selected topics will be analyzed for their temporal changes using the topics_over_time method of BERTopic. This method calculates the frequency values of the selected topics for each fiscal year. We will then compare these frequency values with the descriptions and data related to corporate activities to analyze their consistency.

4 Result

4.1 Result of Extracting News Data

In this section, we present the results of extracting news for the target company, FujiFilm (Company Code: <4901.T>), from Thomson Reuters News for the fiscal years 1996 to 2015. The total number of Thomson Reuters News articles from 1996 to 2015 is 852,941. Using the aforementioned method, the extracted news related to FujiFilm (Company Code: <4901.T>) amounted to 4,517 articles.

4.2 Result of Topic Classification

Figure 1 displays the results of topic classification using BERTopic on the extracted news data. In Fig. 1, the top 13 topics are shown, indicating the prevalence of articles classified under each topic from the highest to the 13th highest.

For example, in the graph for Topic 9, the vertical axis is labeled with "ebola," "drug," and "superbug". These words represent representative terms for the topic, and the numerical values indicate the extent to which each word influences the topic.

Based on the results in Fig. 1, we consider Topic 8 and Topic 9 as distinctive topics for FujiFilm (Company Code: <4901.T>) and proceed to compare them with the annual reports and production numbers of products.

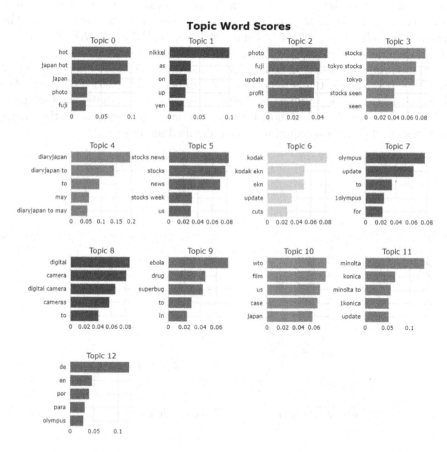

Fig. 1. Result of Topic Classification(Company Code:<4901.T>)

4.3   Comparison with Annual Reports and Production Numbers

Analysis of Topic 8 (Digital Camera). Topic 8 is represented by the words "digital," "camera," and "digital cameras." From these words, it is evident that Topic 8 pertains to FujiFilm's digital camera, one of its main products.

Figure 2 presents the observed dates and frequencies of Topic 8. The horizontal axis represents the year and month, while the vertical axis represents the frequency, indicating the count of times the topic is observed. From the graph, it is apparent that articles related to Topic 8 are concentrated around 2006 to 2008.

Figure 3 illustrates the trend in the production volume of digital cameras in Japan. The production volume data was obtained from the Camera & Imaging Products Association website[1] The horizontal axis represents time (years), and the vertical axis represents the production volume of digital cameras. The production volume was 63,575,987 units in 2006, peaked at 121,766,943 units in 2010, then declined to 23,853,572 units in 2016.

Comparing the trends in news articles and the production volume of digital cameras, it is evident that the peak in the number of news articles precedes the peak in the production volume of digital cameras. This analysis result suggests a lead time in news articles, though various factors may contribute to the timing of news article releases, requiring further detailed analysis[2].

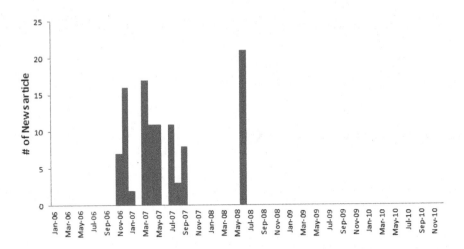

Fig. 2. Time evolution of Topic 8 (Digital Camera)

---

[1] For detailed data, refer to the Camera & Imaging Products Association website at https://www.cipa.jp/e/index.htm.
[2] The delivery of news articles could be influenced by various factors. Further detailed analysis is a future task.

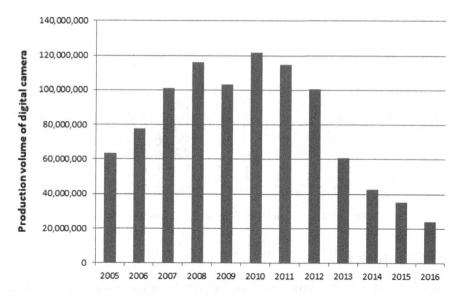

Fig. 3. Transition of Production volume of digital camera

Analysis of Topic 9 (Pharmaceuticals). Topic 9 is represented by the words "ebola", "drug", and "superbug", indicating that it pertains to the pharmaceutical topic.

Figure 4 displays the observed dates and frequencies of Topic 9. Similarly, the horizontal axis represents the observed year and month, while the vertical axis represents the frequency, indicating the count of times the topic is observed. From the graph, it is confirmed that numerous articles were distributed around 2006 to 2007.

Upon reviewing the content of the annual securities reports, no specific reports in the context of pharmaceuticals were found until before the fiscal year 2007. However, in the fiscal year 2007 report, there is a mention of expanding into the medical pharmaceutical business. In the fiscal year 2009 report, the entry into the development of a new influenza treatment drug is described. In the fiscal year 2010 report, the development status of new drugs is documented. Additionally, a component called "favipiravir" included in the antiviral drug "T-705" developed by FujiFilm is noted to be effective against "ebola," and in the fiscal year 2016, it was adopted as emergency aid materials for Guinea's Ebola hemorrhagic fever prevention.

This topic illustrates a case where it took a medium to long-term period for news articles to gain attention in Japan after distribution. The analysis result suggests that the content of news articles is closely related to future significant corporate activities. News articles cover a wide range of topics from short-term to long-term perspectives. Detailed analysis considering these time perspectives is identified as a future task.

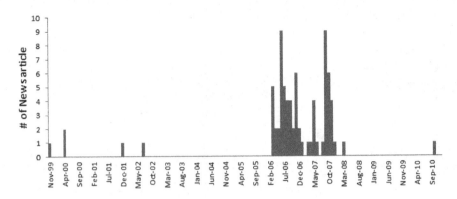

Fig. 4. Time evolution of Topic 9 (Pharmaceuticals)

5   Conclusion

This study attempts to extract corporate trends from news data. Particularly in this analysis, utilizing BERTopic, we categorized news containing various topics into several groups and conducted an analysis on the relevance between topics related to products and corporate activities. The results of the analysis revealed (1) the capability of BERTopic to classify target news into multiple groups and (2) the potential to efficiently obtain information about future corporate activities from the content of the news. These findings suggest the possibility of obtaining timely information about corporate trends through the analysis of news headlines using BERTopic. A more detailed analysis, expanding the scope of the subjects, is a future task.

Acknowledgments. This research was supported by Telecommunications Advancement Foundation, JSPS KAKENHI Grant Number JP20K01751and Keio University Academic Development Funds.

References

1. Brealey, R.A., Myers, S.C., Allen, F.: Principles of Corporate Finance. McGraw-hill, New York (2014)
2. Chan, W.S.: Stock price reaction to news and no-news: drift and reversal after headlines. J. Financ. Econ. **70**(2), 233–260 (2003)
3. Antweiler, W., Frank, M.Z.: Is all that talk just noise? The information content of internet stock message boards. J. Finan. **59**(3), 1259–1294 (2004)
4. Goshima, K., Takahashi, H.: Quantifying news tone to analyze the Tokyo stock exchange with deep learning. Secur. Anal. J. **54**(3), 76–86 (2016)
5. Ryan, B.: The Impact of News on Stock Market Investors, SSRN (2021). https://ssrn.com/abstract=3908662
6. Nishi,Y., Suge, A.,Takahashi, H.: Text analysis on the stock market in the automotive industry through fake news generated by GPT-2. In: Proceedings of International Workshop Artificial Intelligence of and for Business (AI-Biz2019) associated with JSAI International Symposia on AI 2019 (IsAI-2019) (2019)

7. Nishi, Y., Suge, A., Takahashi, H.: Construction of a news article evaluation model utilizing high-frequency data and a large-scale language generation model. SN Bus. Econ. **1**(104), 1–18 (2021)

8. Yanashita, Y., Johtaki, H., Takahashi, H.: Analyzing the influence of head-line news on the stock market in Japan. Int. J. Intell. Syst. Technol. Appl. **12**(3–4), 328–342 (2013)

9. Zhang, X., Zhang, Y., Mao, Y.: Corporate research and development strategy and stock price crash risk. In: Proceedings of the 2021 3rd International Conference on Economic Management and Cultural Industry (2021)

10. Matsumoto, Y., Suge, A., Takahashi, H.: Analysis of the relationship between technological diversification and enterprise value using patent data. Inf. Technol. Manage. 1–24 (2023)

11. Yonemura, T., Matsumoto, Y., Suge, A., Takahashi, H.: Constructing a decision-making system using patent document analysis. In: Jezic, G., Chen-Burger, J., Kusek, M., Sperka, R., Howlett, R.J., Jain, L.C. (eds.) Agents and Multi-Agent Systems: Technologies and Applications 2021. SIST, vol. 241, pp. 275–283. Springer, Singapore (2021). https://doi.org/10.1007/978-981-16-2994-5_23

12. Chen, Z., Matsumoto, Y., Suge, A., Takahashi, H.: The visualization of innovation pathway based on patent data—comparison between Japan and America. In: Jezic, G., Chen-Burger, J., Kusek, M., Sperka, R., Howlett, R.J., Jain, L.C. (eds.) Agents and Multi-Agent Systems: Technologies and Applications 2021. SIST, vol. 241, pp. 265–273. Springer, Singapore (2021). https://doi.org/10.1007/978-981-16-2994-5_22

13. Okazaki, H., Takahashi, H.: Nowcasting of corporate research and development trends through news article analysis by bertopic: the case of Japanese electric company. In: Proceedings of the International Conference on Electrical, Computer, Communications and Mechatronics Engineering (ICECCME) 16-18 November (2022)

14. Okazaki, H., Takahashi, H.: BERTopic study on the acquisition of information on business activities through news analysis: a year-by-year analysis. In: International Workshop: Artificial Intelligence of and for Business (AI-Biz2023), Associated with JSAI International Symposia on AI 2023 (IsAI-2023) (2023)

15. Grootendorst, M.: Bertopic: neural topic modeling with a class-based TF-IDF procedure (2022). https://doi.org/10.48550/arXiv.2203.05794

16. Devlin, J., Chang, M.: Lee, K., Toutanova, K.: Bert: pre-training of deep bidirectional transformers for language understanding, arXiv preprint arXiv:1810.04805 (2018)

Do Young People in Regional Cities of Japan Really Shift Away from Owning Automobiles? – From an Empirical Study and a Semi-structured Interview

Akiko Ueno, Yuko Okiyama, Nozomi Masuda, Ken-ichi Yamaga,
Aino Yamagata, Kazuto Yoshioka, Arata Abe⬤, Koichi Kitanishi⬤,
and Takashi Yamada(✉)⬤

Yamaguchi University, 1677-1, Yoshida, Yamaguchi City, Yamaguchi 753-8541, Japan
{a_abe,kitanisi,tyamada}@yamaguchi-u.ac.jp

Abstract. The objective of this study is to see whether young people in regional cities of Japan have really shifted away from owning automobiles. To accomplish this, the authors firstly analyze empirical data about driver's license statistics and consumer confidence survey to make clarified whether young people living in such places have really become not to drive. Then the authors implement a semi-structured interview to show whether and how their views to automobiles have changed. From the empirical analyses, although there is a trend away from having a driver's license in terms of both the nationwide average and that of regional cities in Japan, the ratio in regional cities are still much higher than the nationwide average. On the other hand, from the fieldwork, (1) the current young people do not consider having an automobile as high-status and (2) the views to having an automobile can be classified on the basis of three factors, necessity, interests, and whether s/he had an automobile at that time, into five types: aspiration, future, untouched, tool, and heavy users.

Keywords: Views to having an automobile · Empirical analysis · Semi-structured interview · Text mining

1 Introduction

It has been often pointed out that the younger people in Japan have become not to have their own automobile for the last decade or so. Although such a phenomenon has not been strictly defined, it involves the facts that the younger people do not obtain a driver's license or that they do not want to have an automobile. In addition, such a phenomenon is applied not only for automobiles

The authors thank Prof. Dr. Setsuya Kurahashi, Prof. Dr. Hiroshi Takahashi, and two anonymous reviewers for fruitful and helpful comments and suggestions. This study has been financially supported by Toyota Corolla Yamaguchi Co., Ltd.

M. Bono et al. (Eds.): JSAI-isAI 2023 Workshops, LNAI 14644, pp. 226–241, 2024.
https://doi.org/10.1007/978-3-031-60511-6_15

and trips but also for various goods, services, or behaviors. In other words, they have not behaved as the elderly generations had done. Possible reasons include: economic recessions for the last three decades leading to smaller wages and/or diversification of values among the people. To tackle this economic and social issue, joint efforts between industry and academia have been done. However, since there are the differences of public transport between urban cities and local ones and people in local areas are forced to buy and use automobiles as the daily transformations, whether such a phenomenon can be uniformly applied is an open question.

Research on the issue has been done by automobile industries and academics. Among these, the trend survey of vehicle market by Japan Automobile Manufacturers Association, Inc., issued on a biennial basis, have dealt with the views of young people to owing an automobile for the last few years. According to the reports published between 2015 and 2021, about 40% of young people in Japan had interests in buying and having their own automobile and thus this does not support the phenomenon [1]. On the other hand, Ohta (2015) has argued that the reason why the younger people have not had their automobile is that the Japanese market including automobiles has become plentiful, which is due to the long-standing economic recession [2]. As a result, their minds have shifted from having their own automobile to just using a car. On the other hand, some people own an automobile because having an automobile and/or driving is a kind of hobby [3]. Such a phenomenon can be observed in many developed countries/regions. For example, Silvak and Schoettle (2012a) have reported that over 80% of young people at their age of 19 have a driver's license in 1983 while only about 70% of them did in 2010 [4]. One of the reasons is that buying and having an automobile is too costly (Silvak and Schoettle, 2013). Similar situations have occurred in Switzerland and Australia [5,6]. But, that does not hold for worldwide because Silvak and Schoettle (2012b) report that in several countries the ratio of having a driver's license has increased [7].

Apart from this, several researchers have tried to clarify whether younger people really have become not to use automobiles by analyzing the data about travel behavior. Kohno et al. (2019) analyzed the trend of travel behavior by younger people in capital area of Japan and found that the usage of automobiles did not decrease but they went out less frequently [8]. Doi et al. (2013) analyzed the person trip data in terms of the people living in Kinki district and found that the younger people are the more preferable to stay home rather than to go out they would be and that the frequency of using automobiles is positively related to the population density [9]. Likewise, Doi et al. (2015) have reported that the younger people in Kinki district became not to go out by making comparison between 2000 and 2010 [10]. But, since these earlier studies have paid attention to rather larger cities, it is still unclear whether such findings are also true for smaller cities[1].

Based on the trends and the findings, the objective of this study is to see whether young people in regional cities of Japan really shift away from owning automobiles. Here, the authors take up Yamaguchi Pref. to progress the research. To accomplish this, the authors firstly analyze empirical data such about driver's license statistics, and then implement a semi-structured interview to show whether and how the younger people's views to automobiles have changed by using text-mining techniques. The reason is, many of people in regional cities have their own automobiles as will be explained in the sequel but that does not mean they really want to have them. This cannot be explained by revealed preference theory.

The remainder of the chapter is organized as follows: The next section empirically analyzes how many young people in Yamaguchi Pref. acquire a driver's license and have an automobile. Section 3 explains how our semi-structured interview is carried out and shows the results of how current and past young people have a view to having an automobile by text-mining approach and manual analysis. Finally, Sect. 4 concludes.

2   Empirical Facts in Yamaguchi Pref. or Related Areas

Figure 1 shows the ownership ratio of driver's license[2] for the people at the age between 20 and 29[3] in the nation and Yamaguchi Pref. between 2008 and 2021. The data are from Driver's License Statistics which is annually published by National Police Agency, and FY2001 edition or later are currently available [12]. On the whole, the ratio in Yamaguchi Pref. is higher than that in the nation. More precisely, in 2008, while the nationwide ratio is 86%, that in Yamaguchi Pref. is 93%. Then the nationwide ratio gradually decreases and the value is around 80% in 2021. On the other hand, that in Yamaguchi Pref. firstly increased and reached almost 100% until 2013, and then decreased to 90% in 2021.

Figure 2 gives the time series plot of the ownership ratio of automobiles in the nation and Chugoku-Shikoku region[4] between 2008 and 2021. The data are from

---

[1] According to the analyses of the authors from Japanese person trip data [11], female people in regional cities have become to use automobiles more while male have not. For one thing, there have been more needs for females to drive for shopping and commuting. The results cannot be included in the study due to limited space.

[2] This study deals with only class 1 driver's license, the ordinary license for driving a private automobile.

[3] Although people in Japan can obtain a driver's license from their age at 18, about half of them are college/university students and thereby they do not have enough money to do so.

[4] Since the data set is given by local region not by prefecture, the data about Yamaguchi Pref. are not available and the authors thus use those about Chugoku-Shikoku region.

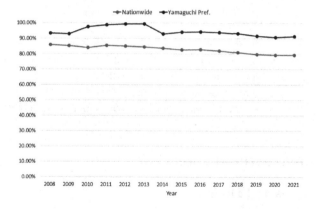

Fig. 1. Ownership ratio of driver's license for younger people in Japan

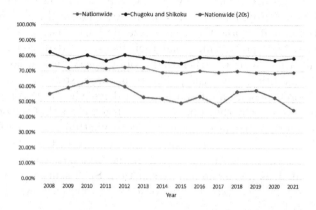

Fig. 2. Ownership ratio of automobiles in Japan

Consumer Confidence Survey which is monthly conducted by Cabinet Office [13]. For Chugoku-Shikoku region, since no data about the people at the age between 20 and 29 are available, only the data about the people of all ages. About three-quarters of people at their age over 18 in the nation have their own car in any given year and the value for Chugoku-Shikoku region is always slightly large. However, for the young people in their twenties, the ratio is apparently smaller: it started about 60% in 2008, went up to nearly 70% in 2011, but then gradually and steadily decreased reaching to 45% in 2021. The possible reasons are economic recession in the last three decades and the over-concentration in the capital area with ample public transport systems, resulting in the facts that they cannot afford to or have become not to rely on automobiles. On the other hand, in local areas like Yamaguchi Pref., the public transport system has become to diminish and the people there thus still need an automobile to commute and go shopping.

Table 1. Experimental design

Subjects	Residents in Yamaguchi Pref. at their age over 20
Number of subjects	30 (about 10 for 20s and about 5 for 30s, 40s, 50s, and over 60s)
Date	Mainly on November 5 and 6, 2022
Place	Main: A car dealer in Shunan City, Yamaguchi Pref.
	Sub: A university and other places in Yamaguchi Pref.

3   A Semi-structured Interview

3.1   Hypothesis and Design

As explained, many of the young people in local regions of Japan still get a driver's license and drive when they go out. But, according to the survey conducted by Japan Automobile Manufacturers Association, Inc., their main purpose of use is commuting and they emphasize 'design', 'space' and 'comfortableness' when they buy one, meaning that their lifestyle and/or consumption style has been utilization-focused rather than hobby-based for the last one or two decades [1]. In addition, since the public transport system in Yamaguchi Pref. has getting poorer, people can do nothing but drive when they commute and go out. Hence the reason why they purchase an automobile is that they regard automobiles as just a tool (means of mobility), not something fun, more technically, high-status. This is the hypothesis of the authors. Note that the 'high-status' means that the owners want to be envied by the others by having a fancy/good automobile, but does not mean self-satisfaction. Such sentiment or the way of thinking includes for example: 'I want to be cool to my partner.' and 'I want to be rich to the others'.

Table 1 summarizes the semi-structured interview implemented in this study. The expected number of subjects for each age is about 5, but since about half of the 20s are the students, the authors collect their views by doubling the number of subjects for that age and equally dividing two sub-groups: students and workers. The 23 subjects of 30 were collected at a car dealer and the others were done elsewhere. Although the authors carried out the fieldwork at the car dealer, a weekend bazaar was open on those days and the visitors came on foot or by car as a designated driver or passengers. Therefore, not all the subjects were the drivers or car lovers.

Table 2 lists the question items asked in the interview[5]. Questions 1, 2, 3, and 5 are to see the attributes of the subject. Questions 4, 6 and 8-a are used to ask whether the subject got a driver's license and bought an automobile. Finally, questions 7, 8-b, 9, and 10 are used to obtain the opinions of the subject about owing an automobile. The interview duration was about 30 min long on average. The subjects received a prepaid card for JPY1K (about 7 USD).

---

[5] The interviews reported in this paper were approved by the Independent Review Board of Yamaguchi University (No. 2022-048-01).

Table 2. Question items in the interview

Number	Question
1	Gender
2	Age
3	Occupation after graduation from high-school (Student, Worker, or Others)
4	Household budget for four years after graduating a high-school
a	Main sources of revenue (multiple selections) (Job, Part-time job, Allowance (fixed), Allowance (as needed), C2C, Yield from investment, Work on an internship, Freelance, or Others)
b	Ownership of an automobile during the period (Yes or No) Yes: How s/he saved money to buy it. No: For what s/he spent
5	Prefectures where s/he was at that time
6	Getting a driver's license during the period Yes: The reasons No: Whether s/he got it afterwards - Yes: The reasons - No: The reasons
7	Willingness to purchase an automobile
a	Whether s/he had it during the period (1: No, 2: Moderately no, 3: Moderately yes, 4: Yes)
b	The reasons
138	Having an automobile
a	Whether s/he bought one Yes-1: The reasons Yes-2: Maker and type s/he bought Yes-3: Maker and type s/he wanted to buy No-1: The reasons No-2: Maker and type s/he wanted to have if any No-3: Whether s/he bought one afterwards No-3-Yes-1: The reasons No-3-Yes-2: Maker and type s/he bought No-3-Yes-3: Maker and type s/he wanted to buy No-3-No: The reasons
b	Top three items s/he emphasize for purchase of an automobile (Gas mileage, Safeness, An exterior view, Interior decorating, Equipment such as car navigation system and/or car audio system, Roomy interior, Trunk capacity, Riding capacity, Status, Price, Brand, Others)
c	The reasons
39	Impressions for the car owners during the period
a	How many friends of his/hers they had his/her own automobile at that time
b	Impressions for the non-car owners during the period if any
c	Mood about having an automobile at that time if any
10	Imagine that s/he had had JPY 10 million at that time and for what s/he would have used (Savings, Investment, Repayment, Buying a home, Hobby, Buying an automobile, Better life, i.e., Purchase of more expensive products/services, Starting a business, Donation, Others)

Table 3. Attributes of the subjects

	# subjects	(#Males, #Females)	Both	Only DL	No
Gender					
Male	16				
Female	14				
Age bracket					
20s (student)	4	(0, 4)	0	4	0
20s (worker)	5	(4, 1)	4	1	0
30s	4	(2, 2)	3	1	0
40s	5	(3, 2)	3	2	0
50s	5	(4, 1)	3	2	0
60s or elder	7	(3, 4)	3	2	2
Occupation after graduating from a high-school					
Student	16	(6, 10)			
Worker	14	(10, 4)			

Both: S/He had both a driver's license and an automobile.
Only DL: S/He had a driver's license but did not have an automobile.
No: S/He did not have a driver's license or an automobile.

3.2 Results

Attributes of the Subjects. Table 3 summarizes the attributes of subjects. Nearly half of the subjects were females/males on the whole, but that was not true for several age brackets. Also, nearly half of the subjects were students after graduating from a high-school. Note that the place(s) in which they lived/are living include Yamaguchi Pref. (19.5), three major metropolitan areas (3.5), and the others (7). The reason why the values in the parentheses are not the integer is that one subject lived in Yamaguchi Pref. and Hyogo Pref. In terms of possession of driver's license and automobile, almost all the subjects have/had a driver's license and all the holders except the current students have/had his/her own automobile. In other words, the subjects at 30s or elder tended to have an automobile as well as a driver's license regardless of whether s/he was a student or a worker[6].

Analysis of the Answers by Text-Mining: Appearance Frequency of Words and Phrases. As explained before, several questions collect the qualitative data about how the past/current/future owners of automobiles have a view to automobiles themselves and purchase of automobiles. By analyzing them, such views can be compared between ages. This interview has three kinds of question types: purchase of automobiles (questions 6, 7, and 8a), status and/or value of owing automobiles (question 9), and points to be emphasized (question 10). To analyze the text data, the authors used both MAXQDA and Python (MeCab and pyvis).

---

[6] A quantitative analytical result is provided in the appendix.

1. Purchase of automobiles (questions 6, 7, and 8a)

   The authors extract related statements on the reasons for getting a driver's license and having an automobile, whether s/he has a plan to buy, and whether s/he had/will have an automobile. Then the authors classify them into eight patterns: status, fun, self-satisfaction, comfortableness, preference to automobiles, necessity, matter of course, and affordability.

   Table 4 shows the number of subjects who mentioned each item in questions 6, 7, and 8a. There are two points to be addressed from this table. The one is, albeit the sample size is relatively small, several elder subjects considered owing an automobile as high-status. For example, a female subject at 60s answered that for young, especially boys, automobiles were really high-status and that thus many of them desired to get a driver's license to have his/her own car. The other is people at 20s, 30s, and 40s tended to regard automobiles just as a tool.

2. Status (question 9c)

   Figure 3 displays a co-occurrence network diagram which shows the frequently addressed words and phrases by the subjects. The size of circles stands for the appearance frequency, the thickness of lines does the co-occurrence frequency, and the distance between the circles does their closeness. By measuring them, one sees how the social trend in owing an automobile was during the several years after having graduated from high-school.

   First, many of the younger subjects at 20s and 30s replied both automobiles/cars and image/impression (panel a). In addition, the words, "status" and "social trend" are also observed and these words are connected to the words "male", "female" and "kei-car/light automobile". Based on them, it seems that some stereotype about automobiles such as "automobiles like this should be owned by females" were shared at that time.

   Second, there are not specific co-occurrence in the replies of the subjects at 40s or elder (panel b), i.e., although each word is connected the word "automobile", the words except for "automobile" are not connected. Moreover, the possible reason why some subjects used the words like "classy car" and "sedan car" is, they experienced a boom in classy cars during the period. But, since the words/phrases "soup up a car" and "popular with men/women" are not inter-connected, the meaning of owing and/or using an automobile may be different from the subjects.

   To this end, while there is a clear impressions and/or social mood in automobiles for the younger subjects, the choice of automobiles varies according to use for elder subjects because they had a more realistic idea to purchase one.

3. Points to emphasize on when buying an automobile (question 10)

   Figure 4 is a co-occurrence network diagram which presents the reasons for the alternatives chosen by the subjects. The younger subjects, at 20s and 30s, mentioned about "exterior view" more and the words, "gas mileage', "interior decorating", and "price" were jointly and frequently used (panel a). The elder subjects, at over 40s, mainly focused on "automobiles/cars" and "gas mileage" which connected to the words, "gas mileage", "price", and "safeness" (panel

Table 4. Classification of statements about views to automobiles by age bracket

	Words and phrases[a]							
	(a)	(b)	(c)	(d)	(e)	(f)	(g)	(h)
20s (student)			1			3		
20s (worker)					1	5	2	
30s					1	3		
40s			1		3	2		
50s	1	1	1		1	5		
60s or elder	1	1			1	6	3	1

[a] The symbols in the table are as follows: (a) status, (b) fun, (c) self-satisfaction, (d) comfortableness, (e) preference to automobiles, (f) necessity, (g) matter of course, (h) affordability.

Table 5. Points which the subjects emphasized by age bracket

	Points[a]											
	(a)	(b)	(c)	(d)	(e)	(f)	(g)	(h)	(i)	(j)	(k)	(l)
20s (student)	2	2	2	1	3					2		
20s (worker)	5		4							5	1	
30s	2	2	3	1	1				1	2		
40s	2		3	1		1	1		1	1	1	
50s			4	2	1		1		2	1	1	
60s or elder	6	3	5	2					1	4		

[a] The symbols are as follows: (a) gas mileage, (b) safeness, (c) price, (d) interior design, (e) equipment, (f) roomy interior, (g) trunk capacity, (h) riding capacity, (i) high-status, (j) exterior view, (k) brand, (l) others.

b). In addition, they said about "mission", "used car" and "loan" which the younger subjects did not address. From this result, while the younger people put more weight on "exterior view", the elder people pay more attention to more realistic elements.

Table 5 summarizes the answers made by the subjects. For all ages, "exterior view" was chosen the most, "gas mileage" came next, and "price" was the third place. In terms of each age bracket, "equipment" was chosen most by the students, "price" and "gas mileage" for workers at 20s, "exterior view" was the first choice for 30s, 40s, and 50s, and "gas mileage" was preferred by the 60s or elder. It can be said that current young generations, unlike the elder ones, more likely to emphasize on costs rather than likes and tastes[7].

---

[7] According to one reviewer, it could be said that "their tough economic situation force[d] them to regard automobiles as just a tool". But, to say so, it is necessary to fully investigate their economic situations and how their leisure has changed. Since this comment is of particular importance, this should be studied in the future.

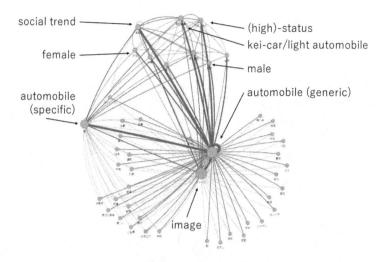

a. Subjects at 20s and 30s

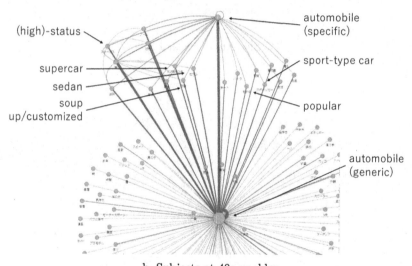

b. Subjects at 40s or elder

Fig. 3. Co-occurrence network diagram on social trends towards having an automobile ("automobile (generic)": general terms of automobiles/cars, "automobile (specific)": particular/specific automobiles)

Analysis of the Answers Based on the Context. The preceding part of the section mechanically analyzes the replies of the subject. This part, on the other hand, manually classifies the subjects into several types by combining their replies and their attributes. By doing so, it may be possible to clarify what kind

236   A. Ueno et al.

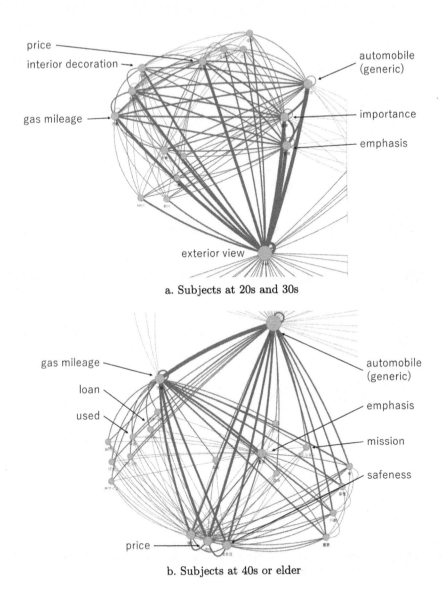

a. Subjects at 20s and 30s

b. Subjects at 40s or elder

Fig. 4. Co-occurrence network diagram on the points which the subjects emphasize when they purchase an automobile ("automobile (generic)": general terms of automobiles/cars, "automobile (specific)": particular/specific automobiles)

Table 6. Types of the subjects

Type	Interests	Necessities	Ownership
aspiration	Yes	Yes/No	No
untouched	No	No	No
future	Yes/No	Yes	No
tool	No	Yes	Yes
heavy users	Yes	Yes/No	Yes

Table 7. Classification of the subjects (60s+: 60s or elder)

	20s	30s	40s	50s	60s+
aspiration	1	0	0	0	1
untouched	0	0	1	1	2
future	0	1	1	0	1
tool	5	1	2	1	2
heavy users	3	2	1	3	1

of views to automobiles each type has and whether each type depends on the attribute of the subjects.

Tables 6 and 7 overview the classification of the subjects. The subjects are divided into five types, aspiration, future, untouched, tool, and heavy users, in accordance with three kinds of criteria: interests, necessities, and ownership of an automobile at that time. "Tool" type, automobiles are simply a tool, is the largest fraction. While two types, "tool" and "heavy uses", exist in all ages, "untouched" type is observed mainly in 60s or elder and "future" type are in 30s, 40s, and 60s or elder.

aspiration type (2 subjects) The subjects in this type did not mention the necessity of automobiles. Instead, they have interests. However, since they are/were not so rich that they gave up purchasing one currently/at that time. For these reasons, once they had an automobile, they were a heavy users. The points they emphasize when purchasing were exterior view and interior decorating, implying that automobiles with good design may attract the interests of such potential users/owners.

future type (3 subjects) The subjects in this type did not address the interests in automobiles, but albeit they had more or less necessity for automobiles they could not afford to do so. All the subjects got a driver's license at that time instead because their friends or others did so, too. Later, they bought a car so that they commuted or dropped and picked their kids up, which led to either a 'tool' type or a 'heavy user' type. From this result, having a car is not (always) high-status for such subjects.

untouched type (4 subjects) The subjects in this type did not have interests in automobiles or necessities for that regardless of whether they could afford. The common feature of this type is, they lived in a place, e.g. Tokyo metropolitan or Okayama Pref., where there were relatively great/good public transport. They did not accordingly have an automobile at that time. Judging from their replies, whether one has something to do with automobiles may be not only due to the social trend but also because of geographical factors. Other than these, the point which the subjects emphasize was "exterior view".

tool type (11 subjects) The subjects of this type did not have interests in automobile itself but felt necessity for that due to geographical reasons. About half subjects of this type were 20s. The points they pay attention to were "gas mileage", "price", and "safeness". In terms of the possession of automobiles, the subjects were divided into two sub-types based on the living place. On the one hand, the subjects in a place with relatively great/good public transport system, e.g. Osaka Pref. and Hyogo Pref., did not need an automobile and neither did their friends and acquaintances. On the other hand, the subjects in Yamaguchi Pref. had necessity for automobiles and they answered that many of their friends and acquaintances had a car. The subjects chose "price", "gas mileage", and "safeness" in question 8b but a certain fraction of them did not have any preference to car type.

heavy users type (10 subjects) The subjects of this type have highly interests in automobiles regardless of whether they could afford and are frequent drivers. Eight of ten subjects were males and seven of ten started to work after graduating from a high-school. There were no imbalance with respect to ages. Although many of them started to drive for commuting, their important points to select automobiles are "exterior view" and "status". In addition, a couple of the elder subjects think that the views to automobiles have varied, i.e. having an automobile was high-status at that time.

4   Concluding Remark

This study investigates whether young people in regional cities of Japan really shift away from owning automobiles. For this purpose, the authors firstly analyze empirical data about driver's license statistics and consumer confidence survey to make clarified whether young people living in such places have really become not to drive, and then implement a semi-structured interview to show whether and how the younger people's views to automobiles have changed. The main findings are in the followings: From the empirical analyses, (1) although there is a trend away from having a driver's license in terms of both the nationwide average and that of regional cities in Japan, the ratio in regional cities are still much higher than the nationwide average, and (2) the travel behavior of younger people in regional cities of Japan depends mainly on automobiles. On the other hand, from the fieldwork, (1) the current young people do not consider having an automobile as high-status and (2) the views to having an automobile can be classified on the basis of two factors, necessity and interests, into five types: aspiration, future, untouched, tool, and heavy users.

Possible future works are as follows: First, since there were only 30 subjects, it would be better to collect more subjects so that characteristics of each type is more clearly identified. This is not only because of lack of the subjects but also the variation of attributes; The places of the interview were only in Shunan City and Yamaguchi City both of which are relatively large in Yamaguchi Pref. Therefore, subjects living in smaller cities or towns may have different experiences and views. Second, something new marketing methods will be derived from the results. In addition, if there were some marketing ideas, it would be fine to test whether they were effective.

A   Statistical Analysis

Since the main part of this paper analyzed how the subjects had the views to automobiles when they were young by text-mining approach, the authors do not deal with statistical analysis for the questionnaire survey as asked in Table 2 so much. Here, the authors statistically analyze only the questions which the subjects chose from multiple options by quantification method of the third type and present the results. In other words, the authors exclude question 9 and those which the subjects were asked to tell the reasons. Note that this analysis with the following discussions are independent of the results in Sect. 3.

Figure 5 shows the result of quantification method of the third type. The points of questions 4 and 10 are omitted. Panel a plots the category scores for the two solutions with the largest eigenvalues[8] and panel b does the sample scores each of which corresponds to a subject. First, while the plots about the affirmative answers for the ownership and purchase of an automobile are observed in the second and the third quadrant, those about the denial answers are in the first and the fourth quadrant. Second, the plot about the subjects at the age of 40s is at $(-0.67, -2.49)$, close to the positive vertical axis, whereas that about those at the age of 30s is at $(-0.96, 3.60)$, close to the negative vertical axis. Consequently, the horizontal axis is considered as whether the subjects have an automobile while the vertical axis is interpreted as age.

There are a couple of points to address from this figure: First, those who were workers and/or lived in Yamaguchi Pref. likely had not only a driver's license but also an automobile while those who were students and/or lived in other places did not need an automobile. In addition, those who had an automobile said that having an automobile was a high-status and that they emphasized on exterior view. Those who did not have an automobile, on the other hand, considered interior view as more important. However, such a tendency does not depend on the age so much. Instead, the subjects at 40s or elder thought brand as more important while those at 30s regarded equipment as more necessary. In terms of gender, it may be that the male subjects had an automobile while the female ones did not so. In short, views to automobiles may depend both on his/her age and on whether s/he drove at that time.

---

[8] Both "Roomy" and "Trunk" in question 8 exist outside of the figure, *i.e.*, "Roomy" at $(-1.25, -6.66)$ and "Trunk" at $(0.21, -4.09)$.

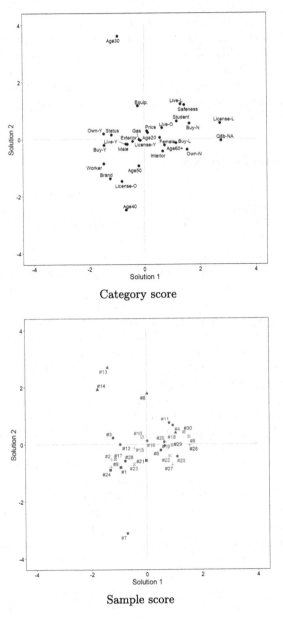

Category score

Sample score

(Age ●: 20s, ▲: 30s, ■: 40s, +: 50s, ⊠: 60s+)
(Gender Red: Female, Blue: Male)

Fig. 5. Results of quantification method of the third type

References

1. Japan Automobile Manufacturers Association, Inc.: The trend survey of vehicle market 2021 (in Japanese). https://www.jama.or.jp/release/docs/release/2022/20220420_2021PassengerCars.pdf. Accessed 5 Nov 2023
2. Ohta, R.: Young people's lifestyle. Jpn. Mark. J. **34**(4), 5–22 (2015). (in Japanese)
3. Asano, S., Daimon, H.: A study on the characteristics of motivation to own a car in local cities. JSTE J. Traffic Eng. **8**(4), A_43–A_50 (2022). (in Japanese)
4. Sivak, M., Schoettle, B.: Recent changes in the age composition of drivers in 15 countries. Traffic Inj. Prev. **13**(2), 126–132 (2012)
5. Rérat, P.: A decline in youth licensing: a simple delay or the decreasing popularity of automobility? Appl. Mob. **6**(1), 71–91 (2012)
6. Alexa, D., Graham, C.: Are changed living arrangements influencing youth driver license decline? Transportation Research Board 92nd Annual Meeting, Washington DC, United States (2013). https://trid.trb.org/view/1240917. Accessed 10 Jan 2023
7. Sivak, M., Schoettle, B.: Update: percentage of young persons with a driver's license continues to drop. Traffic Inj. Prev. **13**(4), 341 (2012)
8. Kouno, T., Anamizu, S., Morimoto, A.: Study on the youth and Womens' long-term change of traffic behavior by utilizing PT survey. In: The 39th annual meeting of Japan Society of Traffic Engineers, pp. 201–205 (2019). (in Japanese)
9. Doi, T., Shiromizu, Y., Nambu, H.: The subject of the transportation planning which became clear by analyzing the result of a person trip survey: consideration from the result of the Kinki district PT investgation. Chuo Fukken Consultants Tech. Rep. **43**, 7–14 (2013). (in Japanese)
10. Doi, T., Andou, N., Shiromizu, Y.: The issues related to mobility and activity of the first of life. Chuo Fukken Consultants Tech. Rep. **45**, 1–7 (2015). (in Japanese)
11. Ministry of Land, Infrastructure, Transport and Tourism: Nationwide Person Trip Survey (in Japanese). https://www.mlit.go.jp/toshi/tosiko/toshi_tosiko_fr_000024.html. Accessed 10 Jan 2023
12. National Police Agency: Driver's license Statistics (in Japanese). https://www.npa.go.jp/publications/statistics/koutsuu/menkyo.html. Accessed 10 Jan 2023
13. Cabinet Office: Consumer Confidence Survey. https://www.esri.cao.go.jp/en/stat/shouhi/shouhi-e.html. Accessed 10 Jan 2023

Author Index

M. Bono et al. (Eds.): JSAI-isAI 2023 Workshops, LNAI 14644, p. 243, 2024.
https://doi.org/10.1007/978-3-031-60511-6

Printed in the United States
by Baker & Taylor Publisher Services